A MANUAL FOR
RESIDENTIAL AND DAY TREATMENT
OF CHILDREN

A Manual For Residential and Day Treatment of Children

By

MILTIADES G. EVANGELAKIS, M.D.

Director of Children's Division
South Florida State Hospital
Hollywood, Florida
Clinical Associate Professor of Psychiatry
School of Medicine
University of Miami

CHARLES C THOMAS · PUBLISHER
Springfield · Illinois · U.S.A.

Published and Distributed Throughout the World by

CHARLES C THOMAS • PUBLISHER

Bannerstone House

301-327 East Lawrence Avenue, Springfield, Illinois, U.S.A.

© *1974, by* CHARLES C THOMAS • PUBLISHER

ISBN 0-398-03118-5

Library of Congress Catalog Card Number: 74-714

*With THOMAS BOOKS careful attention is given to all details of
manufacturing and design. It is the Publisher's desire to present books that are
satisfactory as to their physical qualities and artistic possibilities and
appropriate for their particular use. THOMAS BOOKS will be true to those
laws of quality that assure a good name and good will.*

Printed in the United States of America
C-1

Library of Congress Cataloging in Publication Data

Evangelakis, Miltiades G.
   A manual for residential and day treatment of
children.

   Includes bibliographical references.
   1. Child psychiatry. 2. Child psychotherapy—
Residential treatment. I. Title. [DNLM: 1. Child
psychiatry. 2. Community mental health services—
In infancy and childhood. 3. Day Care. 4. Resi-
dential treatment—In infancy and childhood. WS350
E91m 1974]
RJ504.5.E9   362.7'8'2   74-714
ISBN 0-398-03118-5

PREFACE

Wᴴᴇɴ ᴛʜᴇ ʟɪʙʀᴀʀʏ sʜᴇʟᴠᴇs of the world are groaning under their load of accumulated volumes, anyone who writes a book must ask himself why he should add yet another and look for a better reason than mere intoxication with the exuberance of his own verbosity. My own reason is the attempt to present an operational manual to practitioners who are interested in children's residential psychiatric treatment and would like to understand it better, and also to practitioners whose best intentions for residential treatment are apt to be frustrated by its amorphous complexity; by the conceptual gap between mental and physical, behavioral and dynamic approach; and by the difficulty of stepping into unfamiliar ways of thinking about disease.

The manual is an account of my experiences and successes and some of my difficulties in providing intensive residential psychiatric treatment for severely emotionally disturbed and mentally ill children. It also calls attention to some of the lessons learned over the past several years and to the efforts for a distillation and reduction of what are in fact real and often controversial issues, especially in connection with the programs of residential psychiatric treatment.

The manual was made possible by the cooperation of my coworkers and particularly the directors of the various services of the center. I am particularly grateful to those who never interfered even when called upon for criticism and sensible advice. I should also say that any opinions expressed here are not necessarily to be identified with the views of the psychiatric center with which I am associated.

This manual is not a primer, not an outline, not a text of child psychiatry, nor is it a substitute for any of these. It is written for the student of child care, treatment and education, and it deals with matters of fact and matters of opinion. I have tried to present them as clearly and honestly as I can and whenever an opinion is expressed, to indicate whether it is my own or someone else's.

The manual's intent is a description of my own beliefs in methods of practice of residential treatment and not to measure or evaluate the criteria or standards set by the American Psychiatric Association. The aim has been to provide a fairly concise background of factual information. Naturally, the subjects on which there is general agreement can be described more briefly than those carrying wide differences of opinion, and this explains what may appear to be a lack of balance between the sections. Clinical skills such as the handling of interviews, the function of the group worker, and psychotherapeutic techniques are perhaps better learned by precept and example rather than from books. The fact that they are not described here in detail is not to be taken as an indication that the writer considers them unimportant.

The manual is divided into sections rather than chapters and, in a work of this kind, it is essential to keep the text uncluttered. This manual does not aspire to instruct so much as to remind the reader, not to lead him but only to light the road. The presentation is, of necessity, condensed. While writing it I tried to depart from the usual (and at times unnecessary) practice of including detailed references and often convoluted expositions and critical analyses of other colleagues' methods of residential psychiatric treatment of children. Instead, I have considered the bitter experience of my own early mistakes and have laid stress on those "soft signs" in which the novice is likely to err, either in identifying them or in dealing with them.

The opportunity I have had to work with emotionally disturbed and mentally ill made me decide on the realistic treatment modalities which would help them most. The carrying out of a residential treatment program has emphasized the validity of the old adage that the one steady, consistent factor is that of change. Indeed, my continued experience has led to certain modifications in philosophy and in methods of practice which have given rise to the need for certain changes in administrative organization and clinical structure in a residential treatment center. These changes have to do primarily with quantity and quality of treatment modalities, with staff and their specific job responsibilities and supervision, and with personnel practices. Through these changes, this manual was born and its final spur was the reception given to it by professionals who happentd to become familiar with it.

It is my experience that residential psychiatric treatment of children is particularly dreaded by the general psychiatrist because of its alleged complexities and intricacies. Child psychiatry has a reputation among practitioners as the most abstruse, remote and difficult discipline, full of high-sounding terms, with an elaborate technique of treatment. The physician is ready to tackle any problem in medicine, however difficult, but shies away from a severe child-psychiatric problem; either he recommends endless diagnostic evaluations and educational interventions or "orders EEGs" or treats the child with psychotropic drugs because he believes that "kids should not be treated in mental hospitals."

It is true that modern child psychiatry is highly complex and becomes more so every day. But little is needed by the interested specialist child psychiatrist to be able to establish and develop a workable residential treatment program for disturbed children. And this little is not complicated. I even dare to say it is simple. For residential psychiatric treatment of emotionally disturbed and mentally ill children—as it is exclusively described in this manual—in addition to the adequate housing, maintenance and good food, one needs specialized and dedicated staff, the five senses (sharpened by the gift of observation), and a sixth (common sense).

There is a growing and deplorable tendency to overload residential psychiatric treatment and education programs with mechanical, chemical, behavioral and other laboratory procedures and to overemphasize their importance. The child psychiatrist in charge of the treatment of these children is more and more inclined to base his treatment program on the availability of these mechanical, chemical and behavioral procedures rather than on the availability of the quality of the personality of his staff.

The art of treating children with the eyes, ears and one-to-one relationship is steadily losing ground. Too many neophytes in the field long for standardized, foolproof group methods as a substitute for the one-to-one human relationship. They expect from behavior modification charts and from other laboratory-computerized procedures a mathematical formula which will give them the treatment results as a *deus ex machina*.

Again, the busy child psychiatrist overworked and pressed for time, uncertain about the diagnosis, confused by the results of the preliminary diagnostic evaluation is apt to "pass the buck" to a neurologist, psychologist, special education teacher, child guidance counselor, or a recreational therapist just to gain time and to postpone his decision on grounds which seem reasonable to him. If this be criticism, it must also be directed against me, since I, too, have been guilty of such practice. This practice has attained such proportions that one can, with some reason, speak of "mechanized child psychiatry."

It is expected that this manual will fill the gap at the moment for an elementary account of only a few of the important controversial problems under consideration in this new area of specialization. I can only hope that future revisions of this manual will include an updated and more comprehensive approach to the residential treatment of psychiatric disorders of children. Suggested improvements from all readers are encouraged. These will be reviewed and hopefully included in future editions of the manual.

M. EVANGELAKIS, M.D.

Hollywood, Florida

THE RESIDENTIAL TREATMENT CENTER

BACKGROUND

REPEATED STUDIES HAVE LONG indicated that the treatment of emotionally disturbed and mentally ill children has a high priority in almost every area of the nation. The development of psychiatric treatment techniques geared specifically to disordered children is of fairly recent origin and is still in process. In fact, residential psychiatric treatment itself might still be considered an innovation as a source of therapy for emotionally disturbed children. It has been reported that it would be difficult to ascertain reliably when and where children began to be admitted to publicly sponsored psychiatric hospitals (1, 2). My own research has not found a definitive article on the history of residential treatment centers. It is possible that the first center which provided residential treatment was established in this country in 1920, when the Child Guidance Home of Cincinnati was founded as a study home for children with emotional problems. Also, in 1920, a children's ward was opened in the Psychiatric Division of Bellevue Hospital, New York City, as a result of the epidemic of lethargic encephalitis following World War I. There became a need to care for children with postencephalitic behavior disorders who were neither mentally retarded nor delinquent. After evaluation, some of these children were transferred to a separate children's service at Kings Park Hospital which opened in 1924 from which Gibbs published an excellent report in 1930 (1).

In 1952, the Child Welfare League of America (3), conscious of its responsibility to the child care field to provide data on effective new ways of helping children, conducted a study of twelve pioneering residential treatment centers whose purpose was the treatment of children with severe emotional disorders.

ix

The study provided a description of residential treatment in the United States and also hoped to provide sustained consultation service to communities and agencies interested in developing such a program. The results of the study were invaluable as those responsible for the children's care and treatment sought more effective treatment methods.

Hylton's book (4) is the report of an administrative study of twenty-one residential treatment centers and two therapeutic day schools, conducted under the auspices of the Child Welfare League of America, Inc. The primary focus of the study is the cost of care and treatment of the emotionally disturbed children in these centers, although the periphery of its coverage extends to the centers' operations, the populations they serve, and the administrative concerns of the persons charged with their direction.

Weber's and Haberlein's edited book (5) contains twenty papers by specialists in their respective fields and also presents the rationale of residential treatment of emotionally disturbed children and its various components which include intake and diagnostic procedures, individual and group psychotherapy, education, group living, recreation, arts and crafts, and the administrative procedures which integrate the program.

DEFINITION

In more recent years, the number of requests for information concerning the organization of such centers has increased. The few residential treatment centers in the country have been deluged by requests from social agencies in communities asking for guidance in establishing similar programs.

Though published literature in this field has dealt extensively with many facets of the theoretical base upon which residential treatment centers have been set up, it is apparent that there are few comprehensive descriptions of their actual operation. It is apparent also that these centers have differing viewpoints and have developed variations in methods that mark any new and experimental approach to the problems of treating human ills. The American Association for Children's Residential Centers has so far specifically shied away from developing overall policies regarding organization and procedures for the treatment of children in residential centers.

According to the 1969-1970 report of the National Institute of Mental Health on mental health facilities, residential treatment centers for emotionally disturbed children are defined as "institutions providing inpatient services, usually under the supervision of a psychiatrist and primarily to persons under eighteen years of age, who by clinical diagnosis are moderately or seriously emotionally disturbed."

The recent (1971) publication on "Standards for Psychiatric Facilities Serving Children and Adolescents" by the American Psychiatric Association is an attempt to develop firm "criteria" or "standards" and to set forth some basic principles in the care and treatment of children and adolescents with mental or emotional disorders, mental retardation, or both. My intent is a description of my own beliefs in methods of practice and not to measure or evaluate the criteria or standards set by the American Psychiatric Association.

Considering the varieties of definitions of the residential psychiatric treatment center given by persons active in this field, it would not be inaccurate to say that at present there is no general agreement as to what a residential treatment center is. This is not surprising, since, from a historical viewpoint, residential treatment is an innovation in the process of caring for emotionally disturbed children. Although the concept "emotionally disturbed" is widely employed, its limits have not yet been definitely formulated. For my purposes, I assume that most of the children in need of residential treatment have emotional problems that, although not severe enough to require closed institutional care, could not be treated adequately on an outpatient or day treatment basis.

Residential treatment is still occupied with such matters as determining what the nature of its programs and services should be, what the functions of its various staff positions are, and what types or degrees of emotional problems are best handled in a residential treatment setting.

The experience of child guidance clinics and private psychiatric treatment resources has demonstrated clearly that many severely emotionally disturbed and mentally ill children cannot be adequately treated while they remain in their homes or in the community (6, 7). Direct psychotherapy is not sufficient to meet their needs, and a new gratifying living experience in a therapeutic milieu is required. Some neurotic children cannot be helped without intensive direct individual psychiatric treatment and a benign and positive living experience in a controlled situation. Also, some children with educational deficits and specific school problems require a controlled therapeutic school situation. In a residential treatment setting, the therapy is total with an attempt to provide for direct psychotherapy, education, relationships with numerous accepting adults, group activities planned according to the dynamics presented, creative occupational and recreational therapy, and above all, a milieu that the child knows will tolerate deviation and help him in his attempts to deal with his problems.

At the present time, the treatment programs that are called "residential treatment" differ considerably among themselves in the types of children they accept, size of plan, administrative direction, background, etc. There is actually no universally accepted definition of a residential treatment, although there are many similarities that characterize the residential treatment settings in contrast to group care and hospital type institutions for children. Using descriptions of these distinguishing similarities rather than attempting any formal definition, the following composite picture of a residential treatment center emerges.

A residential psychiatric treatment center is an institution for severely emotionally and mentally ill children who, because of their disturbed relationships with other persons, cannot remain in their own homes for treatment and need the more controlled and therapeutic environment the center provides. It is an "open" setting in that the children have the freedom of the plant and grounds; upon occasion they go out into the community for additional educational, recreational or medical services.

COST—STAFF RATIO

In recent years the persons working in the field of residential treatment, and even more so the parents and the organizations that have been providing funds for the care and treatment of children in such settings, have become concerned about the rising cost of residential treatment. These programs are among the most expensive in the mental health field, and questions are being raised as to: Why is the cost of residential treatment so great? Do costs differ because of the types of children accepted? What does the size of the plant have to do with the cost per child? Could costs be lowered by increasing or decreasing the number of children in care?

Although residential treatment centers do supplement their services through use of community facilities, most centers are largely self-sufficient in providing for the children in treatment. A high ratio of staff to children, particularly child care staff, is characteristic of residential treatment services. Because of the special problems presented by these children, the centers must also supply specialized educational and recreational facilities.

RESIDENTIAL MILIEU

Ideally, residential psychiatric treatment must provide a therapeutic milieu or environment for the children under care and treatment. This practice is predicated on the belief that the daily living experiences of the children—their relationships with adults and with each other—may be as significant for their emotional growth as the hours of direct psychotherapy or the special education they receive. In such a therapeutic environment, therefore, the elements of understanding and therapeutic planning play an important part in even the most casual contacts of staff with the children.

The clinical services of a residential psychiatric treatment center for children must also bring together specialists of various professional arts and skills in mental health and education. Thus, the therapeutic goals of the residential treatment program require the services of child psychiatrists, child psychologists, social workers, teachers, adjunctive therapists, and a psychiatrically oriented nursing staff. Modern child psychiatric treatment is a process in which the specialists must apply their skills concurrently. The term "team approach" includes this concept, but unfortunately it does not quite adequately define it. The particular type of team organization which we consider to be consistent with principles of child psychiatric treatment is one in which each participant has authority and freedom to select and use his own therapeutic tools within the general framework of treatment prescribed by the medical director of the center and his advisory council.

The philosophy of a residential psychiatric treatment center for children must also be responsible for a unique system in which dual and multiple controls and supervision of the staff are the rule rather than the exception. Also, the organization of such a center must be unique in another respect, that of the residence structural and functional plan. The size of each residence should be such that permits the child to be received, treated and able to complete his treatment through the medium of a single group of nursing staff, each of whom would know all of the other members of the group. This should be planned to work to the advantage of the child whose improvement is so highly dependent upon the evolution of his interpersonal relationships. Moreover, the living arrangement of each child should be carefully planned, both with regard to its physical aspects and to the composition of the group with which the child will be most intimately associated.

From experience, I have found that adequate residential treatment is interrupted or set back if the children are exposed to any experiences which they are not ready to master. Therefore, in order to protect them from exposure to situations which cannot be controlled outside the center and to provide the necessary and continuous therapeutic services within the center, no reliance should be placed on any external resource such as schools, recreation facilities or the homes of parents or relatives. These must be used only as therapeutically indicated and when the resource is known to be reliable. In practice, however, the treatment milieu is a modified one because there are such events as weekends, holidays and vacations which some centers overlook when they talk in terms of "continuous treatment milieu" as their main therapeutic modality. I believe that if environmental therapy is the basis of treatment, then it can no more be interrupted under the pretext of weekend, holiday or vacation than the emotional or mental disturbance is interrupted (6). The children have to count firmly on the daily events of their life that should occur in regular succession and without fail.

The center's staff must insist on a certain degree of firmness because the children not only need a fixed, uneventful predictable schedule, but they also need the comfort and security afforded by strict rules of behavior. A mild degree of reasonable permissiveness common to everyday living should characterize a therapeutic milieu; however, certain behavioral manifestations should be frowned upon and others should be encouraged. This quality of firmness that expresses itself without excessive disciplinary action by a friendly, but sound, attitude should indeed be always present in the nursing staff as well as in other staff members. No child should ever be reprimanded in anger; firmness should be compatible with love and interest. With such methods of management and control, it is hoped that children who have been admitted for assistance will eventually be taught to accept a minimum of life's frustrations compatible with that of a normal environment at home and the community. There are other children who will need from time to time to return to a controlled environment or will need to live in a different setting where treatment efforts will have to be continued for a longer period. Only prolonged treatment and evaluation will allow for a prognosis of what the future of these children might be.

REFERENCES

1. Gibbs, C. E.: Behavior disorders in chronic epidemic encephalitis. *Am J Psychiatry, 9*:619-634, 1930.
2. Editorial Comment: *Am J Psychiatry, 121*:925-927, 1965.
3. Reid, J. H., and Hagan, H. R.: *Residential Treatment of Emotionally Disturbed Children: A Descriptive Study.* New York, Child Welfare League of America, 1952.
4. Hylton, L. F.: *The Residential Treatment Center, Children, Programs, and Costs.* New York, Child Welfare League of America, 1964.
5. Weber, G. H., and Haberlein, B. J.: *Residential Treatment of Emotionally Disturbed Children.* New York, Behavioral Publications, 1972.
6. Evangelakis, M.: De-institutionalization of patients. *Dis Nerv Syst, 22*:26-32, 1961.
7. Evangelakis, M., and Sigurdson, W.: A five-year report on the services of the child study unit of the Kansas Neurological Institute. *Ment Retard, 6*:1, 22-27, 1968.

CONTENTS

A MANUAL FOR
RESIDENTIAL AND DAY TREATMENT
OF CHILDREN

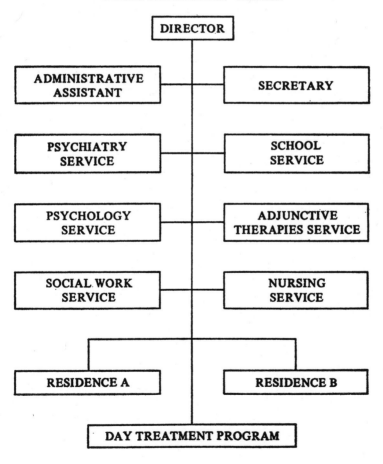

SECTION A

RESIDENTIAL AND DAY TREATMENT CENTER

RESIDENTIAL AND DAY TREATMENT CENTER ORGANIZATIONAL CHART

DIRECTOR

ADMINISTRATIVE ASSISTANT — SECRETARY

PSYCHIATRY SERVICE — SCHOOL SERVICE

PSYCHOLOGY SERVICE — ADJUNCTIVE THERAPIES SERVICE

SOCIAL WORK SERVICE — NURSING SERVICE

RESIDENCE A — RESIDENCE B

DAY TREATMENT PROGRAM

FORM OF ORGANIZATION

THE CENTER IS A RESIDENTIAL and day treatment center for emotionally disturbed and mentally ill boys and girls between the ages of six and twelve years.

Its residential treatment program with a forty-eight-bed capacity serves children who are emotionally or mentally disturbed. The day treatment program with a capacity for thirty children serves primarily the surrounding communities. It is offered to those children who can remain in the community but who are in need of intensive psychiatric, educational and social assistance. It also serves as a transitional program for some residential children as they move toward outpatient services.

PHYSICAL PLANT

The physical plant is located on eighteen acres of landscaped ground and consists of seven buildings of modern, contemporary design with facilities to make the children's stay as comfortable as possible. The center is an open unit and has no walls or fences surrounding it. At the east end of the complex are the children's living quarters consisting of two residences and the service area. Each residence is divided into two units of twelve beds each, thus enabling children to be placed, whenever possible, with their peer group. The ratio of male to female is 3 to 1. Each residence unit includes bedrooms for one, two or three children, a living room, a family room, nursing office, and a large enclosed outside patio. The service building includes the infirmary, medical examination facilities, two dining room areas, and the kitchen.

At the west part of the complex is the school, the day treatment building and recreation building. The school has classroom settings for instruction in the various academic subjects as well as home economics, library, industrial arts and occupational therapy. The maximum number of pupils per class is five enabling individualized prescriptive instruction.

The recreation building has offices for the adjunctive therapies (recreational, musical and industrial) and includes an auditorium with a stage. Here, social functions, movies and indoor sports are held. Outside are areas for playgrounds, ballfields (basketball, baseball, football, soccer), farming, and picnic grounds as well as areas for volleyball, roller skating and bicycling. In the center part of the complex is the administration building, containing administrative offices, clinical staff offices, therapy playrooms, testing rooms, educational classrooms, conference rooms, the professional library, medical records and archives room, and the education and research office.

GENERAL ORIENTATION—ROLE OF THE CENTER

A residential treatment center is conceived as a directed network of programs, each delegated to function within a sphere of autonomous control and thereby able to retain distinctive or unique features which are kept in minimum conflict by constant communication among the directors of the services and their various programs. This authority structure prevents the concentration of the director's role in one person and in one central office.

The treatment programs are formulated and supervised by the director of the center in collaboration with the child psychiatrists, psychologists, social workers, school teachers, adjunctive therapists, and nursing staff.

By and large, psychodynamic concepts are utilized diagnostically and therapeutically. In general, the treatment programs aim at developing social skills and interpersonal relationships which, in turn, seem to influence intrapsychic processes rather than the reverse procedure.

The center's credo is focused attention and direct involvement in what a child is feeling, thinking or doing. The staff believes that the opposite of love is indifference, not hate. It combines the focused attention with psychological safety, i.e. listening to what the child is saying and entering into his experience. In trying to understand his feelings and how he experiences the world, the staff believes it creates an atmosphere in which he is able to accept new information, and with that information he can change his own feelings.

Even though the center's staff is anti-authoritarian in large measure, it insists upon structure, on visibility and openness, and on teamwork. Their belief is that maximum coordination of the total programs must be achieved if the staff members are to be most effective and have equal weight.

The center's philosophy does not subscribe to the stereotypes of "total approach therapy," "therapeutic educational experience," or "programs specifically tailored to the child's individual strengths and weaknesses" as parts of a whole. The prescription of chemotherapy for children is not encouraged, nor are the theories and practice of the "blue," "quiet," "timeout" or "seclusion" rooms and other "isolation therapies" in the name of "recompensation of defenses!" Computerized behavior modification is not prescribed, and there is no review of the literature or statistical analysis on the "cures" obtained in other centers. Nor is there any belief in the self-interest serving and grandiose research results reported by various "investigators of behavioral sciences" whose projects are supported by grants from the public health service and/or pharmaceutical companies.

The psychiatric treatment programs as developed in the center are based on the child guidance process into which has been introduced the factor of residence for the child.

The children are not viewed as "kids," "youngsters," "subjects," "clients," "trainees," "students," "masters," "young men," "young ladies," or "patients." They are just children.

The kinds of treatment given to children at the center are described as modified, dynamically oriented, supportive individual psychotherapy; group psychotherapy; family therapy; education; counseling; group work; and recreation, industrial and music therapy. The treatment programs are also oriented to that part of the theories of dynamic psychiatry adaptable to casework practice. The parents are actively and responsibly engaged.

The goal of the treatment programs is to provide individual and group treatment and education for each child that will enable him to achieve maximum development within his capacity to change; also to provide some means for furthering his emotional growth and development, as well as to prepare him to return to his home and community.

The center's general orientation is that severely emotionally disturbed and mentally ill children can be effectively treated but only under certain optimal conditions. After their removal from the environment to which their symptomatology was related, they are provided with an environment which is not only sympathetic, unprejudiced, fair, understanding and consistent, but which is at the same time so arranged as to enable the proper regulation of management and controls to be set up for each individual child. Avoidance of physical punishment is assured, and in its place provision is made for the direct relation of consequences to causes. The emotionally disturbed children are treated in this environment which calls attention to the slightest successes that they achieve. It is a consistent environment which helps them to meet certain requirements while sustaining them as they become more able to meet ordinary pressures. Through this kind and firm environment, the children are enabled to identify with accepting adults, to become part of a group of peers, and to give free expression of their hostile and pent-up feelings. The children are helped to find a way out of the unhappy entanglement of emotions which cause their disturbances. To this end, the total atmosphere of the environment has to be child-centered.

Since the children admitted represent various levels of emotional development and behavior, the treatment programs are flexible; however, realistically they are not planned to meet the individual needs of each. In spite of some children's severe illness and the frequency of regressed development, many attempts are made to force children into a scheduled program of activities. Staff are encouraged to work with each child on the basis of his current level of behavior. Although the goal is understood to be helping each one attain a more adequate level of adjustment by developing his interests and independence, encouragement towards conformity is not avoided. My personal experience indicates that emotionally disturbed children cannot be treated in an environment which is permissive. Thus an attempt is made to provide adequate external controls for the acting out, aggression-inhibited group.

The reality demands made upon the child in the living situation are modified or intensified in such a way so as to supplement or activate the therapy process. If it is known that he is carrying all the burden he can assimilate, treatment demands are reduced. If he is dawdling in therapy, they can be increased. If his guilt becomes dangerously persistent, restriction can be set up for small infractions to help him regain some stability from vicarious retribution. Likewise, the child can utilize the relationships in the center to live through or relive essential growth experience. Infrequently, a large part of treatment takes place in the living situation techniques by which the nursing staff reinforces the child's confidence in the casework staff and vice versa. The nursing staff supplements casework treatment by furnishing those actual situations in which a child can work out his problems. Their daily reports also give background material helpful to the psychotherapist's individual interviews with children.

The children are provided with planned and supervised activities on a group basis which teaches them to react in a socially acceptable way within firmly set controls. I believe that this type of program is also helpful for the insecure and anxious child who handles his anxieties by excessive acting out. Planned activities are used as a means of giving the child a feeling that he belongs and that of easy identification. A routine and a progression of activities also offer a protective device for warding off anxiety and panic. The use of closely supervised groups with scheduled activities permits a greater degree of permissiveness than would be possible without the limitations set up by such a structured situation.

I believe that children need more than a benign or kind and stable environment which provides custody, healthful care, training and education. In a residential treatment center, the treatment programs are not set up as a series of disconnected services to a child. They are integrated into a healthful and therapeutic milieu in which the facilities and staff merge into one collaborative treatment effort designed toward encouraging healthy personality development and return to normal community living. Also, they do not provide merely a group living experience where group living by itself is supposed to socialize the unsocialized child. Rather, they are a collaborative service given by staff, in which living, treatment and education are integrated. Group living at the center is conceived as a controlled environment where children live within limits in which they can comfortably fit.

Thus, treatment is a three-fold process combining psychotherapy, education and planned living. It is not confined to psychotherapy (the interviewing process) or to the strict academic work. Instead, it is based on the use of psychotherapy and the utilization of all the living experiences of a child in accordance with his treatment needs as understood psychiatrically. The objective of the treatment program is to integrate the living experiences with the treatment and education. This integration includes (1) the kind of relationships he is to experience, (2) the intellectual stimulation to which he is to be exposed, 3) the groups he is to join, (4) the recreational activities in which he is to participate and (5) the staff member he is to see. This involves using planned therapies and fostering healthy and meaningful relationships with adults and peers. It also requires that the child's physical and intellectual development be taken into consideration and that opportunities for creativity be provided. All these are coordinated through continuous psychiatric evaluation and treatment. In order to achieve these objectives great care is taken in evaluating each child's needs; in spite of great difficulties special efforts are made to individualize the program and to adjust and adopt the facilities of the center in accordance with those needs.

Admitting children to the residence is considered an incident in the total therapeutic work with the family. It is at this time where the parents' and child's tolerance for each other may be strained to the breaking point by the conflict that admission to the residence is sought, suggested and advisable, but not for the child's sake alone. Treatment, therefore, consists of a carefully integrated combination of family therapy for parents and child with his therapeutically directed living experiences. Directly related to this purpose is the work that is done with the parents or other persons in the child's "home" environment since they, too, are involved in or affected by the child's problems.

I believe that the child derives an ultimate sense of security from the knowledge that there is an active, sustaining relationship to his parents. If this cannot be adequately provided by resident staff, the child sees his placement in residence as a long-term foster placement. Therefore, it is important that the parents or responsible legal guardians have an active association with the child during his stay in residence so that the very meaningful tie with resident workers does not easily take on the aspects of a parent-child relationship. For it is the very meaningfulness of the parents' or guardians' association with the child in residence which allows the resident staff to be completely free, warm and accepting of the children who are with them. Thus, the resident worker is not placing himself in the position of being the providing parent who will care for the child indefinitely.

BASIC ORIENTATION

The staff's orientation concerning the etiology of childhood emotional disturbance places emphasis on the child's phylogeny and ontogeny, both pivotal factors in the development of his personality and in the etiology of his emotional, mental and behavior disorders.

We are all aware that we are living in a world blessed with material gains and in times marked by great scientific progress. Yet it is indeed paradoxical that we continue to have so many problems which reflect the incidence of mental illness in varying degrees.

Our communications media are filled with reports of children who are mental health casualties, school dropouts, delinquents, neglected and abused. These children cannot raise their voices to complain on the paucity of quantity and quality of clinical services for them and their families, nor can they raise any question on social, legislative and educational approaches for the prevention of emotional, mental and psychosocial disorders.

I believe that the majority of these disordered children are the products of biological and environmental disharmony and contradiction and of harassed idealistic or pragmatic parents whose crisis of identity is a part of the history of our times.

In my work with parents, I found that for years they had been watching many problems with their child go on and had been standing on the sidelines feeling impotent. Some of them felt "an expert was needed" and that "because they did not know enough about child psychology" or "because they had read the baby-book" they could not take a stand. Others felt that their parental authority had been weakened by the overunderstanding of their child and the psychological and sociological overorientation which made them so aware of the problems and pressures of children that they let their child put them in a position of no position.

I often found these parents to have overtly or covertly been a party to their child's problem by not paying attention, by letting the child lie to them, by bailing him out of trouble, and by getting at earnest to clean up the mess. Of course, their ultimate stand, the bottom line, was showering the child with "rewards" for good behavior and "aversion therapy" for misbehavior—prescribed by behavior modificators and other "therapists"—or tossing the child out of the home and providing him with financial support, use the police and the courts, or other measures.

It is realized that children today are exposed to a variety of pressures and influences. Some are taught to be ashamed of their parents and their traditions and their country's record at home and of its role in the world. Besides that and the high price the parents are paying for their overunderstanding and sociological overorientation, their belief also is that there is a pill for whatever ails them. Better emotional living through chemistry. Television advertising, as well as advertising in magazines and medical journals, promotes drugs to cope with their tensions of everyday living.

It is my firm belief that parents can and should take a stand. It is natural for them to learn and understand the loneliness, the sadness, conflicts, and all the pressures a child goes through and still take a stand and set firm limits. When the parents take a gutsy position, nine times out of ten it is a tremendous relief for the child who wants guidelines. Far from being lost, the child ultimately grows closer to his parents.

Therefore, a child without firm and consistent guidelines in his various life experiences finds it extremely difficult to respond to the biological, psychological and social demands of his developmental stages; frequently he tries to compensate by adaptive attempts which prove to be ineffectual and only partially satisfying or they are experienced internally as distressing symptoms. These, as outer signs of the child's difficulty, may be manifested in behavior which is socially unacceptable and disturbing to others and often disguised as severe emotional disorder or mental illness requiring residential treatment.

In order for these children to learn to adjust to their family and community, it is thought important for them to learn to develop a sense of autonomy and to create new configurations of positive and negative identities. Also, most importantly, they must develop a capacity to learn to hope in a milieu which offers them a convincing world view, and within it specific hopes on how to form and assimilate normal associations while under professional supervision and treatment.

For the accomplishment of this task, careful selection, in-service training and education of the staff is of tremendous importance. Only with such efforts is it possible to raise the staff's value of common sense to the level of high art which will provide a soft wall between these children and the world. For with a staff's distorted common sense, the "weak" children, in these times of profound cultural upheaval, would continue to become confused in their identities and either withdraw in isolation or abandon themselves to a mob identity.

In a residential treatment center, the professional staff members are presumably disciplined persons with self-awareness and a knowledge of the structure of personality and the dynamics of behavior. This background is believed to provide the skill to understand behavior in residence in such a way that it contributes to the total treatment objectives. An understanding of the dynamics inherent in behavior also enables the professional staff members to recognize pertinent material which needs to be brought before the total staff for psychiatric evaluation and interpretation.

The staff members are valued for their person and their competence rather than their academic degrees. They do not see themselves as being on a team which plays the decision-making game by vote; they do not seek to function autonomously. They know that the leadership of the team rests with the child psychiatrist when the team is functioning in a medical facility. They also know that he has the responsibility as a supervisor of the whole host of assistants who may or may not have less training but do expect their service to be used and their opinion to be heard.

By treating and teaching and by examples, the staff is trying to further the understanding and attainment of mental health. In so doing, the center divides its work into diagnostic, therapeutic, educational and applied aspects grouped together in eight services and departments. These are made up of people working together and interacting within and without the organization.

The staff lead individual lives, of which their worklife is a part. And since they hold that one's working habits and experiences are an important indication of his mental health, it is important that their working programs give the maximum satisfaction to the maximum number of people within the organization as well as accomplishing its specific purpose.

The role of the staff is two-fold: (1) to enable the child to use the various facilities and services the center provides for the purpose of ego building and the development of self-confidence and (2) to help the child through insight to recognize his behavior patterns, the genesis of his disturbances and the part which he, himself, can play in order to overcome them.

The staff is oriented to the philosophy that it is trying to adjust the child in treatment and education at the center and to the traditional American family and community life and not to an ideal fantasy world in which it might like to have him live. In every area the programs are geared to give a valid expression of accepted family and community standards as the child will encounter them outside the center.

Staff is chosen with the belief that all children need to learn to live with both men and women and to know adults of different personality types. Through employing men and women of various ages, I believe children are enabled to meet their needs for companionship from adults who are not parents, but more like friends or brothers and sisters.

In a residential treatment center, the staff's work begins satisfactorily at the time of admission and does not wait for the children to "actively utilize their treatment time with a psychotherapist." Accordingly, the children are introduced into the school and adjunctive therapy situation even before they have made an adequate beginning in psychotherapy. From the first few weeks they are in residence, they are urged to make an unusual effort to achieve in the preparatory program. Since the children have been entered in residence for the purpose of participating in all available programs and not only in psychotherapy, there are many important requirements placed upon them. They are helped to form a series of relationships within the resident setting, attend school, and have an opportunity to make friends and be active in the setting. Successful achievement in social or school relationships is accepted as an index of a successful beginning for a child.

Nursing staff are seen as the focal people in the child's life in the center. They are responsible for carrying out such functions as health care, shelter, clothing, feeding, discipline, teaching of good living habits (i.e. cleanliness, work habits), and enforcing respect for rules and regulations, for property and the rights of others, participating in planning the use of the child's time within the residence and in leisure time activities outside the residence, the observance of religious teaching and services, and the establishment of good relationships of children to adults and to one another.

All staff are involved in the milieu therapy of the children. Even though maintenance, kitchen and office personnel are not encouraged to have contacts with the children on an individual basis, such staff are involved to some extent with the children, the usual pattern being for the professional staff to keep them informed in a general way regarding the problems of the children and of the importance of their attitudes toward them. Some of these nonprofessional staff are unusually perceptive and warm and are more closely involved in the treatment of the children. They are often a source of emotional satisfaction and support in their passive relationships for those children who, at first, are not able to relate to others. To provide this, such staff members are exposed to in-service training and they are integrated into the total therapeutic milieu after they have recognized their role with the child and the therapeutic implications of the relationship.

In terms of staff versus morale, there is a sense of excitement in getting off the jaded, common well-beaten path of the traditional approach. For many of the professional staff, this becomes a point of discovery for which they so long yearned. In introducing a close day-by-day exchange with the disciplines of psychiatry, psychology, social work, education, adjunctive therapy, group work and nursing, the staff finds considerable stimulation in the process; this bears out a point professionals have made in connection with the great stimulation as possible in involving themselves with other disciplines or other professions. In their programs, a staff member can visit or observe a class, moving freely in a time of crisis; evaluate at first hand a child's interaction with an adult or other children; or share with a child's school teacher, psychiatrist, etc. any presentation and re-evaluation of a therapy or education plan.

The center's therapeutic milieu is carefully planned to reduce the child's anxiety, to meet some of his oral needs, to help develop ways of coping with problems, and strengthen rather than beat down his ego. The child begins to find gratification in learning as a teacher is able to apply specific techniques in education which have been worked out creatively with the clinical staff and that are geared to the child's individual psychopathology. In the center, the integration of the school into the clinical program is most gratifying in increasing the adaptive capacity of the children and in returning children to community schools after their period of residential treatment.

OBJECTIVES

The objectives of the residential psychiatric treatment center are:

1. To secure at all times medical direction for the administration of the center and the entire care, treatment and education of the children.

2. To provide and keep up-to-date written policies, organization and procedures; clinical records, personnel policies, and employment records; and a system of self-assessment measured against its defined objectives, programs and plans set by the director and his advisory council.

3. To secure an adequate number of qualified professional

and nonprofessional administrative and clinical personnel, properly supervised to work directly with children in a therapeutic manner, maintain confidentiality, and respect the rights of the children and their parents.

4. To achieve and maintain the highest possible degree of continuity and consistency among residential staff.

5. To provide a physical plant appropriately constructed, with adequate space for activities and for the comfort and safety of each child.

6. To develop services for diagnostic evaluation, selection and admission of children, not only to beds but to programs as well.

7. To develop comprehensive treatment programs: medical (pediatric, psychiatric, neurologic), dental and laboratory services, psychotherapeutic (individual and group psychotherapy, family therapy), therapeutically designed living experience (treatment in residence, group work), remedial education, adjunctive therapies (recreational, occupational, industrial and music therapy); direct and indirect casework with parents, visiting friends program; preparatory program, and volunteer program. These should provide the child:

a. an opportunity to be observed and treated in an environment in which he is free of the pressures and tensions which exist in his usual family and community life where a true evaluation of all the factors that contribute to his problems is difficult or impossible.

b. a place where his conduct can be assimilated and an opportunity to receive psychiatric treatment, education, group living experience, and other types of treatment.

c. an environment sufficiently supportive and therapeutic so that he can work through some of his maladjustments and develop for himself valid forms of functioning.

d. a realistic discharge plan to enable him to return home or to be placed in as near a normal situation as possible, there to be followed on an outpatient basis by local child and family oriented professionals and agencies.

8. To provide in-service education and training for professional and nonprofessional staff by utilizing the expertise of senior

staff members as well as visiting speakers from related fields of mental health and education of children.

9. To make the center available as a professional education and training resource to students from schools of nursing, education, psychology, social work and medicine (psychiatry).

10. To develop and carefully supervise and coordinate research projects always with adequate safeguards (parental consent, responsible staff, maintenance of proper balance among clinical service, training and research components of the overall program).

11. To provide consultation service to individuals and community and state agencies interested in developing residential treatment services for emotionally disturbed and mentally ill children.

12. To become a pacesetter for the children's residential psychiatric treatment and set standards of excellence in its procedures which will form the models carried away by young professionals entering the field who will themselves later shape residential psychiatric treatment of children.

ADMINISTRATION

DIRECTOR

THE DIRECTOR'S ADMINISTRATIVE, clinical and education duties and functions are to initiate, devise, organize and supervise standards for the program of children's treatment (treatment being construed as the selection, admission, diagnosis, treatment, discharge of patients) within the limits and purposes expressed in the state's statutes (if it is a state facility) or the policies and procedures determined by the advisory board (if it is a private or county facility); to select, assign, and supervise the clinical staff of the center in those aspects of its work which are related to the treatment of children; to confer and collaborate with the director of education with the view of integration of the treatment programs with the teaching and training programs.

The director is responsible to the director of the state mental health division (if state facility) or chairman of the advisory board (if private or county facility) for carrying out the duties described above.

All personnel in the administrative and clinical services are ultimately responsible to the director for activities concerned with the treatment of the children.

The director communicates upward to the state director of mental health or chairman of advisory board verbally, by memoranda, conferences or other means which may be necessary.

ASSISTANT DIRECTOR

The assistant director's administrative, clinical and educational duties and functions are to assume the responsibility for the treatment program in the absence of the director; to confer and collaborate with the director with the view of selection, assignment and supervision of the clinical staff of the center.

As director of education and research, the assistant director's responsibilities are to initiate, devise, organize and supervise standards for the programs of education and research at the center.

The assistant director is directly responsible to the director for carrying out the duties described above.

All personnel are ultimately responsible to the director of education and research for activities in the field of education and research.

The assistant director communicates upward to the director of the center verbally, by memoranda, conferences or other means which may be necessary.

The director of the center and the director of education maintain close lateral communication in order to accomplish the integration of their respective programs. They also communicate laterally with the administrative assistant on matters relating to personnel transactions, accounts, supplies, budgeting and the like.

All professional personnel have a responsibility for participation in teaching and training in addition to the performance of their clinical duties. The director of the center and the director of education and research establish such lines of communication within the services that insure the progress of the center's respective objectives. Such lines of communication recognize the established structure and organization of the clinical services, table of organization and the chain of authority in the various branches of the clinical services.

SECRETARY TO THE DIRECTOR

The secretary to the director is under the direction and supervision of the director of the center. She also performs secretarial duties for the director of social work services, director of psychology services and coordinator of the child study unit (admissions office). Her duties include the following:

Acting as office receptionist; answering telephones; greeting, announcing and routing visitors.

Taking and transcribing dictation; composing correspondence.

Receiving and reading incoming mail.

Typing memoranda, reports, correspondence and confidential material for the director, directors of social work and psychology, psychiatrists and child study unit.

Making travel arrangements and keeping the director's and directors' of social work and psychology calendars by scheduling appointments and conferences.

Taking and transcribing legal dictation of ordinary complexity and preparing and processing legal documents and records (notary public).

Maintaining control records on the incoming correspondence and action documents and following up on work in process to insure timely reply or action.

Maintaining alphabetical and chronological files and records of office correspondence, documents, reports and other materials.

Assisting in expediting the work of the office including such matters as asking the administrative assistant to take care of fluctuating workloads.

Assembling and summarizing information from files and documents in the office or other available sources for the director's use on the basis of general instructions as to the nature of the information needed.

Routine (Daily)

Certain number of copies of gains and losses, forwarded to Director's Office of Division of Mental Health, Statistician, Accounting, Medical Records, file (if it is a state facility).

Certain number of copies of daily report forwarded to Director of Division of Mental Health, file (if it is a state facility).

Report items for Director, Assistant Director, Directors of Social Work and Psychology, and Child Study Unit for daily bulletin.

Typing for above offices.

Routine (Weekly)

Administrative conference—take minutes.

Copies of weekend pass lists to Dietary Department, notifying them of any additions or cancellations as they occur.

Routine (Monthly)

Prepare monthly statistical reports for Director of Center, Statistician, file.

Prepare requisition once a month for office supplies.

Admission Day

Prepare forms. Notify dietary, marking room, post office, chaplain, accounting of admission (name, d/o/b, county, number). List information in statistics books, tablet, cards.

Notarize papers, if necessary.

Secure necessary "patient number."

Discharge Day

Prepare discharge papers and issue social security card for parent or guardian.

Notify departments (as previously named for admissions).

Child Study Unit

Set up files for new referrals, file new information on established files.

Type "follow-up" letters, close files when necessary.

Upon absence from office of coordinator, answer phone and take messages.

ADMINISTRATIVE ASSISTANT

The administrative assistant is directly responsible to the director of the center. He is a member of the advisory council. Following are his administrative duties and functions.

1. *Account and Reports*— (accounting, fiscal office, property control, Children's Fund).

2. *Supplies*—procurement, warehousing, issue, delivery, etc.

3. *Personnel Regulations*—Recruitment of personnel, payroll and related functions, time cards, leave (sick time, vacation time, etc.), resignations, retirement plan, Blue Cross-Blue Shield, Workmen's Compensation.

4. *Dietary*.

5. *Laundry*.

ORGANIZATIONAL CHART

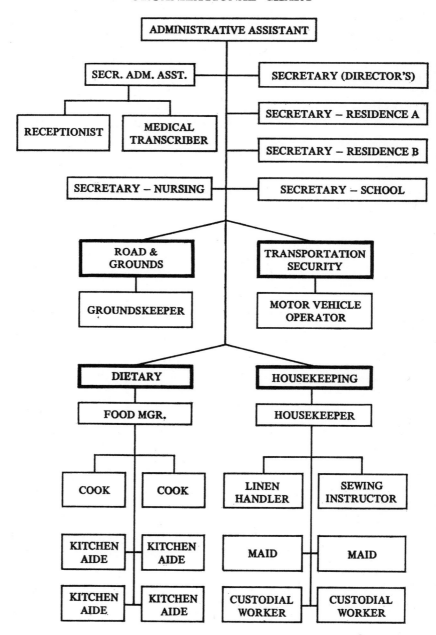

6. *Engineering*— (grounds, building repairs, new construction or remodeling, power house, etc.).

7. *Housekeeping.*

8. *Security*— (fire protection, traffic control, night watch patrol).

9. *Post Office.*

10. *Telephone Service.*

11. *Transportation of Patients.*

12. *Steno Pool.*

13. *Duplication.*

14. *Medical Records, Archives and Professional Library.*

15. *Budget Preparation, Fiscal and Federal Grants.*

16. *Supervision* of receptionist, secretarial and clerical staff.

17. *Admissions*—Financial arrangement with the parents for child's care and treatment.

18. *Coordinator of Volunteer Services.*

The coordination of certain activities and programs among the various services of the center is another important aspect of the administrative assistant's responsibilities. Included in his administrative duties and functions are the following:

1. *Work orders.* Adequate control and follow-up of all work orders submitted to the maintenance department to insure that the work is being accomplished. Any work which can be done through the industrial therapy program of the adjunctive therapies service of the center is planned and coordinated through the administrative assistant.

2. *General stores requisitions.* Each service of the center forwards to the administrative assistant a general stores requisition (expendable items). He orders requested items with particular attention to the need of the item and current existing inventory of the item.

3. *Physical inventory.* The physical inventory (chairs, desks, etc.) of the center is inspected periodically to insure that it is in good repair.

4. *Secretarial and clerical staff meetings.* The administrative assistant plans and schedules meetings of all secretarial and clerical staff of the center in order to discuss such issues as current

administration projects requiring additional typing, new procedures or policies affecting clerical responsibilities and ideas or suggestions which will add to clerical efficiency, and other relative issues pertaining to the proper functioning of the center.

5. *Provisions for clerical staff replacement.* The administrative assistant arranges the work schedule of all clerical staff in such a way as to insure that each clerical position will have a clerical staff member available as "replacement." This "replacement" is required to familiarize herself with the general operation of a service and be held responsible for the clerical operation of the service in the event of illness or vacation of the regularly assigned clerical staff member.

SECRETARY TO ADMINISTRATIVE ASSISTANT

The secretary to the administrative assistant is directly responsible to him for carrying out the following duties:

Supervises medical transcriber and receptionist

Evaluates work and proof reads all typing done by medical transcriber and receptionist

Substitutes for medical transcriber and receptionist (illness, vacation)

Receives and sorts incoming mail

Answers telephone and takes messages

Acknowledges receipt of letters

Posts material on bulletin board

Uses Xerox® machine

Distributes miscellaneous typing

Does payroll for the center

Keeps attendance, computes checks

Calls nursing service twice a day for information on attendance

Keeps record on monthly promotions

Informs supervisor when ratings and raises are due

Compiles all necessary data when employee enters or leaves

Completes necessary information on insurance forms

Prepares social security forms on new patients

Checks in and distributes supplies to services

The Secretary maintains a file of

All personnel
Correspondence
Memos
Personnel actions
Job specifications
Equipment transfers
Purchase orders
General supply requisitions
Workmen's Compensation
Insurance forms
Slot numbers
Payroll timesheets

Unit timesheets
Budget
Federal grant
Admissions and discharges
Day sheets
Leave of absence slips
Yearly timecards
Incident reports
Work orders
Monthly report
Annual report
Volunteer services

The Secretary's typing includes

Letters of reference
Memos
Personnel actions
General information on
   insurance forms
Payroll sheets
Unit timesheets
Yearly timecards
Work orders

Monthly report
Annual report
Volunteer services report
Letters of thanks to volunteers
Sign-in sheets
General supply requisitions
Purchase requisitions
All related work of
   administrative assistant

MEDICAL TRANSCRIBER

The medical transcriber is directly responsible to the administrative assistant and is supervised through the secretary to the administrative assistant for carrying out the following duties:

Transcribing-Typing

Transcribes dictation for center
Types drafts that have been transcribed into final form
Does other typing
Keeps daily record of typing completed

Medical Records

Prepares medical record for newly admitted children
Files clinical and other reports and notes in medical record

Maintains medical records in order

Keeps daily log on records removed and returned to Medical Records Library

Reports to administrative assistant any overdue medical record

Maintains accurate daily count of all medical records for present and discharged children

Prepares monthly list of admissions and discharges

Arranges for a child's photograph to be included in medical records

Archives

Maintains properly organized archive sections on all services and departments

Receives all clinical and administrative papers, reports, notes, etc., not in use from all services

Places all material in each section assigned to service or department

Reports to the administrative assistant any removal of material from the archives.

RECEPTIONIST

The receptionist is directly responsible to the administrative assistant and is supervised through the secretary to administrative assistant for carrying out the following duties:

Reception Room

Maintains order in the reception room

Observes activity in the parking area

Is responsible for opening the safe

Receives visitors, parents, new admissions, children for their scheduled appointments

Signs outgoing children's passes (psychotherapy, etc.)

Occupies young children when their parents are in session

Talks to children when waiting for their appointment

Asks visitors to sign the visitor's book

Asks parents to sign responsibility book before taking child for off-grounds pass

Directs personnel to facilities on the campus

Reports children in unauthorized areas.

Telephone

Reports children in unauthorized areas.

Takes messages if person is not available at time of call

Informs psychotherapist when child arrives for appointment

Calls residence or school or A.T. (adjunctive therapy) if child has not shown up for his appointment or left the administration building very upset.

Filing-Typing

Maintains file of day sheets

Keeps psychotherapy attendance chart up to date

Types and distributes daily bulletin

Types miscellaneous material given only by her supervisor.

Professional Library

The Receptionist is a member of the Professional Library Committee; she

Keeps a list of new books and donated books

Stamps all professional journals

Orders books and journals (after authorization from director of education)

Lacquers all books

Attends and maintains center's scrapbook

Maintains a file on authors, books, journals, pamphlets

Maintains a file on purchase orders

Checks outgoing and incoming books

Contacts personnel with overdue books

Reports personnel with overdue books to director of education

Conducts inventory twice yearly

Types the yearly report.

PERSONNEL POLICIES
Recruitment of Staff

1. The directors of services are basically responsible for recruiting their staff members. However, they are helped by other staff in regards to referrals and recommendations.

2. The applications and reference documents are submitted to the administrative assistant for clearance on qualifications and reference checks.

3. All candidates for employment may have an appointment with the director of the center. Final decision is made with the three persons involved (director of service, administrative assistant, and director of the center). The director of service communicates the decision to the prospective employee.

4. Any prospective students or trainees before being accepted are interviewed by the assistant director (director of education).

Professional Staff's Time Schedule

A usual weekly schedule is kept by every professional staff member to keep track of his time spent daily. The purpose of such a policy is for improvement of job performance and statistical purposes. Forms are available at the office of the directors of services.

Staff Performance Evaluation

Each staff member's performance is evaluated at least annually and rated either unsatisfactory, conditional, satisfactory, above satisfactory or outstanding.

The purpose of periodic staff rating is:

1. To improve job performance.

2. To afford the administration an opportunity to make known to staff the objective of the center and explain what is expected of them in this regard.

3. To indicate the need for disciplinary actions.

Each staff member is rated by his immediate supervisor and all ratings are reviewed and approved by the director of the center. The results are furnished the staff member by his supervisor after the rating has been finalized at all levels.

The staff member is required to acknowledge with his signature receipt of the rating even though he may not agree with it. However, each staff member is afforded an opportunity to make written comments on the rating form.

The administrative assistant or the supervisor furnishes the staff member with a copy after it has been reviewed and approved by the director of service and the director of the center.

The administrative assistant holds periodic orientation sessions for supervisors to train them in the techniques of a uniform and effective staff performance evaluation program.

Staff's Relations with News Media

Any staff member who is called to give information on the center is alerted to the following:

1. He should write down the inquirer's name, who he works for, his questions, etc.

2. He should know that there is no law saying he has to talk to newsmen and that there are circumstances in which it is perfectly justifiable to refuse to talk to newsmen.

3. He is simply not the man best qualified to discuss a particular subject.

4. He cannot stop the reporter from going after a story. In most cases the reporter has an assignment which he must complete.

5. As a matter of good press relations and plain courtesy, he should always give a polite and reasonable explanation for refusing to divulge information or grant an interview.

6. He should not make statements he would not want quoted.

7. He should assure the reporter that he or someone else will get back to him as soon as possible.

8. He should discuss the call with his supervisor, who in turn should refer the call to the director of the center for the purpose of securing coordination of action.

MEDICAL RECORDS LIBRARY AND ARCHIVES

The medical records provide a method of integration, a tool in supervision, and a documentary account of the service given to each child.

The contents of the medical records are confidential, "privileged" materials. Thus, at the center every effort is made to prevent disclosure of information acquired by the staff. Medical records, therefore, are not made available to any person other than the attending psychiatrist and staff members who are directly concerned with the treatment of the child. The psychiatrist may disclose a portion of the record to other personnel where this knowledge is necessary and desirable in treatment planning and implementation.

Therefore, the center establishes policies and procedures to

organize the medical records library by providing for a person responsible for the medical records, and a special room where medical records are kept in locked files

devise an appropriate system of filing

establish rules and regulations governing the use of the medical records.

Policies-Procedures

The child's medical record is the responsibility of the psychiatrist to whom the child has been assigned. The administrative assistant and the medical records librarian share this responsibility.

The medical records librarian is directly responsible to the administrative assistant for the enforcement of the following.

The medical records library is open from 8:00 AM until 4:15 PM daily except weekends and holidays. No medical records are checked out after 4:15 PM. No one is permitted in the medical records library during closing hours except in an emergency when access becomes the responsibility of the officer of the day (O.D.).

No medical record is taken out of the administration building, and no medical record is removed from the grounds of the center. Confidentiality is stressed to all staff members when using medical records.

Only the medical records librarian, or designated substitute, removes records and returns them to the files.

No reports are removed from the medical records at any time, by anyone other than the medical records librarian or her designated substitute. Materials needed for duplication purposes are pulled by the medical records librarian. The material is returned as soon as duplication is completed.

A notation of the medical records checked out is kept with the date, name of child, the name of the person taking the records, time out and time in. A medical record is not kept for more than eight hours.

Only authorized personnel are allowed to check out medical records. Authorized personnel are psychiatrists, social workers, psychologists, administrative assistant, and the secretary to the director of the center. Other staff members of the center who are directly involved with the treatment of a child may study in the presence of the medical records librarian.

Unauthorized personnel of the center are not permitted to check out medical records either for themselves or for anyone else without a written permission from the director of the center.

The Office of Administrative Assistant notifies the medical records librarian when an employee is hired who has a member of his family or relative in treatment at the center.

The medical records library is locked with a special key which is kept by the administrative assistant.

All medical records are kept in locked files in the medical records library.

Filing Procedures

Filing is the responsibility of the medical records librarian.

All correspondence to or from the center, reports from other agencies and physicians stapled to cover letters, parents' or legal guardian's agreement, application for admission, discharge form, financial statement, authorization for treatment and face sheet are filed on the left of the record. The application is filed at the bottom and the face sheet is always on top.

All other filing material (except resident chart material) is filed in date order on the right of the record with two exceptions: (1) laboratory slips are taped to a laboratory sheet and filed at the bottom; (2) pictures, if any, are stapled to card stock paper and filed directly on top of laboratory sheet.

Residence material is filed in date order in a separate folder from the clinical filing. It includes nursing notes, TPR's, doctor's orders, progress notes, weight charts, home visit permits, clothing cards, etc.

Clinical reports, copies of letters, etc. in which corrections in handwriting have been made, are returned to the responsible staff member for review, retyping and signature.

Archives

The archives of the center are kept in specially designated sections in the medical records library. Each director of service is responsible for the selection and placement of files of all unused reports, notes, daily bulletins, rough draft copies of papers, etc.

The medical records librarian is responsible for the supervision of the archives sections and reports to the administrative assistant any staff member who removes material from the archives sections.

Directors of services are permitted to remove archives material from their own sections, only after written permission from the director of the center.

PROFESSIONAL LIBRARY

In order to place in proper perspective the value of the professional library and its role in the development of an atmosphere of learning at the center, the following policies and procedures are established.

The professional library functions administratively under the Office of the Administrative Assistant. The medical records librarian is responsible for the coordination of all activities of the professional library. She always utilizes the consultative services of the director of education and research.

Procedures

GENERAL BORROWING OF BOOKS. Books may be checked out of the library for a two-week period, except those in popular demand which will be checked out for a one-week period. Certain books and references are kept in the library, and they are not to be borrowed or removed from the library.

OVERDUE BOOKS. An overdue notice is sent if the book is kept beyond the due date. If the book is not returned, library privileges are withheld for a three-month period and payment collected for the book. The charge will be double or triple the price of the book if it is out of print or difficult to obtain.

INDEFINITE LOAN. Only books which are used frequently or regularly are borrowed on the indefinite loan plan and are signed for by the individual. Approximately every four months the librarian sends a list of books on indefinite loan to the individual asking for a review of the books. Those not in use are returned to the library. Directors of services may request a re-evaluation of classroom textbooks or work books to see if they should be reclassified as equipment rather than library material.

INTER-LIBRARY LOAN. Requests for material not in the center are handled through the librarian (Administrative Assistant's Office) who requests the material from other libraries where it can be obtained. The librarian notifies the individual when the material is available and to pick it up at the library. Individuals are notified if the material is not available.

BOOK INVENTORY. An inventory is periodically made of the existing books in the library. Copies are sent to the directors of services and the director of the center.

NEW BOOKS. The name and author of new books arriving in the library is posted in the daily bulletin. The librarian keeps a list of books and journals which are requested and are not available at the center library so that a record may be kept of books which are most frequently in demand and should be purchased for the library (submit title, publisher, year of publication and price).

The librarian also keeps a list of books requested which are on indefinite loan so that if there are frequent requests for a book, a second copy be considered for purchase for use in the library.

JOURNALS. These are circulated among directors of services for discussion with the staff to consider which articles might be of interest to the center's personnel. Staff members who do read useful articles are encouraged to send the name and location of the articles to the librarian and also to describe, in one sentence, the nature of the article. These brief abstracts are published in the daily bulletin.

PAMPHLETS. The librarian properly files all pamphlets and reprints of interesting articles related to the mental health field.

VOLUNTEER SERVICES

Objectives

To assist the center's staff in defining their special needs for volunteers and goods.

To develop and marshal available community resources for the betterment of the care and treatment of the children at the center.

To develop community understanding of the center's objectives, available services and methods of treatment.

To plan, develop and utilize the services and material goods which are voluntarily offered to the center by the community.

Attitudes Toward Volunteers

The volunteer program is viewed as a potent and valuable public relations service. Volunteers are welcomed into the milieu of the center for the purpose of enriching the clinical programs.

The staff assumes the obligation of providing volunteers with necessary instructions, equipment and supervision to perform their assigned tasks properly.

For a volunteer to be of real help, he must be ready to work in a manner and in an area that is prescribed. Volunteers are not replacements of paid employees.

Procedures

Services and material goods that the community has to offer are accepted by the volunteer services if they will benefit the children. The staff does not feel obligated to accept whatever is offered nor is it felt that the community is obligated to offer whatever volunteer services or items are needed.

All inquiries for volunteer services and donated items to the center are referred to the Office of the Administrative Assistant of the center.

Staff members of the center assist the office of the Administrative Assistant in the recruiting of the volunteers and on the acceptance or rejection of donated items.

The directors of the services keep a monthly list of volunteers' inquiries and items received from the Office of Administrative Assistant.

The administrative assistant submits to the director of the center a monthly list of (a) the names of volunteers and addresses, (b) the donated items received.

A letter of appreciation is written by the administrative assistant and sent to the person or organization which offered its services or items to the center. The social worker-coordinator of the Visiting Parents Program keeps in close contact with the administrative assistant.

SECTION C

METHODS OF INTEGRATION

THE PHILOSOPHY OF THE CENTER is that treatment and education is effected through the total experience of the child in residence or in the day treatment program. Various methods have been devised to integrate scheduled activities, educational experiences, psychotherapies and relationships into a total plan of treatment. These include the advisory council, the psychotherapy board, the various committees, the communication system, the formal group and individual conferences, and meetings and informal meetings.

ADVISORY COUNCIL-PSYCHOTHERAPY BOARD COMMITTEES

1. *Admissions Committee*   weekly
    Members: Psychiatrist (Chairman)
    Director of Psychology Service
    Director of Social Work Service
    School Principal
    Coordinator of Child Study Unit
2. *Psychotherapy Board*   twice a month
    Members: Psychiatrist (Chairman)
    Director of Social Work Service
    Director of Psychology Service
3. *Education and Research Committee*   twice a month
    Members: Director of Education (Chairman)
    Director of Psychology Service
    Director of Social Work Service
    School Principal
    Director of Nursing Service
    Director of Adjunctive Therapy Service
    Coordinator In-service Nursing Training

4. *Advisory Council*   once a month
    Members: Psychiatrists
          Directors of Services
5. *Committee on Playrooms and Toys*   once a month
    Members: Director of Nursing Service (Chairman)
          Administrative Assistant
          Psychiatrists
          Director of Psychology Service
          Director of Social Work Service
6. *Visiting Friends Program Committee*   once a month
    Members: Director of Social Work Service (Chairman)
          Social Worker in Charge
          Psychiatrists
          Director of Nursing Service
          Administrative Assistant

ADVISORY COUNCIL

The advisory council is composed of directors from the eight services and one department: administrative assistant, child study unit (admissions office), psychiatry, psychology, social work, education, adjunctive therapy, nursing.

Not all members of any service participate in the advisory council. Recommended staff members are invited to participate in the advisory council whenever their special knowledge and skill on a subject under discussion is recognized.

The chairman, vice-chairman and secretary of the advisory council are elected every year. They constitute the executive or "steering" committee which meets separately each week and prepares the agenda for the full council meeting.

The members of the council meet regularly at a specific time and conduct their business whenever a quorum of one half of the members or more, is present.

The council shares responsibility with the director of the center for formulating all operating policies and procedures, approving all programs, new and old, proposing innovations and disapproving others. It carries its share of these responsibilities by (a) becoming informed about the existing programs of the center and their interrelationships and (b) making recommendations to the director not only on questions brought to it by the various members but also questions which it discovers on its own initiative.

Recommendations of the advisory council are presented to the director of the center who may favorably accept them or return them to the advisory council for further study and reconsideration.

COMMUNICATION SYSTEM

1. *Telephone.* All services and individual offices have a telephone which is connected directly to the central switchboard or through the receptionist's desk. Collect calls are prohibited.

2. *Dictaphone.* There are several individual dictaphones available for use by key staff members. Also, there is central dictaphone service connected with the medical transcriber's desk (typing pool) in the Administrative Assistant's Office.

3. *Memos.* Memos are strongly discouraged in the center.

4. *Daily Bulletin.* The daily bulletin is the responsibility of the Administrative Assistant's Office. Staff members submit information to be announced through the daily bulletin to the receptionist by 3:00 PM.

5. *Reports (Monthly-annual).* The directors of services submit, by the first week of the month, the monthly report on their service for the previous month. For the uniformity of the monthly report, a form is available at the office of the director of the center. During the first two weeks of July, the directors of services submit the annual report on their service. Both monthly and annual reports are submitted to the office of the director of the center.

6. *Working Papers.* Periodically, professional staff members prepare working papers on administrative and clinical subjects of interest. These are submitted to the director of the center for approval and are distributed to the directors of services.

7. *Manual.* The center's manual (Part I and Part II) are assigned to each psychiatrist and each director of services, the co-

ordinator of child study unit, and the coordinator of in-service nursing training.

In addition, each residence nurse is assigned one copy of Part II of the manual. Removal of pages from the manual is not allowed, and persons assigned manuals are responsible for keeping them in good condition. Since the success of the entire program of the center is highly dependent upon the organizational and functional structure of the center, each staff member is encouraged to familiarize himself with the policies and procedures and the description of the programs.

Future revisions of the manual depend on suggested improvements from all staff members. These are reviewed by the advisory council and after the approval of the director of the center are forwarded to the person responsible for the manual. Any pages cancelled are forwarded to the secretary of the director of the center.

8. *Official Correspondence.* For the purpose of uniformity of correspondence in the center, it is necessary that all staff members follow the accepted pattern as outlined in forms that are available at the Director's office.

Any secretary receiving *incoming official correspondence* stamps the receiving date, preferably on the lower right hand corner of the cover letter which is initialed by the staff member who reads it. The envelope is always kept with the correspondence. All official correspondence is sent out with the initials of the director of the center on the carbon copy indicating his approval and with the signature of the individual writing the letter according to this example:

Sincerely yours,

. . . . M.D.

Director

. . . .

Name of Person who writes letter
Title of Person who writes letter

All correspondence to individual children assigned to a psychiatrist is sent out with the initials of the psychiatrist on the carbon copy indicating his approval and with the signature of the individual writing the letter according to this example:

Sincerely yours,

. . . . M.D.

. . . .
Name of Person who writes letter
Title of Person who writes letter

The office of the director of the center is always consulted in case the incoming and outgoing official correspondence refers to major issues effecting established policies and procedures.

9. *Recording.* All reports are typed on official forms which are available through the office of the administrative assistant. If forms are not available, reports are typed on plain white paper. For ease in differentiating among reports from the social work service, a yellow color of paper is used for social work reports.

For purposes of uniformity of recording and better communication, all reports are typed as follows:

RESIDENTIAL AND DAY TREATMENT CENTER
RESIDENCE A (OR B)

Child Name (last, first, middle)
Date: . . . .

or DAY TREATMENT PROGRAM
or PSYCHOLOGY SERVICE
or SOCIAL WORK SERVICE
or NURSING SERVICE
or SCHOOL SERVICE
or ADJUNCTIVE THERAPIES SERVICE
or ADMINISTRATIVE SERVICE
or PSYCHOTHERAPY SERVICE

Names of Reports—Number of Copies

MONTHLY REPORT	2 copies
ANNUAL REPORT	2 copies
ADMINISTRATIVE CONFERENCE	15 copies
ADVISORY COUNCIL CONFERENCE	10 copies
PSYCHIATRIC EVALUATION REPORT (for CSU)	2 copies

ADMISSION NOTE	2 copies
INITIAL DIAGNOSTIC AND APPRAISAL CONFERENCE	2 copies
PROGRESS DIAGNOSTIC AND APPRAISAL CONFERENCE	2 copies
FINAL DIAGNOSTIC AND APPRAISAL CONFERENCE	2 copies
PSYCHOLOGICAL EVALUATION REPORT	2 copies
EDUCATIONAL EVALUATION REPORT	2 copies
SOCIAL WORK REPORT (yellow)	1 copy
SCHOOL PROGRESS REPORT	2 copies
DISCHARGE NOTE	2 copies
INITIAL PSYCHOTHERAPY NOTE	2 copies
PROGRESS PSYCHOTHERAPY NOTE	2 copies
TRANSFER PSYCHOTHERAPY NOTE	2 copies
FINAL PSYCHOTHERAPY NOTE	1 copy
GROUP PSYCHOTHERAPY NOTE	2 copies
FAMILY THERAPY NOTE	1 copy

CONFERENCES—MEETINGS—SEMINARS

Achieving integration of the total treatment at the center is complicated by the number of children under intensive treatment and education and the large staff necessary to attend them continuously and effectively. Therefore, it is not possible to have certain conferences and meetings with full attendance.

Procedures established for coordinating the programs of all services and for integrating the various facets of treatment and education include formal group conferences (administrative conference, diagnostic and appraisal conference and interpretation conference) and group meetings (admission committee meeting, treatment team meeting, advisory council meeting and education and research committee meeting).

In addition to the formal group conferences and meetings, a rather extensive schedule of individual conferences and meetings among the members of the various services has been set up in the attempt to effect more time-saving staff integration. These individual conferences and meetings are used on a regular basis, i.e. individual psychotherapy supervisory conference, and also when the need arises, for getting information quickly to the various people concerned with a child when it will be helpful in their handling of him.

Considerable importance is attached to the value of frequent informal meetings involving all staff members, as there are many opportunities for staff to talk informally about the children and their management. These seem to offer valuable means of integration.

Administrative Conference

The administrative conference is used to unify the various parts of the program. Through this conference the director and those responsible for different types of treatment and education keep each other informed of what is happening in their services and obtain better understanding of each other's problems and viewpoints.

This conference also provides an opportunity for the director to interpret administrative policies and the reasons for them.

The administrative conference is scheduled for one hour weekly and attendance is limited to the psychiatrists, directors of services, and coordinators of the child study unit and in-service nursing training. The secretary of the director of the center keeps the minutes of the conference, types the conference notes and forwards a copy to each member.

Diagnostic and Appraisal Conference

The children admitted to the center have often been discussed primarily in terms of unmet needs. They have been ousted from public schools and rejected by the neighborhood and community. Many of these children have so baffled the ordinary attempts of psychiatric treatment that their diagnoses have been relegated to the catch-all nosological wastebasket. They are labeled with functional disorders, hyperkinetic reactions, unsocialized aggressive reactions, withdrawing reactions, runaway reactions, and other obscure and nonverifiable behavior disorders.

Starting with admission, and after the initial orientation in the residence, each child is introduced to the preparatory program. For a period of three weeks, he is not enrolled in prescribed activities. During this time, he is regularly seen by the psychiatrist in charge of coordinating the various facets of the diagnostic evaluation.

A week or so after admission, as the child has more or less adjusted to the new environment, he is referred by his psychiatrist for psychological, educational and adjunctive therapy testing. Although he is participating in the preparatory program, he is often accompanied to individual scheduled appointments and is interviewed by the diagnostic evaluation team members.

As the third week after admission approaches, and depending on the child's progress of adjustment, he is sent unaccompanied to the school and adjunctive therapy activities where he is gradually exposed to structured class environment.

Although the focus of the diagnostic evaluation is on the child, he is studied as an integral part of his family. His ability to function, adjust and progress are considered in relation to his parents. Thus, the social worker, adhering to the basic premise that the physical separation of the child from his parents does not alter the fact that the unit must be treated as two parts of the same problem, conducts a series of regularly scheduled interviews with the child's parents or legal guardians.

In general, the Diagnostic and Appraisal (D&A) Conferences take place twice weekly (Tuesday and Thursday for Residence A, Monday and Thursday for Residence B). They are scheduled for one and one-half hours and are so timed that both the day and evening shifts of the nursing staff can attend. They are presided over by the psychiatrist, and attendance is limited to the professional staff of the center who have contributed to the evaluation and treatment of the child and to the staff who will be working with the child. Any other professional person who has worked with the child before admission to residence or who may work with him after he leaves is invited to attend the conference. I feel that the widespread practice of having all staff members attend this conference needs re-evaluation because I believe that its importance as a teaching device is overrated except in the case of students.

During the D&A conference, only one child is discussed. The child is not brought into the conference, as the staff does not subscribe to the opinion of those who claim important gains from such demonstrations.

Before the conference, the team members prepare their formal summary reports (the original copy of the D&A report is filed in the child's medical record and the second copy remains in the service file). The treatment team member (in his absence, a staff member representing the service which has worked with the child) reads the summary report. Thus, the social worker who is working with the child's parents reviews the background material, including the developmental history of the child's problems; his behavior before admission, at home and in school; and his adjustment with other children. The social worker also describes the family situation, including the relationship of the mother and the father to their parents, to the marital partner, to their other children and to the child under consideration. The personality makeup of each is described and the trend of the casework interviews.

The psychologist summarizes and evaluates all psychological tests the child has received, including those before admission. The school principal summarizes the educational tests and the child's school adjustment and achievement. The adjunctive therapist describes the child's choice of activities and his response to them.

When the child was admitted to the residence, a new factor entered into the picture, namely his relations with the nursing staff who care for him. Therefore, the residence nurse or the child's group worker reports on the child's physical and mental status, his ability in interpersonal relationships, and his day-by-day adjustment in residence.

The child's psychiatrist reports on his interviews with the child, on significant findings on admission or in subsequent examinations, including clinical laboratory work. He makes an evaluation of the problem and gives his own diagnostic impression. When all material has been given, the psychiatrist initiates a discussion on the dynamics of the child's illness, diagnosis and needs of treatment from a psychiatric point of view rather than what residence contributes in treatment. This discussion also covers highlights and recommendations.

The psychiatrist usually concludes the conference and either confirms the diagnosis made or suggests an alternative one. He summarizes the final recommendations which may include continuation of residential treatment, day treatment or return to a community outpatient service, or inpatient treatment in another institution. After the conference, the psychiatrist prepares a formal D&A summary report, the original copy of which is filed in the child's medical record and the second copy is forwarded by the medical records office to the residence chart.

Even though D&As provide an opportunity for discussions on significant divergence of diagnostic opinions and of treatment recommendations among professional staff members, every effort is made to avoid verbalizations resembling college campus debate. With staff members insufficiently secure to participate in these discussions, any negative criticism or discussion of personal feelings is taken up in individual conferences.

INITIAL DIAGNOSTIC AND APPRAISAL CONFERENCE. At the end of the three weeks after admission, the Initial Diagnostic and Appraisal Conference is scheduled for the child. The object of the Initial D&A conference is to

—diagnose the child and discuss aspects of differential diagnosis.

—determine whether the child will benefit from residential or other kinds of treatment.

—reconsider additional evaluation studies if needed.

—begin the plan of treatment.

—provide a blueprint for the entire staff regarding their roles in the treatment plan.

—outline the direction the social worker should take in her interviews with the parents and how to coordinate casework or family therapy with the child's treatment in residence.

—outline the direction the schoolteachers, psychotherapists, adjunctive therapists, and nursing staff should take in their treatment and education efforts with the child.

—project the need for a change in the direction of treatment.

—prognosticate the possible trend of treatment and the child's and parents' reactions to it.

—project the frequency of periodic reappraisal of the child's and parents' progress.

—project discharge plans according to the parents' and child's readiness.

PROGRESS DIAGNOSTIC AND APPRAISAL CONFERENCE. During the last week of the month, the child's psychiatrist, in collaboration with the members of the treatment team, prepares a list of eight children who are due for D&A conferences the following month. This list is given to his secretary and is communicated to the staff through the daily bulletin.

The Progress D&A conference for each child takes place at least every three months and, in some instances, monthly. Although the aim of the staff is to have the cases reviewed every three months, it is both the needs of the child and of the staff which determines whether conferences will be more frequent.

During the Progress Diagnostic and Appraisal Conference, the same procedures are followed as those of the Initial Conference. In addition, psychotherapy progress reports are given by the child's individual and group psychotherapist as well as by the family therapist.

The object of the Progress Diagnostic and Appraisal Conference is to reappraise

the treatment goals

the child's and parents' progress

the probability of the child's being able to benefit from further treatment at the center

the need for a change in the direction of treatment (refocus of treatment)

the help each staff member needs as to how he shall proceed both with his own responsibilities for the child and in relation to the other areas of treatment

the readiness for the child's return to home, school and community.

Interpretation Conference

The Interpretation Conference is considered as an integral part of the diagnostic and treatment efforts.

After each Diagnostic and Appraisal Conference, the social worker, in collaboration with the psychiatrist, arranges an interpretation conference with the parents or legal guardians. Other staff members may be included whenever this is deemed advisable by the child's psychiatrist.

The diagnostic findings and recommendations of the professional staff are presented in such a way that the parents are able to understand and weigh their questions. When agencies are involved, the same is valid. The parents may be "led" to do most of the verbalizing and arrive at most of the "answers" of their own or the information might be presented in a somewhat academic factual fashion.

At the end of the Interpretation Conference and after the departure of the child's psychiatrist, the social worker remains for a while with the parents to evaluate their reactions and answer other questions the parents may have "forgotten" to ask. The social worker includes in her "Progress Social Work Report" the highlights of the Interpretation Conference.

Treatment Team Meetings

Routinely on Mondays and Thursdays, a one-hour treatment team meeting is held in each residence. It is chaired by the psychiatrist and is attended only by staff working for the children of this residence (social workers, psychologist, adjunctive therapist, schoolteachers and nursing staff). Individual and group psychotherapists are encouraged to attend the meeting. Directors and coordinators of services are invited to attend the meeting; however, their role is that of a guest.

The meeting is usually conducted in an informal manner and no formal report is filed. Its unique function is to focus primarily around discussion of residence problems or management and administrative matters. Children who have presented particular problems are reviewed first to insure that those about whom the nursing staff are most concerned are covered.

Nursing staff may also bring up problems about other children and are encouraged to describe their behavior and comment on its apparent significance. They may also describe any problems parents have presented during visiting. These meetings afford an opportunity for staff to discuss their own personal interaction and feelings about the children and to suggest a tentative method of how they might be managed more effectively. From a careful detailing of the child's behavior and emotional reactions and the staff's reactions to the child, it is believed the following is made clear: (1) that the child's motivation is often made evident not only by observing all possible details but also by noting the feelings evoked; (2) that the nursing staff member is not only "the eyes and ears of the treatment team members and often their best assistant, but is often the only person who may be able to understand and deal effectively with the child's attitude at the moment; (3) that perhaps the most important clues as to treatment may become manifest in such incidents.

Discussion may also focus on the children's current behavior in school, adjunctive therapy and psychotherapy. The social worker may discuss the parents' response to casework and other related matters.

The psychiatrist makes suggestions as to how situations might have been managed differently. He may briefly review the other members' efforts, point up the dynamics of the child's behavior, and evaluate them with the present members of the team. He may also indicate and discuss errors of both omission and commission in the treatment and management efforts which include ways nursing staff can give more help to the children and any new direction the other team members should take in casework, education, adjunctive therapies and psychotherapies.

Intraservice Meeting

Each director of service conducts a weekly one-hour meeting with the staff members of that service. During this meeting, administrative and clinical matters pertaining to the techniques and the quality of the work of the service are discussed, as well as the relationships of the staff members to the treatment team members with regard to the application of their work to a particular child.

Special Program Meetings

Group work program, preparatory program, "Visiting Friends" program.

Psychotherapy Seminar

The psychotherapy seminar takes place weekly and is led by a psychiatrist on a three-month rotating basis. The seminar's attendance is limited to the staff engaged in individual and group psychotherapy as well as in family therapy. Outsiders are not invited to psychotherapy seminars. The seminar is focused on techniques in psychotherapy.

Individual Supervisory Conference

Individual supervisory conferences are also seen as ways of better integrating the total treatment program.

These include:

supervision of psychotherapy
supervision of director of services by director of center
supervision of staff members by director of service

SECTION D

CHILD STUDY UNIT
(ADMISSIONS OFFICE)

THE PURPOSE OF THE CHILD STUDY UNIT is to receive all inquiries for information about the residential and day treatment services, the admission criteria, and basic procedures, and to coordinate procedures for the pre-evaluation, evaluation and postevaluation process on children who are considered for admission.

All inquiries for admissions to the residential and day treatment programs are processed through the Office of the Coordinator of the Child Study Unit. Any parent, legal guardian or professional in the fields of health, education or welfare can inquire about the services of the center.

COORDINATOR-DUTIES AND FUNCTIONS
(Also see "Procedures")

The coordinator of the Child Study Unit, with the active participation of the director of the center, the team members (psychiatrists, psychologists, social workers), and the school principal, is given the authority and responsibility to coordinate the pre-evaluation, evaluation and postevaluation processes for children referred for residential or day treatment. He reviews all ongoing evaluation charts, and if there has been no contact during a period of one month, he notifies the applicant that the case is being closed, with the explanation that an application can be resubmitted in the future if the basic criteria for admission are met.

The coordinator prepares the monthly and the annual report on the Child Study Unit's activities and submits it to the director of the center.

The coordinator also participates in the weekly administrative conference.

50

ADMISSIONS COMMITTEE

To insure that efficient and reliable administrative and clinical procedures be developed and adhered to in implementing the admission policies, the director appoints a committee which is known as the "Admissions Committee." It is composed of the psychiatrist-chairman, the coordinator of the Child Study Unit, the director of psychology, social worker and school principal. The committee members meet weekly at a specific time.

As final decision for the admission of children to the center rests with the director of the center, recommendations of the admissions committee are presented to the director of the center who may favorably accept them or return them to the committee for further study and reconsideration.

General Orientation

Considering the American Psychiatric Association DSM-II diagnostic criteria, approximately 40 percent of the children referred to a residential center are diagnosed as psychotic, 20 percent as severely neurotic and personality disordered and 30 percent as behaviorally disordered. The remaining are scattered among nonpsychotic organic syndromes.

My view, however, is that the above classification of children's disorders is inconsistent with current knowledge and confronts us with the minutae of overlapping diagnoses and inconsistency of socio-legal labels. I believe that the psychiatric diagnostic classification of children cannot be an abstraction, reduction or modification of established adult psychiatric formulation with regard to etiologic considerations of adult psychopathology. Thus, emotional disorders which have their onset and symptomatic manifestation during childhood years must be viewed within the parameters of a developmental scheme, as they are very different phenomena from the classical conceptualizations accommodating adult psychiatric disease.

It is true that the majority of referred children to residential treatment centers (RTCs) do have previous psychiatric workup. However, points of genetic, dynamic or diagnostic import are not sufficiently clarified by the time all the required referral material has arrived. Most of the referrals indicate that the child is "schizophrenic" or "borderline psychotic" and they "strongly recommend" that the child is in need of a residential treatment program.

In my experience, many professionals in the field, in spite of years of living and working with children, planning and administering varied children's treatment programs, referring and placing children, they still tend to parcel out children to institutions essentially on the basis of diagnostic labels that neither describe the child nor offer a sound prescriptive base for treatment. In their practice, they still concentrate more on those children likely to produce more positive results than on those which are a challenge to the members of the mental health team. Their responsibility for the mentally and socially disabled child is seldom clear, often decided by circumstance, diagnosis, or a social or legal label.

The admissions committee is often confronted with many differential diagnostic problems which can be solved if a screening process is available, that is, a diagnostic evaluation in person.

As a rule the recommendation that the child should be admitted into the residential or day treatment program is made after a very difficult decision, a decision which on the one hand admits that other treatment methods have failed or that the child must be removed from his usual living situation in order to be helped. On the other hand the decision suggests that the residential or day treatment can and will do better. Thus, a broad consideration of the recommendation for residential or day treatment is broken down into four complex and interlocking areas which lend themselves as criteria for the arriving at the decision for residential or day treatment: (1) the severity of the child's emotional problem, (2) the severity of the child's problem in terms of the family, (3) the severity of the child's problem in terms of his school performance, and (4) the severity of the child's problem in terms of the community.

In order to systematically evaluate all the above criteria during the admissions committee conferences, it is preferable to avoid labels which do not describe the child and his family in terms of their treatment needs. Instead, an effort should be made to use determining factors of common denominators of treatment and care programs applicable to a certain range of behavioral difficulties, psychiatric disorders and psychosocial needs. Also, an encouragement of simple definitions in operational terms is applied uniformly and systematically so that one can know what to recommend. In other words, the staff should try to work on a framework of comprehensive diagnosis, always considering an attempt at going beyond just a diagnostic label, e.g. etiological diagnosis when possible, differential diagnostic impressions, functional and educational diagnosis, diagnosis of associated medical and emotional findings, social diagnosis of the total family and of the community situation.

Admission Policies

The admission policies of the center are governed by provisions of the mental health statutes of the state (if the center is a state facility) or by the criteria established by the advisory council of the center. Final decision as to the admission of children to the center rests with the director of the center.

Eligibility for Admission to Residential Treatment Program

Children are admitted irrespective of race, religion, or social status. To be eligible for admission to the residential treatment program, a child must meet the following criteria:

1. He must be between six and twelve years of age.
2. He must be potentially capable of functioning within the normal range of intelligence.
3. He must be within normal physical range and without medical and neurological handicaps, such as blindness, deafness, juvenile diabetes. Those children with minimal defects which would not interfere in the treatment program will be considered.
4. He must be severely emotionally disturbed or acutely psychotic. Children with chronic psychosis, chronic brain damage, or primary sociopathic disturbance are excluded.

Eligibility for Admission to Day Treatment Program

To be eligible for admission to the day treatment program a child must meet the following criteria:

1. He must be between six and twelve years of age.

2. He must be unable to function adequately in the regular school environment.

3. He must be within normal physical range and without medical and neurological handicaps, such as blindness, deafness, juvenile diabetes. Those children with minimal defects which would not interfere in the treatment program will be considered.

4. He must not be chronically and/or severely psychotic, a severe acting out behavior problem, mentally retarded or drug addiction problem.

5. The parent or guardian must be able to provide daily transportation to and from the program.

The determining factor for admission is the child's diagnosis, his ability to be integrated into existing residential or day treatment groups, and his ability to function within the program on at least a minimal basis. Children admitted are assumed to have the capacity to use the psychiatric modalities, educational programs and the group experiences offered.

The date on which the child is admitted depends upon (a) the available beds, (b) the composition of the group in residence, (c) the distribution of clinical problems in the group. This distribution has been found to be of major importance in the total treatment program.

Suitability of children for residential or day treatment is also determined by the parents' potential for becoming involved in the child's treatment program and for working through their own problems to the extent that the child could sustain treatment again after returning home. The responsible parents, foster parents, or agencies must agree to take an active part in the treatment through visiting the child and participation in ongoing casework or family therapy as indicated. They must assume as many parental responsibilities as is possible during the child's treatment period. The center is not obligated to keep a child for treatment whose parents refuse to cooperate.

Procedures

Pre-evaluation Period

The inquirer usually contacts the coordinator of Child Study Unit (in his absence, the designated substitute) either by phone, letter or in person.

All staff members at the center are instructed to refer all inquiries to the Office of the Coordinator of Child Study Unit.

The coordinator fills out the preintake date sheet and makes a log of entry and chart folder (See Appendix A).

The coordinator advises the inquirer (by phone, letter or in person) on the residential and day treatment services of the center and on the criteria of eligibility. If the child does not qualify, the inquirer is so advised. He is still offered a data questionnaire if he requests it.

When eligibility is established, the coordinator confers with the director of the center on the case and forwards to the parents or legal guardian the application form, brochures, data questionnaire, legal forms and authorization for release of information. When the inquirer appears in person, the coordinator takes the social history (See Appendices B, C, D, H).

The coordinator also requests that the parents ask all physicians who have examined the child or worked with him therapeutically to send a summary of their impressions and work with the child to the director of the center. The request includes loans of EEG, X-rays and reports of hospitalizations; physical, neurological, etc. examinations; psychological testing or other special tests such as hearing (See Appendices E, F, G).

Any material sent to the Child Study Unit by parents, physicians, hospitals, teachers, psychologists, institutions, and agencies is received by the Secretary of Child Study Unit, is stamped *date received,* and is presented to the coordinator of the Child Study Unit who initials and reviews it and presents it to the director of the center for advice.

The coordinator receives all pertinent data and checks for the child's photograph and physician's and parent's signatures. All pre-evaluation material for a given case is gathered in the Child Study Unit and remains here until the evaluation is completed.

Evaluation Period

When the application and other pertinent data is received, the coordinator acknowledges the receipt by a letter which is signed by him.

EVALUATION IN ABSENTIA. If it is decided that the case will be evaluated in absentia, the pertinent material is shared with the other members of the admissions committee for advice on the need of more or better information and on the recommendation for admission or no admission.

EVALUATION IN PERSON. If it is decided that the case will be evaluated in person, the coordinator forwards a letter to parents giving the date and time schedule for the one day or more of evaluation appointments. He asks for confirmation by phone or letter, and when confirmation is received he informs the members of the admissions committee of the date.

In the morning of the first evaluation day, the evaluation team members hold their conference in the psychiatrist's office. The case is briefly reviewed and the members meet the parents and child at the lobby and observe the family's interaction. The parents are seen by the social service and the child by the psychiatrist, followed by the psychologist and school principal.

Post-Evaluation Period

EVALUATION IN ABSENTIA. The coordinator notifies the parents of the admissions committee's recommendation and the director's decision as to admit or not to admit the child.

EVALUATION IN PERSON. Shortly after the initial evaluation, the members of the admissions committee hold their conference. At this time, they present their reports (psychiatric, social work, psychological test, educational test, special examinations, etc.).

Following the completion of the evaluation the psychiatrist assembles the material from all reports and prepares the case summary in which he includes the findings of the evaluation and recommendations.

The psychiatrist writes to the referring professional source (physician, juvenile court, etc.) and the coordinator to the parents or any interested agency, informing them of the evaluation findings and recommendations in such a way that will be most helpful to the child and to them.

Whether the child is accepted or not, any material gathered during the evaluation is kept in the Child Study Unit master file, except the loaned data which is returned after the evaluation.

If the child is accepted for admission, all data originating from the child study unit is transferred to the medical records library of the center. Date of admission is secured and the parents and agencies as well as the residential or day treatment team members are notified by the coordinator.

SHORT-TERM INPATIENT EVALUATION AND TREATMENT

Due to a number of requests made by parents and by community agencies for inpatient diagnostic evaluation and treatment, the center can develop a policy that a child who is in critical need can respond readily and can benefit from "short-term inpatient evaluation and treatment" be admitted to the center providing that all admission criteria for residential treatment are met.

The parents or legal guardians of such child are early advised that the child's stay in the center may be short; that emphasis would be more upon the immediate problem, for the purpose of diagnosing and determining needed treatment and helping the parents to mobilize their interests and abilities.

While in residence the child is exposed to all treatment and education programs which (it is hoped) will help him accept relative responsibility for himself. Evaluation, treatment and parental counseling are aimed at the specific problem—the crisis which caused the child's breakdown in good functioning.

Regular meetings are held with both parents, the child and the social worker. This is not to be construed as family therapy.

After a stay of two to three months the child may continue with inpatient or day treatment at the center or be discharged for further treatment on an outpatient basis in the community or be transferred or recommended to be transferred to a state institution.

CHILD PSYCHIATRIST-RESIDENCE CHIEF

T programs of treatment and care for all children assigned to
  HE PURPOSE OF THE RESIDENCE is to conduct the comprehensive
the residence within the framework of existing policies and procedures developed by the center and approved by the Director of
the Division of Mental Health (if it is a state facility) or the
advisory board.

Both residences function administratively and clinically under
the supervision of the child psychiatrist chief of the residence.

Residence chiefs are appointed by the recommendations of the
director of the center.

The residence chief enters the residence not as a visitor but as
the administrator and clinician in relation to management, supervision, treatment in residence, care of property and similar matters.

The duties of the residence chief include administrative, clinical and educational functions.

ADMINISTRATIVE

He is the official head of the residence and all staff assigned to
the residence for both internal and external functions. He is
charged with the administrative aspects of residential treatment
and care of all children in residence.

He is directly responsible to the director of the center for carrying out the following duties:

—Direct, coordinate and supervise the functional assignments
of staff members as related to their participation in programming within the residence.

—Plan the most effective utilization and maintenance of existing facilities within the center.

—Organize and preside in the meetings of various staff groupings inside and outside the residence relative to the program implementation.

—Communicate with the directors of services (psychology, social work, adjunctive therapy, school, etc.) and encourage the professional discipline representative assigned to the residence to do likewise.

—Share authority with the directors of services (psychology, social work, school, adjunctive therapy, etc.) for discipline assignments to his residence staff; for promotions, demotions, terminations; for coordination of vacations and time off; for performance evaluations; and for salary adjustments.

—Confer and collaborate with the chiefs of residence and day treatment program for the comprehensive integration of the treatment programs.

—Coordinate children's admissions and placements on the residence with the center's Child Study Unit (admissions office).

—Assist in the interpretation and re-evaluation of the center's policies, organization and procedures and prepare budgetary and other administrative requests.

—Submit to the director the monthly and the annual report on the administrative and clinical activities of the residence and recommendations for optional range of the residence's functions.

CLINICAL

—Participate in the preadmission evaluation and selection of patients for admission to the residential treatment program.

—Admit and complete the workup of a new patient.

—Preside at the Initial (and Progress) Diagnostic and Appraisal Conferences and the discharge planning as well as in the treatment team meetings.

—Share the responsibility for interpretation conferences with the parents.

—Prescribe appropriate medical and psychiatric treatment for children.

—Provide psychotherapy (individual, group, family).

—Supervise other psychotherapists.

—Participate in the selection of parents of the "Visiting Friends Program."

—Participate in the operations of the preparatory program.

EDUCATIONAL

—Confer and collaborate with the director of education in developing the education and training programs for professional and nonprofessional personnel of the center.

—Exert whatever effort is necessary to maintain a balance between the creation of new knowledge and the practical application of such knowledge to the delivery of services.

—Provide individualized and continuing education and training for the staff of the center.

—Provide education and training for members from various community mental health and education services.

Generally speaking, and in most instances, the above can be utilized as a guideline for both residence chiefs; however, consideration is given to the fact that each residence within the center is unique in its own right due primarily to the type of child for which they are responsible. Consequently, operational procedures need not be identical in both residences, but close similarity is advisable. To provide for flexible operation, residences can modify their procedures of operation, but only with the written approval of the director which will be given after consultation with all administrative and clinical staff of the center.

Both residence chiefs are responsible for keeping an up-to-date written statement of operational procedures as well as recommendations for maximum range of the residence's functions. A copy of this statement is filed with the director of the center.

THE PSYCHIATRIC TEAM
(Team Concept, Team Work, Team Failure)
Introduction

In various psychiatric treatment centers, the traditional team—psychiatrist, psychologist and social worker as primary supporting players—is still where it was a generation ago. However, it is still considered as essential to diagnosis and appraisal as it is to treatment; in some psychiatric services, particularly those for children, there have been additions to the traditional team, both at professional and sub-professional levels. We now have teachers, adjunctive therapists, nurses, group workers, child care workers and others, all together constituting the larger psychiatric team.

Even though in a general way, the teamwork goes well, I feel the need from time to time to review the team concept, its functional integration, and the causes of team disharmony and failure. In this manual, I am interested in illustrating the value of the team concept and team work and in promoting the understanding and efficiency of the psychiatric team.

As a point of embarkation I believe a good operating team must have a certain fluidity about it. Hence, the best of team operations may threaten its team members' sense of professional identification if the latter is too rigidly conceived. I also believe that the desire to remain within the limits of one's traditional professional orientation may at times hamper what a team can and should be doing. Granting that we cannot go merely on traditional definitions of a profession nor cast aside the very reason that we need multiple knowledge and skills from several professions, we try to solve the problems by agreeing that each team participant has authority and freedom to select and use his own therapeutic tools within the general framework of therapy prescribed by the center. This presupposes both that each member of the team has substantial knowledge of what each of the other members has to offer and that he understands and respects the limits of his own contributions.

In the center, the implementation of the treatment programs is based on dual and multiple controls and supervision of the staff; for example, the schoolteacher is responsible for the techniques and for the quality of schoolwork to the principal; but for the application of schoolwork to a particular child, the schoolteacher is responsible to the child's psychiatrist. The smooth operation of such an arrangement depends fundamentally upon general agreement as to purpose and methods, and secondarily upon clear and continued vertical and lateral communication.

The disturbed or mentally ill child frequently has come to us from a family in which the roles of authority have been ill-defined or erratic, where a pathological system of interaction between family members is commonplace and for whom doubts exist about how responsibilities develop.

I believe that confusion of roles among those who care for the mentally ill child fortify his traumatic experiences caused by the pathologic system of his family members' interaction. Also that a team's decision formulated and based on a model of majority rule, often creates a double bind for the child whose past experiences are so contradictory. It is often presumed that the child, as an infant, was subjected to a single authority who decided on eating schedules, bowel control and the time for sleep. However, when a decision as to the eating of an extra dessert was to be made, the child's mother did not tell the child she must put off the decision until she could confer with the father and siblings after which a decision would be rendered. And when he was in school, if he raised his hand for permission "to go," the teacher did not tell him he must wait until he had a vote from the other teachers and the students.

The center's primary commitment is to induce and maintain healthy change (or personality realignment: structural, characterological, or defensive rebuilding or whatever one chooses to name it) (1). The center is conceived as a set of component functions each of which strives toward its own legitimate goal at the same time as working to fulfill the overall goal of the therapeutic effectiveness. The ultimate beneficial effect on each child rests equally upon the effectiveness of every component modality applied by the staff representing these functions and upon the successful coordination of each with the other. An effort is made to place no limit either to the essential importance or to the development of the effectiveness of any component part. It is also recognized that while training and discipline reduces the possibility for error, human frailties are part of the system and must be accounted for in some open and systematic way (2).

I believe that psychiatric treatment is attained when we make it a goal in itself; it comes about only when several efforts are made by every treatment team member. By treatment I mean promoting efforts for physical and emotional growth as well as remedial efforts of which education is often paramount, including such modalities as remedial reading, speech therapy, occupational therapy, recreational therapy, and music therapy according to the special needs of the child. In the center the treatment programs do not subscribe to the claims of the therapeutic effectiveness of the "attitude therapy" and "behavior modification." Also, the center is not considered as "a place to hold the patient while he undergoes psychotherapy." Instead, the staff strongly believes in methods of regulating staff interaction.

The psychiatric and educational programs are based primarily on the principles of planned ego development. Because most of the staff members are psychodynamically oriented in their psychiatric education and training, they have the advantage of integrating the psychodynamic concepts and models into common sense thinking. By and large, they utilize psychodynamic concepts diagnostically and therapeutically in the rationale of the residential and day treatment, in the school and in the adjunctive therapies. In addition, the group work program, as part of the nursing service, focuses on the development of social skills and interpersonal relationships which in turn do influence intrapsychic process enhanced by individual and group psychotherapies.

The teams include people from various disciplines because it is recognized that the child is not merely a biological organism, not merely a psychic entity, not merely a concatenation of social variables, but rather that he is all of these and much more. In order to be understood, he has to be comprehended in terms of the interaction of a host of biological, psychological, social, and many other forces. The functional representatives in the center are the child psychiatrist, psychologist, social worker, schoolteacher, nurse, group worker, child care worker and adjunctive (occupational, recreational, industrial, music) therapist. Their formal communication is regulated by several types of meetings which are moderated by the child's psychiatrist and are attended by the majority of the nursing staff, teachers, adjunctive therapists, and the social worker, psychologist and psychotherapist involved with the same child. This involvement of many disciplines, however, presents problems of organizing these large groups of team participants for efficiency of action. The need for efficiency at times can cause the emergence of an authoritarian approach. In the treatment team, although there is an hierarchy of authority communication is free and open among the members of the team; this very pattern of communication seems to bring individuals closer together for purposes of concerted thinking and action as a team.

The structure of the psychiatric team is built upon the mutual appreciation by the individual team members of their different functions and skills and upon the fact that authoritative differences in function do not necessarily imply a fixed hierarchy of functions. Their relative importance varies as the focus of the team changes while it maintains its overall therapeutic goal. Thus, at times the function of the social worker will become crucial, while at others, for instance when a question of differential diagnosis must be settled, the psychologist's function or diagnostic testing may predominate.

Team Concept

The psychiatric team concept emerged out of the recognition that the patient is too complex to be fully understood through the eyes of a single discipline, let alone through the eyes of a single individual.

Human beings cooperate one with another on the assumption that they can accomplish collectively what they cannot separately. Small, organized groups of people with specific or limited goals are sometimes referred to as "teams." Some equate team with every member of the professional staff within a specific unit of the psychiatric setting. Others tend to term any combination of two or more people whose work in a psychiatric setting has a remote connection with that of others and is somehow related to patients as a psychiatric team. The word "team" has more recently been used to describe

1. a number of people associated together or a group of peo-

ple each completing one set of operations as part of a total project;

2. a group of professionally and scientifically trained people brought together for a common goal, namely understanding and treatment of a patient, with each individual of the team contributing uniquely from his own background of training and experience toward that common goal;

3. a vehicle for integrating multiple understandings for the benefit of the patient's treatment;

4. an educational seminar where the focus is on the conscious use of information rather than on transference phenomena.

Others, disillusioned and disappointed with the team prefer to call it

1. one of those mythical, multiheaded creatures which lurk everywhere in our imaginations under the generic name of teamus psychiatricus, or more commonly, "psychiatric team";

2. a group of people working together toward a common goal and against each other;

3. a distinct entity entirely apart from the individuals who comprise it.

I believe a psychiatric team is a group of various professional and nonprofessional individuals in the mental health field who share a common purpose, meet together to communicate, and share knowledge and individual opinions concerning patients from which decisions and plans are made for the present and projected therapeutic possibilities for the future.

I also believe that the decision as to which therapeutic action, by whom taken and when, follows the control pattern selected by the team leader; and that when the team is functioning in a medical facility the leadership rests with the physician.

Perhaps no concept in mental health activity is subject to more ambiguity and disagreement than is the concept of the team. In fact, there is little doubt in my mind that this very ambiguity of the concept may be playing a significant role in the central problem with which many are concerned, namely the failure to effectively integrate the team in psychiatric treatment centers.

I am aware that considerable lip service is given to the concept of "team approach" in psychiatric treatment centers, but I am equally aware that this has not become a guide to action in such centers and that the members of the "team" have themselves continued to perpetuate the myth that the team is functionally integrated, when in reality this is an objective yet to be realized. What is frequently realized is that many disciplines are represented in the treatment setting, but being housed together under the same roof does not in itself constitute a team.

I also see in the "treatment team" concept many of the problems of psychiatric fads. This concept makes many heroic assumptions that often obscure basic mental health problems. The patient does not necessarily benefit by having a single important person, whether a physician or child care worker, replaced by a faceless "group." More than that the team concept does not really take the authoritativeness of expertise into account. It submerges a good deal of this authoritativeness under "democratic" pretention and in that way pits the scientific content of psychiatric expertise against good intentions and a romantic social ideology. In the long run this can be destructive to the very values which the treatment team methods hope to maximize.

Another outgrowth of the treatment team concept is the development of subtle forms of competition within the team in which virtuosity with jargon becomes important. Exotic interpretations take place among the team members and most of these are ploys and counterploys in the game of professional competition. The jargon actually obstructs the common sense use of psychiatric systems.

Also, mental health professionals, particularly those in children's psychiatric treatment settings, tend to spend too much time diagnosing one another, analyzing the "pathology of their superiors' motives" and the "neurotic traits of their subordinates." Also, in some administrative human relations, there is the tendency to substitute unnecessary psychiatric attitudes for "horse sense."

Finally, a number of psychiatrically trained professionals tend to confuse "mental health" with the democratic attitude. Yet I know definitely that many nondemocratic cultures are psychiatrically quite well off. This attitude among professionals creates indiscriminate hostility to such a concept as "supervisory responsibility," notions that may seem "authoritarian" in tone. For opposite reasons, they uncritically embrace every "democratic" fad that comes along, e.g. equal rights amendment, mystique feminine, rap group. The "team concept" unfortunately has something of this fad quality about it.

With all its disadvantages, however, the team concept and teamwork may be the only way to reach certain goals if the concept, the role of the team members, and the potentialities for the team's disharmony can be clearly understood.

Team Leader

I believe that the teams are only as good as their leadership. To function adequately the leader must possess supervisory skills, technical knowledge of his own field, and awareness of contributions that other disciplines can make. He should be able to see to it that team meetings, when related to decisions about children, should be limited to discussions about those children where sufficient uncertainty and indecision about management and treatment warrant team decision making.

Who makes decisions? To say that the team is the decision-maker may at first seem too abstract. The decision involves the representatives of several treatment modalities: the psychiatrist; the social worker; the psychologist; the psychotherapist; the schoolteacher; the nursing staff; the occupational, recreational, music and industrial therapists respectively representing medicine-psychiatry, casework, psychology, psychotherapy, education, residential life, arts and crafts, recreation and music. Each representative must perform his function to the best of his skill and ability while at the same time giving careful thought of how his part contributes to a cohesive whole of thought and action. Thus, authority resides in the team because no one functional representative can decide alone and because each acts ultimately in the child's behalf. The team's authority can become chaotic without the respect for each other and loyalty to the team process.

Frequently, by "team supervision" is meant the supervision of individual professionals by the team leader when and only when that leader is also the physician-psychiatrist. I believe it is doubtful that an individual from one profession can supervise an individual from another profession without some blurring of professional identities. The danger in advocating team supervision is that it ultimately leads to no supervision. Directors of the involved professionals often feel that they will lose supervisory control over their people. Indeed, some of their people are accustomed to taking things directly to their directors or supervisors and resent having to deal with team members with less status. Others are lured into the error of bypassing their own professional hierarchy for that of the team. The team, however, is likely to be short-term goal oriented and is not apt to be concerned with the individual's professional development, particularly if this is not of the immediate concern to the team.

There are situations wherein formal and administrative authority remains with the supervisor of the individual profession while the informal authority is held by the team leader. The resultant danger is that an aggressive individual uses this bifurcation of authority to obtain independence of supervision from any source.

Teams are often conceptualized as democracies in miniature. Members of such teams will state that decisions are arrived at through the democratic process, i.e. after hearing all the possibilities, members of the team vote on a course of action. However, this notion of the majority determining a plan of action or treatment borders on the illogical, and possibly on a perversion of professional roles when carried into specific areas of treatment.

I have often encountered reference to the "team captain," in which the team seems analogous to the crew of a ship or the members of a sports organization. Captain or leader appears a poor choice of terms for whatever is meant by leadership of a team, since this use frequently carries a surplus meaning which includes a fixed hierarchy and patterns of interaction within this hierarchy.

All teams are dependent upon leadership for integration. In order for any team to function effectively, it must share responsibility in keeping with some plan for a physiological division of labor. It is important to recognize that the physician's medical responsibility to the patient has been established by law. The physician in the team is expected to be the leader and to have the privilege of delegation of authority, but not of responsibility. Leadership and responsibility have tended to become equated, with the result that all responsibility for the patient's welfare has been placed under the rubric of medicine. Thus, the phrase "delegation of responsibility" is often used to mean that the individuals constituting the team are given permission to assume responsibility for the performance of tasks that clearly were the responsibility of those professions in the first place. Such circularity has occurred because of confusion as to what constitutes medical responsibility to the patient.

There is distinction between authority as the legally and socially sanctioned power to make decisions, authoritativeness as the expertise necessary to make sound decisions, and authoritarianism as an arbitrary method of decision-making. Without leadership this distinction cannot be made and this would be tantamount to anarchy. The mental health team has traditionally been a "thinking" team, i.e. it is concerned with understanding and conceptionalizing the patient in terms of his problems, needs, conflicts, etc. and the implications of those for his treatment. This, of course, does not minimize the importance of the team in "doing," i.e. in treatment, but clearly the latter is based primarily on this "thinking through" process.

Team Members

Some psychiatric settings designate as a team member every person who has contact with patients. Others include in the team only persons who are the most important to the patient. I regard a team member as a person who is prepared to share his knowledge, values and philosophy with other members of the team, while at the same time he becomes cognizant of the knowledge, values and philosophy of other professions and displays a readiness to receive the contributions of others and the capacity to carry out decisions. Unless he assumes responsibility for defining his areas of responsibility, authority and competence, and unless he recognizes the responsibility, authority and competence of other team members, his designation as a team member is a myth.

Often a team member withdraws from full participation and falls back upon his own professional group to preserve the inflated notion of his own importance by sharing in his profession's narcissistic image of itself. In this way, he fails to acquire an appreciation for the skills and knowledge of other disciplines and thus loses much of his effectiveness as a cooperating member of the team.

Clearly the significance of the professional training and background must be reconciled with the evolving role of each team member. In my past experience it was far easier to let the phantasm of professional training interfere with team functioning than it was to utilize professional training properly. In the center the professional images of the psychiatrist, the nurse, the psychologist, the social worker, the schoolteacher, and the adjunctive therapist still have a charismatic as well as a rational-legal and traditional authority. However, unlike many psychiatric centers, the bulk of the authority for direct child care is given to the nursing personnel; it is from them that the child receives much of his help.

Obviously, it is imperative that the professionally trained staff share their knowledge, skills and responsibility effectively with the nursing personnel. The child care workers have an advantage in that they are not burdened with the rigidity or status quo consciousness which so often stems from the extensive professional training of some of their team colleagues. The psychiatrists make special effort to allow nursing personnel and all other team members to share their knowledge of children effectively with the entire team. By stressing the value of open communication and by being alert to phenomena symptomatic of blockades to communications, I believe that a therapeutic climate in the center is created.

Team Work Structure

Treating children in a psychiatric setting requires something akin to a team effort. The team members' efforts and functions for which they stand must somehow be coordinated. The coordination of all the essential but differing treatment modalities must be based on codified principles (2).

Some professionals in the child psychiatry field think of teamwork as doing something to the child; others think in terms of teamwork as ways of increasing collaboration between services; others think of temporary associations between professionals to provide services to a child that anyone of them singly could not do; others are sick and tired of hearing about the teamwork and would like to outlaw the term.

Sometimes in teamwork team members appear to exercise an extensive "blurring" of roles, i.e. they seem to have the same duties, make the same decisions, assume similar responsibilities, and, in general, function interchangeably within the team, regardless of their professional group and, to a large extent, of their background. In reality, by proper teamwork integration, this "blurring" of roles can be de-emphasized. A clear distribution of the lines of responsibility, when possible, according to the skills proper to each discipline, often proves to be more satisfactory to the staff and does not seem to be any less effective in the operation of the therapeutic milieu. Although at times there is overlapping in the functions of the different disciplines, an effort can be made to promote a certain degree of specialization according to disciplines or to individual talent or inclination.

One of the interprofessional relationships which is particularly involved with the team's function is that of the psychotherapist (psychologist, social worker, psychiatrist) who sees the child for definite appointments and of the child's psychiatrist who is responsible for his residential or day treatment and management. If ever there is a need for closely integrated teamwork it is between the functions of the psychotherapist and the child's psychiatrist. The failure of teamwork in this area is so apparent because it is one which is particularly sensitive even to minimal incoordination. The particular source of difficulty stems from the apparently contradictory functions expected from the psychologists and social workers. In the center they are, as psychotherapists, clinically subordinate to the child's psychiatrist who bears the medical responsibility for the child. Yet, in functioning as psychologists and social workers, they are certainly not professionally subordinate to the child's psychiatrist. They are in the position of playing a predominant role in the treatment of the child, but without the administrative responsibility for their work. This makes for a highly complex team structure which must be recognized in the formal arrangements among the team members.

The organizational hierarchy sees to it that maximum authority is vested at the various services and particularly the nursing staff which makes decisions and acts promptly in the course of their every day duties. This decentralized and delegated management authority to the treatment team seems to prevent demoralization and stagnation of the staff.

The center's organization is also designed to promote the assumption of responsibility by the child to whatever extent he can and to enlarge or decrease his area of responsibility as indicated. Each child is encouraged to accept whatever responsibilities he can, however small or however great, and to turn to another person whom he knows and trusts for help when he has reached the limit of his own resources. Thus, he may turn to another child, to a nurse, to a child care worker, a schoolteacher, a psychologist, a social worker or to his psychiatrist. This process allows for problem-solving and social learning at the time and in the place where the problem occurs, not at some scheduled or indefinite future time. Such immediacy frequently is of more value to a child with seriously restricted ego than the process in a didactic relationship child-therapist. In the latter, insight is more often the means of experiential learning rather than problem-solving, which is left to the child to work out in the extra-therapeutic situation. Thus, when the child reaches an impasse, however minor or great, he learns to consult with someone, another child or staff member on the team. Eventually the team leader may consult the directors of services or the director of the center for advice, counsel and assistance. The functions of the director and the directors of services are to encourage and guide, rather than to hamper by overvigilance or overrestriction of the team's initiative, creativity and therapeutic inventiveness.

The staff is able to give optimum help to such a large number of children by expanding its roles to capitalize on each child's functioning skills and assets. Each staff member contributes what he can, not what is prescribed out of some stereotyped, preconceived job description. It is expected that each person's contribution is from the self, not from his training alone. The contribution of the self is shaped and guided, I feel, by a person's training, whatever it may be. Formalized background is allowed to blend inseparably with the personal background, each mutually supporting the other to make the full, functioning team member.

An awareness of the structure of which the differences in function give rise to team disharmony can be used to define in some formal fashion the relations between the team members in their various roles and in terms of the various services which the team offers.

Unilateral actions are typical of settings in which the team structure is poorly understood, and they frequently create consequences which are far more harmful to the therapeutic purpose. While it is true that certain administrative arrangements are, in a sense, vehicles to convey and maintain or implement structure, they are not identical with what we mean by it. Team structure is a psychological rather than an administrative concept and basically refers to the feeling of the participants that they are working together and have assumed responsibilities toward each other for a common purpose. It would be a mistake, however, to confuse the administrative arrangements to implement structure with the structure itself. I strongly feel that administrative arrangements without recognition of the mutual responsibilities, or the structure which gives them meaning, might be psychologically destructive rather than helpful. It is the acceptance of structure which creates workable roles, not roles which create structure.

It is imperative, therefore, for the team members to be aware of the concept of structure and to show how it could be used. The individual team members need to re-evaluate their intrateam functioning when the lack of integration is made clear in supervisory conferences. The members are helped to see the extent to which they are making full professional use of each other and how the limited awareness of structure interferes with this. The well-known superficial politeness and professional "distance" which masks the lack of integration, gradually makes it clear that individual participants have not used each other effectively and have not been sufficiently aware of the professional functions and capabilities of their team members. An unmasking of the implicit structure the team has among its effects is the freeing of energy and a clarifying of functions which permit more constructive work than is previously possible.

Quite often unconscious processes with the team become the focal point of attention. It is true that unconscious determinants, e.g. transference, play a part in team relationships, but it is the responsibility of the supervisors or directors of the professions involved to provide ways of dealing with these phenomena. The structure, organization and modus operandi of the team can be so designed that these phenomena occur less frequently and with less intensity. It should be remembered that transference can be reduced if the team members are oriented to the need for conscious use of knowledge, values and philosophy; if all team members are free to contribute and their contributions are received by other members; if the team is not reified (reification of the team precipitates the development of transference phenomena, whereas the concept of the team as a short-term, goal oriented unit, discourages the development of such phenomena); and if keeping individual supervision in the hands of the supervisor of the individual's profession rather than in the hands of the team leader.

Team Disharmony (Friction-Rupture-Failure)

Morrow (2) observes that:

> In many instances when a decision has been made correctly, that is, in the best interests of the child (which may often include considera-

tion of the family), and when the team members have functioned within their roles and in obedience to the overriding goal of team coordination, the authority has rested in the team. . . . When the team process bogs down, when the members find themselves quite at cross purposes and having a more difficult time than usual in coming to a conclusion, several new insights of potential therapeutic benefit come into focus. If the representatives of two or more services see the child differently, this is the time to get together, to work harder to account for the apparent discrepancy. This disharmony in the team when scrutinized provides valuable insights. In the first place, it may reflect a subtle sign of discord and disharmony within the child himself. If so, and if we discover it, not only does a diagnostic but a treatment effect accrue. . . . When the team members can see the child as the only one who is setting them against each other, a serious mistake is made. . . . The team members' failure here to recognize the effect of their own differences on each other and their tendency to put it back on the child as his "fault" only serves to intensify the child's deep conviction of badness, of inadequacy, of defectiveness—all of which he has already had too much. The center makes efforts in setting firm and consistent limits on the child's behavior and inculcates in all staff a maximum anticipatory awareness of the difficulties the child is likely to get us and him into. To fail in these total efforts would confirm the child's sense of badness and destructiveness.

Team member and team process failure may result from an over- or under-estimation of an individual team member's part process. . . . Philosophical biases (which are not precisely reflections of an individual team member's failures) may interfere with team functioning.

Another factor is the psychotherapist himself who is out of step with the team process as at times he tends to lean over backwards in the opposite direction and fails to present strongly enough his opinion or diagnostic assessment. The same may apply with any other team members since they may feel they are nearer the bottom of the administrative or status ladder, likewise may tend to hold back an expression of their opinions.

Sometimes team members respond out of the fear of being left out of the diagnostic and treatment process and overstate their opinion. Others, intimate as they are with the child's daily life, they may also take too conservative a position in pointing out the child's "illness."

Having recognized the possibility for the team itself to generate disharmony, it becomes possible to visualize the solution for such a disharmony by adequately working together and by competent functions to bring about a net beneficial effect. In practice this is accomplished by utilizing four principles of team coordination:

a) Each team member must try to fulfill his particular function to his utmost ability. . . .

b) Each team member must be able to take information from another member's understanding and formulation in order to reach a fuller picture of his own concept of the child at the moment.

c) Full understanding is never gained without data from all significant areas.

d) This data must be integrated into a total formulation.

In conclusion, the helping efforts for the children in treatment definitely require more than one profession, one discipline, one function. A better integration of the team can bring about a better integration within an individual child. While we can never "force" this to happen . . . and while it is quite apparent that the healthy ego integration may not be reached for years in many children whom we wish to help, when we fail to recognize in our relations with each other, and when we fail to formulate accurately the particular nature of the split-plus-externalization of our patients, any nascent integrative capacity within him will have great difficulty in developing.

All of us who wish to help disturbed children are well trained not to be moralistic; but we are, in the best sense of the word, moralists. We are concerned and care about unhappy human beings; we have strong convictions regarding both our wish to help and how we might go about helping. We all know that it is a difficult enough task in the best of circumstances for a healthy child, and especially the early adolescent, to integrate drives and the demands of reality, to reconcile realistic urges and conscience, to sublimate libido and aggression to the task of learning, and to find acceptable outlets for libidinal urges. We cannot afford to make it more difficult for the emotionally disturbed or mentally ill child and for our charges.

ADMISSION
Preadmission

The decision as to which residence a child will be admitted to is made by the director of the center in collaboration with the psychiatrist-chief of Residence A or Residence B. The coordinator of the Child Study Unit informs the parents of the date and time of admission (preferably Tuesday at 10:00 AM). After this is confirmed, she notifies the psychiatrist, who in turn notifies the residence nurse.

The day before admission the residence nurse notifies the nursing staff and the children of the new admission. She also makes arrangements for the child's bedroom, sanitary routine and preparation of the residence chart. The coordinator of the Child

Study Unit during the morning residence staff meeting discusses pertinent information about the child to be admitted.

Admission

I believe that the way in which the child is admitted to the residence is one of the most significant events that will happen to him while he is in the center; also both parents and child are usually under the stress of disturbing preconceptions of "mental hospital." However, I also believe that in order to make the admission process more realistic there is no need to display infringing attitudes such as overcoercion, overindulgence and overunderstanding or to try forcefully to remove the parents' and the child's preconceptions about the "mental hospital."

The process of admission to residence is utilized to emphasize the interrelatedness of child and parents, and every effort is made to prevent psychological separation. Admission requirements include the parents' agreement to maintain a relationship with their child while he is in residence and to be responsible for any after-care plan when he leaves residence. I believe that it is the parents' interest and concern which motivates the treatment process and that a child becomes an active participant only after the parent has become involved in the plan.

Reception of Parents and Child

On the day of admission and at 9:30 AM the coordinator of the Child Study Unit meets briefly with the admitting psychiatrist and social worker to discuss any new developments on the case.

In case the parents and the child arrive earlier than the agreed time, the receptionist notifies the coordinator of Child Study Unit and the nurse who both meet the parents and keep them occupied until the time the psychiatrist and social worker are ready for the admission.

The coordinator introduces the psychiatrist and social worker to the parents and the child. Separation of the child from his parents takes place at this time.

The child remains with the psychiatrist, who either takes the child into his office or escorts the child to the residence while talking and orienting him or introducing him to some children (who usually are aware of the new admission and purposely wait around the water fountain outside of the recreation area to meet the newcomer).

The nurse escorts one parent (usually the mother) to the social work service conference room for the clothing check (clothing record # ..) and signing of the clothing inventory and agreement form. Following this the nurse guides the parent to the social worker's office to join the other parent and the social worker for the initial interview.

The social worker may arrange an appointment with the psychiatrist if the parents have requested it or if they have questions she feels the psychiatrist might answer.

Initial Interview with Parents

During the morning and afternoon initial interviews, the social worker tries in a general way to help the parents with feelings arising out of the child's admission, anxieties about emotional illness, and separation from the child. She does not focus on therapeutic interviews.

I believe that the initial interviews as a therapeutic experience have been overrated by self-styled omnipotent and omniscient, and personality-wise oversensitive and often insecure professionals in the child psychiatry field. In the center, the staff is usually concerned with the following:

1. helping the parents to determine their reasons for coming.

2. helping them clarify their expectations.

3. allowing them to accept or reject the services.

4. introducing them to the feeling tone of a treatment contact and relationship.

5. explaining the center's policies and procedures.

6. assisting them with the completion and signing of necessary forms (parents' legal agreement, general authorization and financial statement) (See Appendices I, J, K).

7. securing additional background and present illness information.

Child's Initial Orientation

While in the residence, the child is introduced to the nursing staff and other children. He is generally oriented to the physical surroundings and is supervised for a shower. He is also inspected for his general physical condition including bruises, eruptions and injuries. The staff listens to anything the child may say, but does not probe. The nurse (or charge aide) explains to him the regulations pertaining to privileges and restrictions. Other routine regulations are explained to the child gradually and are based mostly on his questions.

Child's Examination

On the date of admission, the admitting psychiatrist interviews the child. In the afternoon (between 1:00 PM and 2:30 PM) the psychiatrist, in the presence of the residence nurse examines the child (physical, neurological). He writes orders such as diet, escort status, precautions, privileges, and routine laboratory work (urinalysis, CBS, chest and skull x-ray). Routine lab examinations may be omitted if they have been done within fifteen days before admission. The psychiatrist writes the admission note (identification of patient and problem, background, mental status, physical and neurological examination, diagnostic impression, recommendations).

The psychiatrist's secretary prepares the admission statistics and notifies the office of the director of the center.

DISCHARGE

Discharge Planning

Because leaving the center is in itself an emotionally charged event for the children, careful preparation is required before they return to their own homes or are placed in foster family, group home or other institutional care.

A major problem arises for children who have no parents or suitable homes to which to return and for those whom foster family or other placements must be arranged. Such preparations involve thoughtful selection and planning, for children leaving residential treatment still face a series of adjustments. In many instances, appropriate placements cannot be found immediately, and the children must remain in the center beyond the point at which they are ready to leave.

In our experience, as the treatment staff members, the parents and the child are getting closer to the decision for discharge, more family involvement in the form of increased weekend visits of the child to his home or an increase in parents' meetings at the center is not necessary.

Discharge planning is one of the many goals set at the time of the Initial as well as the Progress Diagnostic and Appraisal Conferences. It includes the home to which the child is to be discharged (family, foster home, etc.), the school he will attend, and the responsibility of a plan for continued treatment after discharge.

The decision regarding the day of discharge is usually made by the child's psychiatrist in collaboration with the treatment team members. In the case of a child with a home, the day is set one month prior to the discharge in order that the social worker has time to prepare the family, child, public school, and community. In case of "dependent" children more time is required to find and prepare a responsible foster home or make other arrangements.

In the center, the majority of discharges occur in June through July, just after the end of the school period or in January, just before the beginning of the second semester, for it is unfair to the child to enter him into a public school classroom situation in which he is unfamiliar with his peers and the work being done by the class. I believe it is much easier for the child to start out in a situation that is new for all children.

Criteria for Discharge

A child is considered ready for discharge if

1. he has shown significant improvement and can function in the home and the community;

2. the family has shown significant improvement and is ready to accept the child back in the home;

3. he has made no progress because of chronicity and has to be transferred to another institution;

4. he has reached the maximum age of fourteen where either return to the home or suitable situation is sought, or if the child is still ill, transferred to another institution;

5. if, after study and diagnostic workup, it is felt that the child will not benefit from the offered therapeutic program and will benefit from a different therapeutic approach, the proper placement is determined and recommended.

Children who are discharged usually

1. are returned to their home and suitable schooling is determined in the local area;

2. are admitted to the day treatment program if the parents live within the immediate area;

3. are placed in a foster home setting if home is not recommended or not existing;

4. are transferred to other institutions.

In the event the parent or legal guardian cannot be found or refuses to accept custody of said discharged child, the child shall be placed in the care and custody of the juvenile court of the county from which the child was originally admitted as a dependent child.

If a child is removed by his parents against the recommendation of the child's psychiatrist, he is discharged "against medical advice."

Discharge Procedures

Psychiatrist

The day prior to the discharge, the child is physically examined. On the day of the discharge the psychiatrist writes the order of discharge, completes his progress note in the child's residence chart and writes the discharge summary which includes identification of the child, reason for admission, initial diagnosis, course during treatment (including physical illnesses and immunizations), final diagnosis, status at discharge (improved markedly, moderately, slightly, not improved), reason for discharge (adjustment sufficiently good to warrant discharge; passed age limit for center; adjustment fair; discharge advised; unsatisfactory adjustment; adjustment poor; transferred to another treatment center, state hospital, or training center; transferred to another type of care by agency responsible for the child; family moved out of state; against medical advice), and prognosis (good, fairly good, fair, fair to poor, guarded, poor).

A copy of the discharge summary is sent to the referring source, to the agency which will continue to provide the child with psychiatric service, and to the family physician, always after authorization for release of information signed by the parents.

Schoolteacher

A copy of the educational summary report is sent to the school to which the child will return.

Social Worker

On the day of discharge, the social worker meets with the parents or legal guardians and discusses with them any changes made in the after-care plans and recommendations. She writes a "Social Work Summary" on latest developments.

Administration

In case of "voluntary" patients, the legal discharge note is signed by the director of the center (or in his absence by the assistant director). In case of "involuntary" patients, the discharge certificate is forwarded to the county judge who originally certified said child and copies are sent by registered or certified mail to the parent or guardian of the child.

A clearance sheet is completed by the nursing service and the administrative assistant before the child is discharged.

Nursing Services

All clothing and valuables are checked with the child's clothing record (Form # ...). The person to whom the child is released signs the clothing card and other suitable release for clothing and valuables taken with the child. Any clothing and valuables not accounted for are listed and dated and the list is attached to the clothing record.

The child's bed and room are cleaned. This includes airing the mattress, washing the bed, bedside table, etc. Residence chart (doctor's orders, doctor's progress notes) includes time of discharge and person to whom the child is discharged. The child's complete residence chart is forwarded to the medical records library.

Continued Treatment After Discharge

The residential treatment experience, while it affords many children an opportunity for resolving their problems and provides a foundation for living in the community, is not an end in itself. Continued treatment both of children and parents is, more often than not, a necessity in the postresidential period.

The center does not provide outpatient services for discharged children and their parents. There is no program of direct continued service. Children leaving the center are usually assisted in obtaining continued treatment through other mental health agencies and private therapists. Also, since many children in residence are from geographically distant counties, they cannot conveniently maintain regular contact with the center following discharge.

For many children leaving residential treatment, opportunities are not available for maximizing the gains they have made in the center; this is a source of deep concern to the staff. Often these are children from deprived social environments who have received treatment and have been able to benefit in many respects, yet have to return to their former living situations and try to get along with their families and others in the community. Although work with the parents of children in residential treatment is, in most instances, recognized as being necessary to the child's functioning after he leaves the center, not all parents are willing or able to be involved in therapy. Some children who were treated at the center and have returned to their homes, are asked in a sense to be therapist to their family. This is a great responsibility for a child, and such situations point up the importance of having sources of continued treatment and support available for these children.

REFERENCES

1. Rinsley, D. B.: Psychiatric hospital treatment with special reference to children. *Arch Gen Psychiatry, 9:*489-496, 1963.
2. Morrow, J. T.: *Respect and Team Loyalty as a Therapeutic Force.* Unpublished paper presented at Professional Staff Meeting of the Menninger Foundation. January 28, 1969.
3. Bowen, W. T., *et al.:* The psychiatric team: myth and mystique. *Am J Psychiatry, 122:*6, 687-690, 1965.

PSYCHOLOGY SERVICE

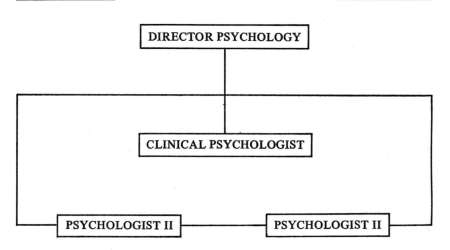

THE PSYCHOLOGY SERVICE is active in three related areas: (a) initial evaluations, re-evaluations and treatment recommendations; (b) individual and group psychotherapy; and (c) education and research.

The psychology staff consists of the director (Ph.D.), the clinical psychologist (Ph.D.), and two psychologists (M.A.).

The director of psychology is directly responsible to the director of the center. He is delegated authority with accompanying responsibility to carry out his administrative supervisory and clinical duties and to develop and maintain the clinical abilities of the psychology staff for the benefit of the entire center.

He is a member of the advisory council, admissions committee, psychotherapy board and the education and research committee.

The director of psychology service submits to the director of the center a written monthly report and at the end of the year the annual report on the psychology service activities.

The clinical psychologist assists the director of psychology in planning and implementing clinical, educational and research programs as well as performing clinical services. Supervisory duties are required.

The psychologist (M.A.) primarily performs clinical duties including psychological testing (evaluation and re-evaluations), individual and group psychotherapy, and other treatment team functions.

The activities of the psychology service include the following areas.

Initial Diagnostic Evaluation

The psychologist administers a battery of psychological tests which help to determine diagnosis, the span and depth of the child's problems, and whether or not a child can profit from the therapeutic programs. The resulting report discusses in detail intelligence and personality factors. The psychologist aids in making recommendations for appropriate residential or day treatment and for aspects pertinent to the education program.

Treatment Team

The psychologist assigned to each residence and day treatment program is an essential member of the treatment team. He discusses the children's functioning in all areas of the center and offers recommendations for their treatment.

Re-evaluation

During the child's course of treatment, it is often necessary that the psychologist makes re-evaluations. These measure progress, delineate problem areas in the personality functioning, and aid in further treatment. Requests for testing are discussed at the treatment team meetings and are requested only by the child's psychiatrist.

Discharge Planning

When discharge is anticipated, the psychologist contributes a report which may be incorporated in the discharge summary. This may contain suggestions for the type of home and school situation that would best meet the individual child's needs and the type of continued therapy indicated for that child.

Psychotherapy

The major focus of the psychology service is in individual and group psychotherapy, performing this function in accord with the psychotherapy policies and procedures of the center.

Education

The psychologists are also available to lecture and conduct in-service training and seminars for the staff and visiting groups. These usually concern the purpose, description and interpretation of tests; psychodynamics underlying interaction among children and between children and staff; the application of learning principles; and any other areas of expertise such as developmental psychology, intellectual and learning processes, and experimental design and analysis. In addition to the in-service weekly programs the staff are encouraged to add to their skills through attendance and participation in lectures and seminars outside the center.

Research

In addition to research conducted by the psychologists, consultant and cooperative services are provided for those interested in undertaking experimental or survey projects.

PSYCHOLOGICAL TESTING
Appropriate and Inappropriate Referrals

In the center, the psychologist is not a psychometrician but an active treatment team member, involved in diagnostics, treatment, education and research. Due to his many duties, the use of routine psychological testing becomes a problem of economics; while theoretically it could add something to every case, it is often not practical or possible for the psychologist to test every case. Hence, criteria are carefully set up to discriminate among referrals as to their relative appropriateness.

The following is an attempt to discuss the circumstances under which a referral for the psychological testing is appropriate and to indicate what a referral source may reasonably expect from a psychological evaluation.

In the usual setting the appropriate circumstances for the psychological testing lie somewhere between the routine referral of all children and the nonreferral of any children. The difficulty with the former is that the psychological test report tends to become so routine that it is inefficiently used. The defect with the latter is that the psychologist's services are not utilized in those circumstances where psychological appraisal could provide pertinent or even essential data for the child workup. Professionals in the field sometimes tend to forget that the psychological testing is no "sacred cow"; there is much that it cannot do. Moreover, it is only valuable or effective as the psychologist doing the workup. The data as such does not provide answers; it has to be interpreted and integrated by the psychologist.

The usual referral for psychological testing should clearly specify exactly what questions or problems prompted the referral, and what the referral source hopes to obtain from the testing. The real value of the psychologist's report lies in the emphasis which it places on answering the specific referral questions. For example, when the question involves a problem of differential diagnosis, ideally the information pinpoints the diagnostic alternatives and those areas of ambiguity which make the diagnosis difficult.

Under situations of inadequate staff it is necessary to limit the testing to the more urgent diagnostic and disposition problems. The more comprehensive and informative the consultation request, the better able is the psychologist to determine the priority with which each case should be dealt.

A further consideration of major importance concerns a need for continuing communication between the referral source and the psychologist. After the psychologist evaluates a child, there is feedback of information regarding the ultimate findings in the case. Such communication facilitates the growth and development of the respective professions around the framework of service to the child.

Psychological testing can offer service in comprising (a) the child's intellectual functioning and (b) his personality structure and psychological dynamics. Of course, I realize the artificial nature of this breakdown as intelligence is, properly speaking, a facet of personality.

Intellectual Functioning

In working with children we learn that there is a considerable variability in the child's intellectual functioning which makes a rigid reliance upon the IQ untenable. It must be remembered that the child can do at least as well as his performance on the intelligence test indicates. How much better he might do if his physical state (e.g. illness, fatigue or effects of drugs) or psychic state (e.g. anxiety or lack of motivation) were altered has to be inferred. However, despite these various sources of error, the range of the child's intellectual capacity can be estimated with reasonable confidence.

As a guide to the kind of functions which are generally considered to reflect intelligence, I mention these:

1. *Mental alertness, attention and concentration.*

2. *Perceptual-motor abilities,* that is, the capacity to coordinate and integrate successfully sensory-motor activity.

3. *Social and environmental awareness* such as accurate evaluation of and sensitivity to everyday situations.

4. *General abstracting abilities* such as symbolizing and perceiving logical relationships, the ability to discriminate between the sensual and superficial elements, differentiating and integrating capacities, and conceptual skills.

5. *The ability to learn,* as reflected by associative skills, the depth and breadth of old knowledge, and the capacity to acquire new knowledge.

While theoretically all of the above information is available in the center, a general request for that information is not ordinarily made unless a specific need would be served.

The following are instances in which a psychological testing for the appraisal of intellectual functioning might be *appropriate.*

1. For making a differential diagnosis, e.g. for legally declaring a child mentally ill or retarded.

2. For making a recommendation for special treatment of a case, e.g. whether a child has the intellectual capacity to utilize certain types of psychotherapy.

3. For evaluating the relationship between a child's current functioning to his potential abilities, e.g. when a child failing in school is felt to have the capacity to perform more adequately.

4. When there is a question of disturbed thought processes, e.g. when psychotic disorder is suspected.

5. For evaluating impairment of, or deterioration in, ability to perform cognitive functions, e.g. when organic involvement is suspected. Here, testing can neither confirm nor rule out a diagnosis of organicity. It can only indicate that certain functions are impaired and that this impairment is consistent with this diagnosis.

It should be stressed that in only the first of these instances, and sometimes in the third, is a formal measure of intelligence absolutely essential. A reasonably good estimate of the level of a child's intelligence may be obtained from an analysis of his performance on many projective tests. These estimates are often sufficient, unless for some reason a more precise appraisal of current intellectual functioning would be appropriate under all of the foregoing conditions does not imply that the measure of intellectual functioning will necessarily be an "intelligence test."

A psychological testing for the appraisal of intellectual functioning is considered *inappropriate* under the following circumstances:

1. when it would be of merely academic interest, e.g. the fact that the child is being presented at a case conference is not in itself a sufficient reason for his being tested. This is not meant to deny the importance of the psychological testing as a teaching or didactic measure. In many instances psychological testing is an intrinsic part of this segment of the center's teaching program. If evaluation of intellectual functioning is important from a learning point of view, then this in itself would justify the referral.

2. when there is low level functioning and no suspicion of higher intellectual potential.

3. when there is superior intellectual functioning (unless the extent of superiority would significantly determine disposition).

Personality Structure and Dynamics

While extensive inferences concerning a child's personality are possible through the use of appropriate psychological tests, it should again be noted that these tests are never infallible; the inferences they generate are of varying levels of probability and a function of the psychologist's acumen, and that their validity is limited by the incompleteness of our current knowledge of the determinants of human behavior. Given these limitations, the following information concerning the child's personality functioning is potentially available through psychological testing.

Structural aspects of the personality including the relative strength, flexibility and efficiency of the child's ego, and the modes of control and expression of his underlying drives and impulses can usually be inferred. These would include the adequacy of reality testing; the specific adaptive or defensive mechanisms characteristically employed; the hierarchy or order in which they appear under conditions of frustration, stress or conflict; and the degree of anxiety present. In addition, it is possible to evaluate the quality (e.g. lability or the control) and the extent (e.g. strength or drive) of the child's emotional responses, the general level of maturity, and the levels of development at which primary motives are fixated or to which regression has occurred.

As well as portraying the structure or framework of personality and accessing the adequacy of its current functioning, it is possible to gain insight into a number of specific factors which fill in the details. These would include specific conflicts, their intensity and their attempts at resolution, e.g. unresolved oedipal striving; the character of the child's interpersonal relationships, his perceptions and the way he views people; and psychological factors in development determining his present condition, e.g. the nature of his perception of early relationships with significant persons.

A request for psychological testing of personality functioning is considered *appropriate* under the following circumstances:

1. for evaluating possible underlying psychopathology, e.g. the suspicion of what appears to be neurotic symptomatology masking a psychotic process.

2. for evaluating the relative strength of different psychopathological trends in a child, e.g. whether a depression observed clinically is primary or incidental to other psychopathology also present clinically.

3. for obtaining information about a child which may be unobtainable through interviews, e.g. the "hyperrepressive" child.

4. for investigating the etiology of a symptom, e.g. the meaning of conversion reaction.

5. for evaluating the advisability of initiating, continuing or terminating treatment, e.g. when there is a question concerning the possibility of further decompensation.

6. for planning a psychotherapeutic approach, e.g. for deciding between supportive or interpretive therapy by alerting the psychotherapist to the forms of resistance and defense mechanisms likely to be employed.

7. for an evaluation of change as a result of the therapeutic process.

The psychodiagnostic evaluation of personality functioning is *limited* when it attempts to predict specific behavior. While the psychological appraisal may suggest the potential for types of behavior under specific conditions, as with other methods of assessment it is unable to provide precise information concerning the future. Therefore, predictions concerning future choice of symptoms or specific behavioral acts can only be answered qualifiedly.

SOCIAL WORK SERVICE

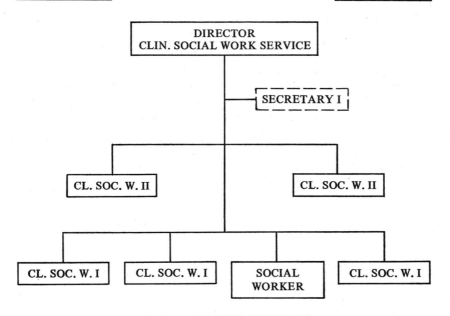

SOCIAL WORK SERVICE

BASIC TO TREATMENT AT THE CENTER is the philosophy that both the child and his family have contributed to the creation of the problems for which help is sought, and that all must share in their resolution. Social work expertise as a part of the interdisciplinary team is focused on maintaining and enhancing this necessary family involvement.

DIRECTOR OF SOCIAL WORK SERVICE

The director of the social work service is directly responsible to the director of the center for carrying out the administrative and clinical functions of social work service. She is a member of the admissions committee, advisory council, psychotherapy board, and education and research committee.

The director of social work service

—plans, organizes, directs and supervises the activities of the social work staff;

—implements and evaluates the social work services;

—develops in-service educational and training programs for the social work staff;

—is directly involved in casework, individual and group psychotherapy, family therapy, and parent discussion groups;

—provides consultation services to the various disciplines represented at the center;

—provides supervision to social workers, psychotherapists;

—sees that the functions of the treatment team are augmented when there is a shortage of social work staff;

—reviews as a member of the admissions committee, applications and referral material for admission forwarded to her by the Child Study Unit (admissions office);

—supervises and provides consultations for the Visiting Friends Program;

—provides staff and consultation to the Child Study Unit (admissions office).

ROLE OF SOCIAL WORK SERVICE

The social work service contributes its particular expertise in the following areas.

Admissions

On the day of admission, the social worker receives the parents or legal guardians and conducts the initial interviews, assists the parents in the completion of all necessary forms, and emphasizes the importance of maintaining their parental role. She also informs the parents of the requirement for their involvement in casework or family therapy programs, either at the center or in their community. The social worker also discusses with the parents all practical matters such as provision for clothing, limitations regarding sending children money directly, telephone calls, and parent's handling of similar matters related to maintaining the child in residence. She also secures any additional background and present illness information.

Diagnostic and Appraisal Social Work

The social worker addresses herself to an appraisal of the child's internal and external environment and attempts to understand the interrelationship between the world from which the child comes and the self that he is.

In order to construct an integral comprehensive profile of the child, the social worker obtains any additional medical, psychiatric and psychological evaluations, plus educational background material. A psychiatric social history depicting family relationships, psychosocial and socioeconomic status in the child's developmental stages is obtained as an essential tool in providing an understanding of the child's total situation.

To complete the diagnosis, an assessment is made of the family's readiness to participate actively in the treatment process and of community resources to insure the child's readjustment to his social environment.

As an aid to assessment and as a bridge to treatment, direct contact with the child's environment is sometimes indicated. This includes possible evaluative visits to the child's home after his admission, as well as conferences with those agencies which have previously known the child. These approaches enhance the objective data already available on the child and his home environment.

The social worker collaborates with all agencies responsible for placement and aftercare of children and encourages them to send representatives to all initial and progress diagnostic and appraisal conferences.

Treatment Teamwork

The social worker is directly involved in the treatment of children and, as a psychiatric team member, is under the supervision and consultation of the psychiatrist. When functioning as the social worker on the treatment team she coordinates the rehabilitative efforts of the center as related to the child in treatment and his family at home. She places emphasis upon the bonds that connect the parents and child so that both the child and his parents are simultaneously involved in the treatment programs. The social worker who is responsible for the child is also the one who works with his parents.

The social worker in collaboration with other members of the treatment team determines the most therapeutic plan for each individual child with regard to visiting on or off grounds, the length and frequency of visits, and/or the use of the Visiting Friends Program. Parents are free to call the social worker between interviews and the worker calls them when something occurs for which they share responsibility regarding their child.

When the parents create difficulties in regard to the child's treatment, about visiting, or problems outside the social worker's area of functioning, the child's psychiatrist or the director of the center is called.

Work with Other Agencies

The social worker maintains contact with the representatives of the agency which is assuring that they follow the same requirements as parents, e.g. to buy the child's clothing, to visit on and off grounds, to provide an allowance, to write letters, give gifts at appropriate times, and to plan with the child throughout his residency for his care after discharge. In addition, the social worker provides the responsible agency with ongoing consultation and support. She sees the agency worker just as she sees parents. My experience indicates that some workers who try to admit children at the center demonstrate little understanding of emotionally disturbed children. Indeed, they seem to need the same kind of help in planning for the children that the parents require. If the agency worker will play an active, responsible and meaningful role in the life of the child, he will have less need to seek out a parent figure in the residence. If he cannot establish a significant association with the foster care agency and he lacks a parental tie, he will eventually tend to find this with one of the staff members at the center. Since such a relationship cannot be maintained beyond the treatment period, it is sounder to encourage such an association with the foster care agency which can carry the child after treatment into foster placement.

Direct Casework

With local children, referring agencies are usually asked not to continue or assume casework with the parents since casework responsibility should be that of the center's.

Local parents are seen privately in regular casework interviews. The frequency of interviews depends on the type of service as well as the parents' accessibility and cooperation. Some are seen on a weekly basis; others less frequently.

The aim of casework with parents is not to provide psychotherapy for them. If it is found that parents are in need of psychiatric treatment for themselves and are accessible to treatment, they are referred to a family agency, a psychiatrist or a clinic.

The purpose of casework with parents is

—to coordinate casework of the parents with the treatment of the child;

—to keep the parents from interfering and to prevent them from jeopardizing the child's treatment;

—to help them recognize, understand and accept their child's problems;

—to understand the interrelatedness of the child's problems with their own and the ways in which these are associated with the child's problems;

—to bring to the parents' attention other conditions in the home environment which need to be improved;

—to help those parents found to be destructive to their child's welfare to accept foster care or adopting.

The social worker directs her work with the parents towards helping them learn more constructive ways of handling their child. This usually develops in response to requests from the parents for such help when home visits are scheduled or when plans are under way for the child's returning home, or when the parents are unable to visualize that he may return home.

In general, the goal in working with the parents is to change the child's home situation so that he can be returned to it or the parents can be helped to accept alternative plans. In some cases the social worker attempts to give the parents an understanding

of their child's disturbance and some insight into their part in
it.

Indirect Casework Consultation with Other Agencies

Since a number of the children in residence may come from
homes located in geographic areas distant from the center, it is
often impossible for the social worker to coordinate the treatment of the child at the center with that of the parents in the
same way that is possible when the family lives closer to the center. In such cases arrangements are made through which a local
agency (public or private) takes the responsibility to work with
the parents of these children.

The social worker serves as a liaison person, fostering communication between the center's staff which is responsible for the
child's treatment and education and the agencies in the community which are responsible for the counseling or casework of the
parents.

The social worker requires that the agencies keep the center informed by correspondence or phone calls regarding the agency's
work with the parents and conditions in the home. In turn, the
center sends regular reports to the responsible agency regarding
the child's progress and initiates any other correspondence regarding specific problems.

The relationship between the center and the local agency ser-
vicing the family is ongoing and is terminated only at the time
of the child's discharge.

Individual and Group Psychotherapy

Although the primary function of the social worker is the relationship of the family in the community to the child in residential treatment, she also provides individual and group psychotherapy to the child. In doing this, the social worker becomes directly involved in the total treatment programs for the child and
his parents.

In order to develop proficiency in psychotherapy techniques,
the social worker, along with the other professional clinical staff,
utilizes the in-service training provided by the education department. Supervisory opportunities are also made available to her

through the director of social work services and through psychotherapy seminars.

The efficiency of psychotherapy services as delivered by the social work service is tested and fully researched to afford objective criticism and provide data for further growth.

The social worker is usually assigned children in individual psychotherapy (their number varying from four to five) and also conducts group psychotherapy sessions with four to six children participating in each group.

Family Therapy

Based on the recommendations of the treatment team members, local parents are asked to participate jointly in therapy whenever there are strong indications of need for direct involvement of any family members in the treatment of the child. First consideration is given to the child's potential need for improvement rather than to insist rigidly on the parents' participation in family therapy when the child is not ready for it.

The purpose of family therapy is

—to provide a direct involvement of parents and child and help them to observe their patterns of communication;

—to provide more direct intervention and clarification of misconceptions, conflicts and separation anxieties;

—to help the parents and child consider their own feelings and tendencies as they operate in intrafamily functioning;

—to provide, through a supportive relationship, a strengthening of the parent's and child's assets and enhancing healthy potentialities;

—to help the parents and child attain insight on a deeper level when they show readiness for it;

—to help the parents and child correct the family relationships which have contributed to the child's problems.

Parent Discussion Groups

It is believed that rehabilitative services are often enhanced by effectively grouping parents for group discussion sessions. For this reason, careful grouping of parents is made and group discussions are carried out on a weekly basis. The number of parents per group varies from five to six (total ten to twelve persons per group).

Interpretation Conferences

The social work service, because of its focus on the family, is responsible for planning, preparing and implementing interpretation conferences as indicated throughout the child's stay at the center.

The interpretation conference is the professional vehicle through which the findings of the multidisciplined team study, evaluation and treatment are shared with the child's family and/or parent surrogates. It is also the place where the significant responsible people raise their questions, give further understanding of the practical nature of the problems, and enter into the contractual agreement to work and cooperate with the center.

Interpretation conferences are formally planned following the Initial Diagnostic and Appraisal, and thereafter following other significant Progress Diagnostic and Appraisals culminating with the final Diagnostic and Appraisal preceding discharges.

Discharge Planning

Inasmuch as discharge plans are projected from the day of the child's admission, rather than as intensive treatment being terminated, early ongoing considerations are made for the eventual return of the child to his home and community. The social worker helps the family and pertinent agencies for the child's smooth transition from the center to the community living. She also provides the treatment team with current information on the child's home and community readiness to accept his return. In addition it is her responsibility to prepare the community agencies (social, educational, legal) which are involved with the child, for their role in the ongoing therapeutic process.

"VISITING FRIENDS" PROGRAM

Purpose and Rationale

The Visiting Friends Program is a service to the children providing family life experiences for children whose parents or guardians are unable to visit and who need an ongoing contact with the world outside the center in order to reduce the side effects of institutionalization. This is particularly necessary for children in the following situations:

1. Children admitted for residential psychiatric treatment and education who come from places distant to the center, an obstacle which often precludes frequent visits with their parents.

2. Some families have multiple problems including financial problems, illnesses, personal inadequacy and are unable to provide visits.

3. Some children are wards of the state and have no family to visit them.

Most of these children will ultimately be returned to their families or family surrogates in the community. Therefore there is a need to develop and maintain their experience of, and skills in family and community living.

Coordinator of the Program—Duties

A social worker is the coordinator of the program, and is directly responsible to the director of social work services for carrying out the following duties:

1. to confer with the child's psychiatrist and other members of the treatment team on the child's need of a visiting friend; on matters pertaining to the matching of the child, his management, precautions, chemotherapy, type and extent of visits, etc.

2. to submit to the director of the social services a monthly report on the census, names (visiting friends and patients), and the number of visiting hours. The report is forwarded to the administrative assistant who is in charge of the volunteer services.

Selection of Visiting Friends

Interested community people are carefully screened and evaluated by designated members of the clinical staff (psychiatrist, social worker) to determine that:

1. they are positively motivated, mature, stable and able to provide appropriate friend and adult models;

2. they are willing to assume responsibility for the child's welfare while he is off-grounds and in their care;

3. they are willing to sign the "Visitors Responsibility Book";

4. they are willing to attend ongoing supervisory, counseling and other planned individual and group meetings when indicated;

5. they are willing to administer prescribed chemotherapy while the child is in their care. In case the child is in chemotherapy, the responsible visiting friends are given prescriptions that can be filled at designated community pharmacies.

Services to Children Provided by Visiting Friends

1. Visits on-grounds.

2. Visits off-grounds (limited—lasting for a few hours, overnight, weekend, or holiday stay) in their homes, or elsewhere.

3. Socializing experiences with the visiting friends.

4. Richer educational experiences.

Dos and Don'ts for Visiting Friends

Do not develop a deep relationship which will be difficult for visiting friend and child to terminate.

Do not view the child as a perspective foster or adoptive child.

Do not over-structure visits with the child but allow for spontaneity.

Do not see the child as "different" but rather as a child with special problems.

Do limit personal contacts to twice a month.

Do share with the social worker any ongoing contacts and experiences with the child.

Do remember that visiting friends serve specific childhood needs for a limited time only and that their relationship with the child will not become permanent.

ADJUNCTIVE THERAPIES SERVICE

A DJUNCTIVE THERAPIES IS THE TERM applied to a group of specialized therapies which are brought together and coordinated into one service because of similarity of aims, functions, methods and goals and for efficiency of administration.

ADJUNCTIVE THERAPIES SERVICE

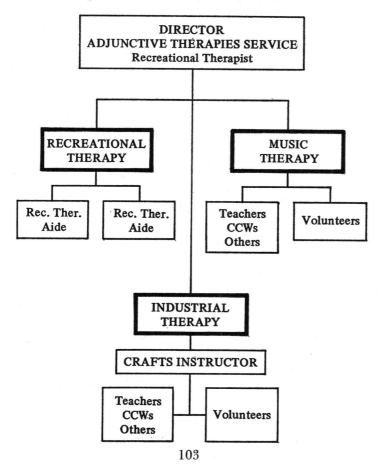

PURPOSE

The adjunctive therapies service with its three major programs of recreational, music and industrial therapies has an advantage over other forms of treatment; it is couched in the concept of fun and play. The child is oftentimes involved in the activity before he realizes what is happening. He is having fun, enjoying himself, and does not think of himself as being in a treatment setting. This sense of freedom and naturalness allows for the complete giving of one's self without the awareness of being on guard.

Because of our western concept that children should play and that opportunities should be provided for play, the center strongly reflects this concept. It provides planned recreational, musical and industrial programs for the children in its care. These programs run the gamut from all kinds of sports to arts and crafts, hobbies, outdoor and indoor recreation; from active to nonactive participation in music; and from group to individual projects in industrial therapy. As used in the center, though, activities are not limited to play "for fun" alone. Aiding the physical development of the children, building their confidence, training them in social values, reaching their education, and utilizing these experiences as therapy for their emotional problems are all part of the adjunctive therapies service.

LOCATION—STRUCTURE

The central recreational area contains a regulation softball diamond, a football field, picnic tables, barbeque grills, swings, a slide, a basketball court, a volleyball court, tetherball, and an outdoor muscle man set.

The auditorium serves as the hub of most of the recreational, and music therapy activities. These activities include shuffleboard, table tennis, billiards, indoor games, tumbling, wrestling, boxing, stage shows, dances and school plays.

STAFF
Qualities of Staff

The staff of the adjunctive therapies service consists of the director of adjunctive therapies service, the music therapist, three

recreational therapy aides, and the industrial therapy aide.
An adjunctive therapist who works with children should have
—knowledge on the normal aspects of children's growth and
  development as individuals and as social beings;
—a fundamental knowledge of the structure and functions of
  the human body;
—knowledge of the normal needs and desires of the child and
  of his varying degrees of emotional, mental and physical
  capabilities;
—understanding of the learning process and how to facilitate
  it, including skill in the use of appropriate leadership techniques with due regard for the different needs of children;
—ability to stimulate the children's maximum participation in
  activities and proficiency in evaluating outcomes of learning
  experiences;
—knowledge and skill in the use of group processes and other
  methods of informal education.

Director of Adjunctive Therapies Service

The director of the adjunctive therapies service is responsible
to the director of the center for carrying out the administrative
and clinical functions of the adjunctive therapies service.

He is a member of the advisory council and of the education
and research department.

He submits a monthly and annual report to the director of the
center on the activities of adjunctive therapies service.

He is responsible for
—planning, organizing and directing the coordination and implementation of a comprehensive adjunctive therapies program for children;
—organizing, directing and supervising the adjunctive therapies staff;
—securing necessary equipment for the implementation of the
  therapeutic programs and activities;
—evaluating adjunctive therapies programs, staff, and facilities
  to determine the strengths and weaknesses in the operations
  of the adjunctive therapies services within the center;
—providing recreational therapy classes;

—augmenting the functions of the adjunctive therapies staff in case of shortage of staff.

RECREATIONAL THERAPY
Characteristics of Recreation as a Therapeutic Tool

The recreational therapy program of the center plays a major role in the treatment of the children in its care. Recreation or the tool for recreation contributes in the development of the child's self-concept, in the learning of acceptable social roles, and in the ability of the child to function within a group situation and to accept the group norms and expectations.

The recreational therapist, as a member of the treatment team, involves himself in observing the child in structured recreational functions and reports his observations to the members of the treatment team. The activities presented to the child are fashioned to help him deal with his basic problems and motivate him toward participation in less protected activities. The activities permit the healthy part of the child's personality to continue to function.

The treatment team uses recreation as a tool to assist in diagnostic and personality evaluation. This is done through the therapist's direct contact with the child when engaged in various adjunctive therapies activities. The manner in which the child participates in certain activities, the choice of activities he makes, his interactions with peers and staff aid in the diagnosis and appraisal of the child.

Recreation provides opportunities for the expression of emotional needs and drives. These are made available to the child through the interpersonal relationship between the therapist and the child. With the recreational therapist the child learns to develop a proper attitude toward the use of leisure time and to develop skills that will allow him to pursue his favorite activities upon returning to the community.

Functions and Therapeutic Effects of Recreation

The need for a child to engage in meaningful activities is acknowledged by the staff of the center which believes that recreation, socialization, and mental health are closely interrelated. Activities are therefore specially designed for the child in order to enhance his feelings of importance and adequacy. Sports activities are used by the therapist as a means of coping with tensions, be it the venting of them or the creation of higher levels of tolerance.

For a child to identify with and to be a part of a group is a goal for the recreational therapist. Recreation contributes to the positive functioning of group membership. Through this activity, the child is drawn from social isolation, discovers a common basis for interaction, and finds that recreation provides valuable supportive and corrective experiences for relating to others.

Field trips play an important role in the recreation experiences of the child. At every opportunity, he is exposed to various functions within the community. The recreational therapist in conjunction with the nursing staff plans various cultural and recreational activities needed by the child.

Admission—Diagnostic and Appraisal Work

When a new child is admitted to the adjunctive therapies program, the recreational therapist takes the child on a one-to-one basis for evaluation and appraisal. It is at this time that the child is evaluated on skills, attitude, coordination and interests. This gives the therapist an idea as to where to place the child in classes that are coordinated with the school's program. For example, a child that is a novice in all activities is assigned on a one-to-one basis so he can learn basic skills functions such as batting, throwing, catching, etc. This would eventually make him skillful enough to play in large groups without receiving criticism from his peers.

Diagnostic appraisal in recreational therapy after admission consists of testing to determine:

Skill (leadership ability, sportsmanship, creative ability, etc.)
Attitudes (towards peers, staff, activities, receiving instructions, care of equipment and facility, etc.)
Coordination (kicking, throwing, catching, running, walking, posture, attention span, eye contact, calisthenics, mixed dominants, etc.)

Interests (hobbies, likes and dislikes in sports, music, drama, nature
lore, special events, preference to large or small groups or individual)

This initial evaluation enables the therapist to properly place
the child with a group that is primarily within his skill level, or
the child may need more of a one-to-one basis before entering into a group situation.

Diagnostic and appraisal work is also done on each child every
three months. This enables the team to review the child's progress
or regression during that period of time.

Recreational Therapist's Duties and Functions

The recreational therapist is directly responsible to the director
of adjunctive therapies service for carrying out the following
duties:

—Plans, implements, and supervises an assigned recreational
program or activity within the center, insuring that the content of the program reflects the desires and needs of the
child.

—Develops and implements within an assigned area a series of
recreational activities based on the child's needs, desires and
abilities.

—Develops and supervises special recreational activities and
events including Christmas parties, Easter egg hunts, social
dances and other related specialized recreational activities.

—Supervises other recreational leaders (other employees or
volunteers) assigned to assist with such activities.

—The director of the adjunctive therapies service assigns one
recreational aide to handle some of the adjunctive therapies
service clerical work. She is directly involved with taking all
incoming telephone calls; typing monthly and annual reports, questions; performs tasks related to clerical work
when required.

MUSIC THERAPY
Introduction

The idea of music as therapy is rooted in antiquity, when activities were more often guided by ritual; because music played

so large a part in ritual, it was but a step from music *in* medicine to music *as* medicine.

Apollo, the god of healing was also the god of music, of sunlight and enlightment, the master of purification of souls and bodies. Apollo, to whom the physicians address the Oath of Hippocrates (the father of Asclepios the physician, the god of medicine), is also the god of the seven-stringed lyre, the musician who outplayed Pan's pipes and Marsyas' flute. Medicine and music were one, or at least the attributes of one god, long before Olympus in the chants and incantations of the first medicine men in the murky deeps of unrecorded antiquity. There seems to have been an attraction between music and medicine ever since.

The Greeks have more especially insisted on the ethical qualities of music and on its moralizing and demoralizing effects. Menander says that to many people music is a powerful stimulant to love. Plato discusses what kinds of music should be encouraged in his ideal state. He only admits two kinds of music: one violent and suited to war, the other tranquil and suited to prayer or to persuasion. He sets out the ethical qualities of music "on these accounts we attach such importance to a musical education because rhythm and harmony sink most deeply into the recesses of the soul, and take most powerful hold of it, bringing gracefulness in their train, and making a man graceful if he be rightly nurtured . . . leading him to commend beautiful objects, and gladly receive them into his soul, and feed upon them, and grow to be noble and good."*

Aristotle takes a wider view of music than Plato and admits a greater variety of uses for it. He accepts the function of music as a catharsis of emotion and seems to have first suggested that rhythm and melodies are motions, as actions are motions, and therefore signs of feeling.

Our ideas of music therapy, it seems, are too often impressionistic. We always recall the time when "David took a harp, and played with his hand; so Saul was refreshed, and was well, and the evil spirit departed from him,"† but forget the occasions

---

* Plato: *Republic—Book III*. Transl. B. Jowett, Classic Club Publ. Roslyn, N. Y., W. J. Black, Inc., 1942, p. 289.
† I Sam. 16:23.

when David's music therapy was less successful and Saul hurled javelins at him. There were at least two such occasions—David's being a courageous fellow, and maybe too slow to take a hint.

The ancient belief in the moralizing influence of music has survived into modern times mainly in a somewhat more scientific form as a belief in its therapeutic effects in emotional and mental disorders.

We are all aware that successes commonly attributed to music therapy can be due to other, perhaps coincidental, factors. The patient is being benefited by the music he hears, by the music he produces, by the rhythm, by the group activity, or by the simple and beautifully symbolic action of continuing to make-believe.

A survey of the literature makes apparent that many of the articles which lauded the efficacy of music therapy were written by people whose knowledge of the subject was confined to an interest in music and who wished to bring to the patient a measure of the relaxation and enjoyment that they themselves experienced when playing or listening to music. Little attention was paid to the medical aspects of the problem.

Recent publications on music therapy include studies of psychological and physiological effects of various employments of various types of music, from experiments with the mentally disturbed to the empirically justified use of music in the operating room. There are vigor, imagination, and an encouragingly wide range of activities in these reports. There are also temptations to hurl psychiatric mud pies at these reports.

When the benefits, if any, were attributed to music itself, the patient was usually a person who was fond of music. However, each report of a favorable influence, no matter what the reason, served to create a seemingly formidable amount of evidence, in spite of the fact that later writers reported the same "cures." These isolated instances were so often reiterated that they came in time to be accepted as proof that music per se is a therapeutic agent.

Yet, the therapeutic value of music still is little understood. One cannot say that music in itself is therapeutic. Other factors contributing to its usefulness are the psychologic and physiologic effects it has on the mood and behavior of the patient. It would seem to serve rather as a way of enabling the patient to make better use of other therapeutic experiences than to be one itself.

We all have become increasingly aware of the growing number of "therapies." The problem being faced today is the fragmentation and dysfunction of our therapeutic resources whereby each novel segment comes to be called "therapy" and may be dignified by being a separate department. Although many activities may be therapeutic, it seems preposterous to "therapize" every step in living.

We have, to begin with, at least a few fine facts by which to justify the use of music therapy. First, there is some variety of disorder of affect in every mental illness. Second, man's whole dealing with music is primarily affective; music is an emotional and an affective experience from the earliest chants of the priest-medicine man to the most sophisticated modern concerto, and from the ancient cadence of the drums and horns which first inspired columns of marching men to Babylon to the contemporary television hit paraders. In historical, poetical and musical annals through the centuries, there is eloquent evidence to this effect. A relationship between music and the course of mental illness is one of those things which many suppose to be demonstrated by ordinary observation, and it probably is. And there is at least a little sound clinical evidence, although not enough, to justify the nature and extent of some of the sweeping conclusions sometimes drawn from it. There is enough smoke to indicate fire somewhere, although the what, how and why of the burning are largely matters of speculation.

All this adds to an impressive case for carefully planned and skillfully directed examination. After several thousand years of talking it is time to learn what we are talking about. The resources to find out are available—musical, psychological, psychiatric—if we can only agree first that our ignorance is considerable and then make the further more difficult determination to do something about it. If music is a universal language, then surely it not only can help to overcome the difficulties of the disturbed and maladjusted child but can perhaps show us the way to overcome the hatred and fear rampant in the world today.

Music has an important role to play in psychiatric treatment, judging from its rise to prominence in the field of adjunctive therapy. Music is both a beautifier and an educator. It can be very exacting as in scale exercises and practice to develop technique; or it can demand very little, as in listening to music for the sheer pleasure of sound. It also may give children an opportunity to do something for themselves, to play the piano or sing in a chorus.

The aim of music therapy must be therapy, not music. The aim is neither to entertain the child nor to educate him to appreciation of good music, although both may be incidental gains; it is to cure him or alleviate his condition. It is my belief that the real purpose of music therapy is to minister to the emotional, intellectual and spiritual needs of the children. Music, more than any other art, is born of the mind itself rather than of the objective world; therefore, it is more independent of the external world and more dependent upon the activity of the creative imagination.

In our efforts to use music as a therapy we must observe the effects of music upon the child's emotional responses, carefully study children at scheduled musical activities, and equally select groups for therapeutic music sessions afterward to obtain resocializing effects by emotional outlets. Also, we should not minimize the cultural, social and individual differences in the backgrounds of the children.

To be effective, music therapy must be individually prescribed on the basis of the child's needs and conflicts and within the framework of the overall treatment goal. It must be prescribed with the same open mind with which psychiatry prescribes psychotherapy, chemotherapy and other treatment modalities. Many therapists are biased in favor of music therapy because they themselves are musical, instead of inquiring into it objectively and assessing it impartially. Since music is from the very heart and soul of man, it rarely flourishes under regimentation. Creative expression, free dramatization, and making-believe with music are important in therapy and almost equally so in education.

Characteristics of Music as a Therapeutic Tool

Source of Information for Diagnostic Evaluation

A valued trait of music therapy rests in the fact that it can be utilized as a source of diagnostic information.

Music has its intellectual aspects, particularly for the musician; for the ordinary listener, it is almost pure affect. The study of this applied affect can be useful for the light it might cast on psychopathology. Thus music can be utilized as a source of diagnostic information. And if something can be learned from a personality test as to musical likes and dislikes of the child, this knowledge can be applied for the scientific selection of music for therapeutic purposes.

Many children who cannot (or will not) talk about their problems; who are too threatened by ordinary examination techniques to be applicable; or who, because of some sensory or motor deficit, are physically incapable of expressing themselves verbally can be studied indirectly by studying their response as listeners to various kinds of music or their participation in music production, alone or in combination with other expressive modes.

Any music therapist today employs "common sense" and rule of thumb selection methods. In music, as in the Rorschach test, there are preferences and forms of expression which point to the principal mental disorders. If we can tell what they are, we may be able to use them to influence the disorders to which they point. Or there might be negative value in pointing towards what to avoid (1).

Low Failure Potential

I feel that music can contribute to the total life—educational and social—of a child, that it can be meaningful in his everyday experiences, and that it helps to build an integrated personality.

In our culture, the school desk and the dining room table are the most likely scenes for the enactment of conflicts between child and parent or between parents about a child's course. Almost all parents expect and urge their children to excel at reading and writing. Not all children are able to excel in academic pursuits, however; and parental urging, in areas where it is inappropriate, can and does sow the seeds of emotional disorder.

The first and most important attribute of music therapy is its low failure potential. This characteristic derives, in part, from the fact that music occupies a unique and enviable position in our cultural value system. Unless a child comes from an unusually musical family, any failure to show aptitude for a particular musical endeavor does not become an emotionally charged issue for the child or for his parents.

Many children, because of the low failure threat involved in music, can permit themselves to be vulnerable for the first time in music therapy. In order to achieve, a child must be willing to make himself vulnerable. That is, he must be willing to place himself in a position which has both failure and success as possible outcomes. Almost all problem children have experienced failure so consistently in classrooms, whether from intellectual impairment or from emotional disturbance or both, that they have become unwilling to try. They avoid the very learning situations which might lead to success because those situations have become too strongly associated with an expectation of failure.

Because music is less emotionally charged for the children of our culture, they may be willing to try in music when they are completely unwilling to do so in any other areas. By assessing their aptitudes carefully and by choosing from the wide spectrum of music only those activities which will guarantee success, quick rewards can be provided. Self-confidence increases with those rewards and diffuses to other subject matter. Thus a child may for the first time become willing to try an activity in another area because his success experiences in music buffer the threat of failure elsewhere.

High Success Value

Because parents infrequently exert undue pressure for musical prowess, a child seldom chooses music as a vehicle for the expression of rebellion, retaliation or hostility towards his parents or their substitutes. For this reason, music is often one of the few areas which are emotionally neutral to a disturbed child. This implies that neither neurotic fear of failure nor neurotic need to fail is strong in connection with music activity; but, happily, it does *not* imply that the rewards of success are meager. Both parents and children can tolerate lack of musical aptitude, but development of musical skill brings high rewards in spite of this fact.

When the first aim of music in a program is therapy, pressure should not be applied for technical perfection. The desire for perfection must stem from the program itself, and the child's desire for better self-expression must be inspired by what he is doing. The program itself must meet the needs and moods of each child and should be one from which he can learn and make progress. Sometimes a change in instruments will help a disturbed child to find release from his worries.

Variety of Skill Levels

The variety of skill levels, instruments, and creativity inherent in music also helps to endow music therapy with low failure potential. The broad gamut from "playing" a triangle in a rhythm band to the participation of a virtuoso in a musical program offers nearly complete assurance that every individual can find some area through music diagnosis and music therapy which will provide an avenue to significant growth and achievement. When the variety inherent in music therapy is viewed from another angle and its range is seen to vary from passive participation in music appreciation to the performance of music and to the creation of improvised or composed music, it is again evident that it holds a niche for almost everyone (1).

Expressive Outlets for Emotion

The range of expressive outlets for emotion provided by music therapy is another vital characteristic which enhances its value as a treatment technique. For the untutored child, simple, direct expression of emotion through improvisation on an instrument or through activity performed to music can provide a nonthreatening outlet for feelings which might otherwise be repressed and find their expression in symptom formation. Even listening to music without motor activity can afford emotional outlet in subtle and nonobservable ways, as all of us recognize from the concept of mood music. At a higher level, of course, music performance and composition provide opportunities for sublimation and self-expression in a socially constructive way (1).

Variation in Structure

Another desirable characteristic of music therapy is the breadth of structure it can encompass. A child may be presented with a musical instrument and given free reign to improvise. Such an atmosphere is conducive to the development of feelings of confidence in the therapist and of acceptance by the therapist, both of which will later permit the introduction of formal structure in small, but increasing doses. This atmosphere also provides the freedom which subtly impels a child to set and strive for his own goals. The child who cannot stand limits, rules or regulations can sometimes discover (for the first time) their utility to him through appreciating how they help him achieve musical goals which he has chosen for himself.

Role Playing Potential (Free Dramatization and Making-believe)

The role playing potential inherent in both instrumental and vocal music constitutes another valuable aspect of this therapeutic tool. Many disturbed children reach a point in treatment where they want to try new modes of response and adjustment; yet old failures linger in their memories and restrict their freedom to experiment with the unknown.

Dreams have been called "the royal road to the unconscious," and certainly a child's musical role playing can be an equally valuable avenue to the discovery of unconscious conflicts. Musical role playing allows such children to sample new techniques in a situation which is not threatening because it is "only playacting." And precisely because it is "only playacting" they can frequently perceive the social stimulus value of a new role and modify it in subsequent therapy sessions until they become comfortable enough to try it in "reality" outside the therapy situation. At other times, playing an exaggerated version of the role they ordinarily assume in their interpersonal contacts may help them to see its maladaptive aspects. Or, by watching another child respond as they might ordinarily respond, they may see how they could modify their behavior in fruitful directions.

Music combined with drama may bring out a child who is too withdrawn to respond to either one alone. We should try to create music and roles for the personality we want to build; spontaneous expression suggested by the music and the character which is being portrayed should be encouraged, rather than the mere recitation of "set lines." Integration of personality is often achieved through this combination of music and drama. For example, one technique used is the singing and dramatization of folk songs. These songs are the unconscious utterances of the people and often an expression of some family, city or national crisis. This type of music can become the unconscious utterance of a disturbed child as well. A child unable to express himself in words may be able to do so in music.

Disguisability

In the center a great premium is placed on the wedding of the therapeutic and educational aspects of music. Far from being paradoxical, there is an advantage of the fact that these two aspects are intertwined, both in action and in the cultural concept of music. Precisely because of this intertwining, music can be prescribed therapeutically, while disguised as sessions, classes, etc. Many disturbed children who desparately need treatment do not accept their own need for it. They may take part in a music therapy program under the disguise of music classes long before they have sufficient ego strength to accept psychotherapy knowingly. In going to a music therapist they can maintain the fiction that they are going to a teacher until they no longer need this defense. In going to a psychiatrist, a psychologist, or a social worker, they would be forced to admit their problems before they could tolerate this admission.

Ability to Combine with Other Treatment and Educational Efforts

The ability of music therapy to combine with other therapeutic and educational tools is another of its broad characteristics. Music therapy can easily combine with singing to increase the effectiveness of both as emotional outlets. Singing is also basic to many applications of speech therapy. In what is seemingly a more educational application, music therapy can be used as a vehicle to teach reading. Dancing and music are obvious therapeutic combinations.

Direct Therapeutic Effects

The above described indirect characteristics of music as a therapeutic tool lend themselves to certain direct therapeutic effects which can be classified under three general headings.

Educational Catharsis

In providing educational catharsis, music therapy allows for socially acceptable expression of the instinctual, unlearned strivings for pleasure which are considered to constitute the unconscious (the id). In addition, music can also encourage expression of learned material which has been repressed and which has thus become a part of the unconscious. That is, those impulses which have been met by the environment with disapproval and which have, therefore, become repressed can frequently find their first acceptable outlet through music.

Ego Growth

Music has always been a tool of communication and in the treatment program is mostly used to promote mental stimulation and imaginative growth. To be effective the music therapy program is planned in terms of the abilities and interests of children of different intellectual and age levels. Music therapy can contribute to ego growth by developing skills for communication with the world of reality, by combining with dance to develop a child's body-image, and by presenting realistic evaluation of the self and of others.

Conscience Growth

Music therapy can also foster growth of the conscience (superego). To a disturbed child, controls, rules and standards (which constitute a major portion of the superego) can often demonstrate their usefulness and necessity more quickly in music than they can in social interaction or other conflict laden areas. Similar effects on personality growth accrue from the application of other therapeutic tools, but few therapies affect all three major facets of personality so directly as music therapy.

In summary, these formulations are mainly based on the orientation that the child's behavior is influenced by the music activity in which he participates. This orientation eventuates in quite different procedures and goals from those which proceed from an expressional orientation in which the guiding principle is that behavior influences music. When impression is the guiding principle, the child is offered selected opportunities to integrate his personality by setting up musical objectives which challenge him to try for such efforts.

Music Therapist's Objectives

Even though there is emphasis on the cultural and psychological features of music therapy I believe it is the therapist's systematic use of a relationship with the child for purposes of personality integration which actually differentiates music therapy from music education. The music therapist, using the flexible medium of her special field, is a therapeutic agent. The atmosphere the therapist creates, the relationship she establishes with a child, and the direction in which she turns his attention changes music activity into music therapy. Therefore I recognize the paramount importance of the child's relationship to the music therapist. In any situation, whether one is performing or listening to music alone or in a group, it has the quality of providing an outlet for feelings. But that provision becomes truly therapeutic when the outlet is planned to suit a specific need, when the intensity of emotion is systematically varied and controlled to achieve a goal, and when the therapist turns the occasion of musical expression to the service of personality integration. This can only be accomplished when the relationship enables the therapist to understand the needs and conflicts of the child and enables the child to abandon neurotic defenses.

The music therapist must develop a program which is creative, spontaneous and stimulating and, at the same time, guarantee success to the slowest child. On the other hand, there are times when it must be soothing and relaxing. There are so many delightful and rewarding things one can do with music for children. Rhythm class, for instance, at the center does not mean counting out whole and half notes, but it means movement, getting into the swing of things, galloping, marching, jumping. The study of different instruments is also important in order that the therapist may discover which sounds best fit the personality needs of children with varying moods and temperaments. Listening for the difference in tone and timbre of instruments and studying the scores of symphonies can make each symphony concert a new adventure in music for the child.

In this frame of reference the following goals have proved useful as guides to the music therapist's operational design.

Aid in Diagnosis and Treatment Planning

Music forms a natural and often a nonthreatening setting for group work which gives the diagnostic evaluation team members a chance to estimate the child's performance level and his enrollment in scheduled activities with reference to the group norms as they become established within the observed situation. Factors considered during the evaluation period include:

Communication Skills: Children often have visual, auditory and verbal impairments which affect their performance in music therapy.

Socialization Skills: Children often interact with other children and adults with extreme difficulty and avoid involving themselves in a group situation.

Orientation and Reality Testing: Children are disoriented and display considerable weakness in reality testing.

Promote Self-confidence

The music therapist often leads children into a sequence of "success experiences" which enable them to change their levels of aspiration.

She can challenge and motivate the children by progressively structuring the musical problems along a gradient of increasing difficulty.

She can often interfere with a child's habitual pattern of failure-expectation, avoidant, inadequate, and/or maladjustive behavior patterns through structuring musical situations and controlling behavior by limit-setting.

She can encourage confidence in the methodology of retrieving better consequences of behavior through choosing new or different alternatives as they are arrayed in the musical situation and through improvising rapport in the relations of therapist and children with all its implied dynamics.

She can induce children to musical activities planned to suit their specific needs and maximize their therapeutic results.

Foster the Development of Skills

Properly planned musical action can facilitate relaxation, improve breathing, strengthen specific muscle groups, encourage better posture, improve coordination, effect some increase in vital capacity, and remove frustrations due to inefficient physical mastery of the environment, thereby reducing internal dissonances in the child's emotional life.

It can also foster the child's growth through his developmental stages, specifically along the dimensions of gross differentiation; integration of knowledge and skills; increasing precision; and using abstractions, rules, principles, definitions and generalizations for better problem solving.

Control Hyperactivity

Musical stimuli can be used experimentally to inhibit the hyperactive child's random responses to them. Also, hyperactivity may diminish when environmental stimulation is minimized as it is in low-stimulus study booths. Surprisingly, a similar effect may be obtained simply by introducing background music (2).

Establish and Cultivate Social Relationships

Musical performance by the child permits the music therapist to work with factors which have become pathological in both the internal and external systems of the child's life-space. Musical activities can also serve to facilitate the early adaptation of the child upon entering the center.

When a child's peer or adult relationships are disturbed, threatening, and anxiety producing, they too, become the objects of avoidance. As a child masters himself, his voice or musical instrument, the expressive techniques in individual music therapy and his enthusiasm naturally lead him toward participation in group music therapy. Sharing interest in music promotes friendly feelings and rewarding social experiences which diffuse to other interpersonal contacts in a rapidly accelerating fashion.

I find that group music aids in the development of leadership, initiative, cooperation and patience. It also furnishes a fine impetus for learning because the group situation itself spurs each one to effort. By its very freedom and gaiety, folk dancing is reflected on the personality; square dancing helps to speed up thinking and learning of the slower children. It teaches patience to the quicker ones while they are in the process of learning. The fact that the music is gay and relaxing creates a happy situation.

Speed Up the Transition from Nonverbal to Verbal Performance Through Musical Action.

For children who have functional speech disorders, music (songs and descriptive storytelling) can be introduced to elicit speech or correct communication.

For children with motor and speech developmental lags, music therapy can help them to learn to use certain concepts or ideas:

Time concepts: Fast, long, delaying, accelerating, slow, etc.

Motion concepts: Swinging, skipping, gliding, stamping, hopping, leaping.

Shape concepts: Round, triangular, linear, square, and combinations.

Number concepts: Using small drums, tapping devices, even hand-clapping.

Opposites: Loud-soft, slow-fast, light-heavy, etc.

Prescription for Music Therapy

The best results of music therapy efforts are attained when they are coordinated with the total treatment and education program. I believe that music therapy is based upon the influence of music upon behavior and that the child's passive reception ("passive" is used only relatively) of music can yield much more field for personality integration. I do not subscribe to the notions which postulate that behavior influences music. I see the child primarily as one who must become engaged in a "being done to" and secondarily in a "doing."

Unique factors about music therapy may justify a psychiatrist's assigning priority to it over other adjunctive therapies as part of the treatment plan. Such factors derive from the capacity of music therapy to

1. use tonal-rhythmic devices to help the child express otherwise unvoiceable feelings;

2. use vocal performance (singing, choir, etc.) to help the child externalize feelings about his self-concept and his basic fears, anxiety, emotional investments, etc.;

3. use club or class meetings, etc. as a communication vehicle;

4. activate the child's ability to understand and behave symbolically through his auditory experiences;

5. enable the child to engage in speech therapy;

6. facilitate the child's growing ability to create;

7. use the meaningfulness of musical experience of the child;

8. glorify, celebrate, and bestow special stature upon a social event, object or idea;

9. further study and understanding of the child.

These factors may paint in rather broad strokes some of the attributes of music therapy which tend to make it "the method of choice" for children from the psychiatrist's viewpoint.

Children's Expectations—Gains

There are some aspects of music therapy to which children themselves appear to attach value. I have observed that once children become involved in the relationship offered by music therapy situations, they expect to make gains, to look for and to expect to find some, if not all, of the following:

1. approval of peers.

2. privilege to occupy a recognized position in the well-ordered (specific rehearsal times, adherence to punctuality), a goal-directed group, with a sense of belonging to it as valued members (raise of self-esteem).

3. association with an understanding music therapist.

4. participation in the joint results of group music therapy and satisfaction from becoming able to contribute to the group goals.

5. identification with an activity whose chief goal is to create.

6. occasional discoveries of new ways to handle personal and social problems.

7. a chance to express unvoiceable emotions through nonverbal inflections of music.

8. opportunities to share this self-expression with others, both within the center and in the community at large.

9. an unfolding understanding that the fundamental usefulness of belonging to the music therapy group is, in a nonthreatening workshop, to explore changes in attitudes, varied skills in social interaction, different levels of aspiration, and more enduring interpersonal relationships.

10. encouragement to continue to develop the musical skills upon their discharge to their home or community.

Staff—Location

The music therapist is administratively and clinically responsible to the director of adjunctive therapies services. She is delegated authority with accompanying responsibility to carry out music therapy duties for the benefit of all children of the center.

She plans, organizes and conducts the music therapy program, participates in the diagnostic and appraisal conferences, and is available to the treatment team members to discuss the use of music with the disturbed children and problems pertaining to specific children.

The music therapy program is conducted in the recreational building, as well as on specified areas on the campus.

Music Activities

The actual activities in the center available under the music therapy program are classified on three levels: individual, group and center.

1. *Music Activities on the Individual Level*
   —Individual instruction in instrumental or vocal perform-ance.
   —Goal-directed listening to music of both serious and light nature (music appreciation class).
   —Composing music, both formal and informal.

2. *Music Activities on the Group Level*
   —Rhythm band, marching, circle games, dance class.
   —Vocal and instrumental ensembles and solos.
   —Club or class meetings; e.g. drum corps, dance combo.
   —Informal "jam" sessions; folk singing, record listening.

3. *Music Activities on the Center's Level*
   —Choirs for Protestant, Catholic or Jewish services.
   —Instrumental groups playing for dances.
   —Vocal groups singing to celebrate holidays.
   —Performing in parts of the center to encourage greater in-terest in music therapy may induce other children to seek participation.
   —Children may attend community concerts or other com-munity activities of musical interest.

INDUSTRIAL THERAPY
Characteristics of Work as a Therapeutic Tool

The industrial therapy program's purpose is to allow children to see themselves in a more positive frame of reference. Emo-tionally disturbed children display a markedly low self-esteem that may need to be enhanced. Children also need a socializing agent to help them learn to interact effectively with their peers and adults.

Industrial therapy is a treatment program of the adjunctive therapies service designed to place children in appropriate work assignments. These consist of eighty minutes of therapeutic work involvement twice a week. The industrial therapy instructor tries to motivate the child through appropriate work assignments toward gaining self-confidence, self-esteem and capability needed during treatment and after his return to his home and community.

Functions and Therapeutic Effects of Industrial Therapy

The industrial therapy program is involved with matters of general maintenance work at the center. Work orders are submitted to the administrative assistant from various services of the center. These work orders are then evaluated by the administrative assistant and given to the industrial therapy instructor for completion.

Industrial therapy involves staff and peer interaction; as projects and work orders are completed successfully, they are seen as positive reflections of each child's contributions. From his contributions he can gain self-esteem; his self-image, pride and respect for property is enhanced.

Admission—Diagnostic and Appraisal Work

When a new child is admitted to the center, it is determined by the treatment team members as to whether or not he should be admitted to the industrial therapy program. The child's psychiatrist notifies the director of adjunctive therapies service of the decision. The director then places the child in industrial therapy. Liaison and coordination take place with the school and other services of the treatment milieu.

The industrial therapy instructor reports on the child's progress in his industrial therapy program to the director of adjunctive therapies service. The instructor also may give an overall review of the child at the D&A meetings. Usually, the industrial therapy instructor reports to the director on the following:

Attitudes (toward peers, staff, activities, receiving instruction, and attitudes toward specific job duties)

Job assignments and hours of active participation in industrial therapy.

Industrial Therapist's Duties and Functions

The industrial therapist is directly responsible to the director of adjunctive therapies service for carrying out the following duties:

—Instructs children individually or in groups in one or more specific craft techniques and skills including painting; photography; plastics; ceramics; and metal, wood, or leather working.

—Instructs and illustrates the skills and proper techniques in the use of tools and materials for specific crafts, projects and minor repairs.

—Supervises the proper use of equipment and facilities of the industrial therapy workshop.

—Prepares purchase requisitions for supplies and materials necessary to complete required work orders.

—Maintains necessary inventory records of supplies and materials.

—Performs related work as required by the director of adjunctive therapies services.

REFERENCES

1. Janson, S. M.: Cultural and psychological features of music therapy. *Bull Nat Assoc for Music Therapy, 8:2,* 1969.
2. Scott, T. J.: The use of music to reduce hyperactivity in children. *Am J Orthopsychiatry, 40:4,* 677-680, 1970.

SCHOOL SERVICE

ORGANIZATIONAL CHART

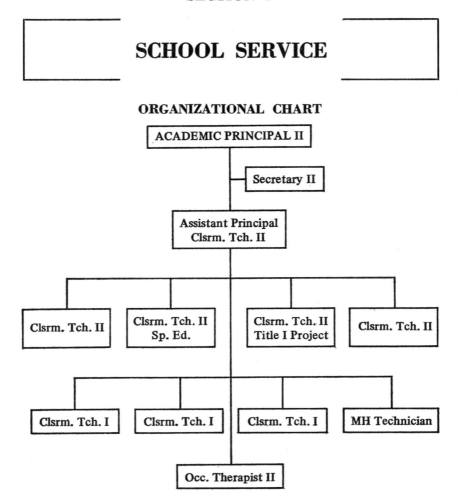

ACADEMIC PRINCIPAL II

Secretary II

Assistant Principal
Clsrm. Tch. II

Clsrm. Tch. II | Clsrm. Tch. II Sp. Ed. | Clsrm. Tch. II Title I Project | Clsrm. Tch. II

Clsrm. Tch. I | Clsrm. Tch. I | Clsrm. Tch. I | MH Technician

Occ. Therapist II

EDUCATION AND LEARNING

CHILDHOOD CAN BE REGARDED as a stage of life in its own right; in that case clues for the establishment of criteria of health must come from what is known in child psychology. Or one can start with the model of the healthy adult and ask which behavior tendencies in childhood hold the greatest promise of health in adulthood. Taking extreme positions in this matter has led to the controversy between the proponents of "progressive" and "traditional" methods of education. This controversy continues to rage bitterly in the absence of facts demonstrating conclusively the impact of either method on the child or the adult-to-be.

Today, a strange Pavlovian reflex takes place; whenever teachers and teaching are mentioned, calumnies against the teachers occur. Teachers' critics resort to irrelevant and inaccurate generalizations about teachers and demonstrate that public expectations of the teacher, education and learning are often unrealistic and absurd. In the end, the teachers are overwhelmed by a public that is ever ready to punish them in self-defense because they come to believe that they have been doubly abandoned in an inexcusable misrepresentation by parents and teachers alike.

Many people think that the mind and the intellect are the same thing; but the intellect is only part of the mind, and it developed late in evolution. It became increasingly important for man because of the wide range of his interests. Developed by proper teaching, the intellect helps us to deal with situations for which our inherited knowledge and skill have not equipped us. Through the process of teaching, one person helps others achieve knowledge, skills and attitudes. At least two persons are always involved in teaching, the teacher and the learner, and teaching creates conditions of leisure and activity that will encourage and stimulate learning. Our word *school* comes from the Greek word for leisure. Of course, reasoned the Greek, given leisure a man will employ it in thinking and finding out about things. Leisure and the pursuit of knowledge: the connection was inevitable, to a Greek.

The older conception of education is based on the assumption that knowledge is power. The child should grow in knowledge as a tree grows, and not as a wall grows, with every brick well and truly laid. As Aristotle put it "children should be taught those useful things that are really necessary, but not all useful things" and that "to young children should be imparted only such kinds of knowledge as will be useful to them without vulgarizing them."*

---

* Aristotle: *On Man in the Universe—Politics, Book VIII*, Classics Club. Roslyn, N. Y., W. J. Black, Inc., 1943, p. 410.

The modern concept of education conceives education to be a process whereby the individual becomes all he is capable of becoming. It looks upon teaching as a process of releasing the creative talents of the individual. Under this concept the learning of practical skills becomes a means to an end and is not seen as an educational end in itself. Under this philosophy of education any knowledge acquired at the expense of personality maladjustment is viewed as an educational acquisition for which too high a price has been paid.

I believe that education is the business of the educator (teacher). It is based on the reality principle and is the imposition of the process of learning of discipline and purpose. The pleasures experienced by children with indulgent teachers who are instructed to touch and, in certain instances, affectionately fondle a child's face, head or arms as a means of establishing a relationship cater only to the pleasure principle. Psychiatrists know that the sublimation of aggressive and sexual needs is not accomplished exclusively by the ego. Superego activity is very much a requirement in the process of sublimation and in motivating a change from pleasure to the reality principle. Also, ego achievements cannot be reached solely on the basis of id motivation (pleasure). Of course, learning can occur under the influence of pleasure motives, but the effort ceases when the pleasure must be deferred and "thinking work" is involved.

We often tend to confuse learning with education. As "there is no royal road to learning," new learning profits from old learning. Learning is a process that goes on everywhere and is the formation of habits of greater or lesser complexity which derive from the experience of living and from social contacts and family. However deeply we may be culture-bound there is no such thing as a unitary culture. Whether we like it or not, certain learning and attitudes fostered by various cultural groups in the country are antithetical to the goals of the modern concept of American education.

Aristotle said that "the object of education is to tame the heart as well as to enlighten the mind." In school, the student is educated; he does not necessarily learn. Education is a classical discipline; it molds the human spirit. School prepares the children for life in an academic way, not in a practical way. Formal schooling is not the best way to help the young mature, or the best way to prepare him to lead a rewarding and responsible adult life. But parents and teachers are telling children so. And the children are angry at them and the school. Joining them in their anger are their parents who assert that both the school and the teacher have failed them. The teachers observe their confusion between education and learning in the community whose hostility they incur because they do not supply the compound services of nursery, babysitter, and vocational counselor. They are not successful parent surrogates.

It has been said that education includes all the ways in which one person deliberately tries to influence the knowledge, skills, habits, values and attitudes of another person. But this is informal learning, not education, and is given by parents, other social groups, newspapers, television, movies, comic books, libraries, museums, churches, camp experiences, business, industry, governments, etc. These are also called "incidental influences," which do not seem to be quite so incidental. This informal learning can be given also in learning centers where programmed learning predominates, e.g. audio-visual materials, instruction and teaching machines which are not a special kind of education (neither do they substitute for reading, writing, telling stories, studying, discussing, or other kinds of formal education activities). They are often contributions of social experiments with students by people who are trying to read the instructions!

MEANING OF THE CURRICULUM

The center holds to the tenet that "every human being is capable of learning and of a lifetime of usefulness and personal fulfillment." The staff, therefore, believes in the part which education plays in creating constructive releases within the framework of the child's capabilities in reality.

I believe that the everyday concern of all teachers and treatment team members in every children's psychiatric center is to develop and to administer a sound curriculum. The concerns about the implementation of a strict and demanding curriculum versus a free atmosphere of inquiry also become problematic.

Indeed, there are distinct problems in planning an educational program which is still therapeutic. The program needs not only to be planned for emotionally disturbed children who are either intellectually normal or brilliant but also to meet the needs of the educationally retarded who may be also emotionally disturbed. From an educational standpoint, the program for the first group should first of all be therapeutic, then challenging and interesting enough to insure steady intellectual and emotional maturation. For it is easier to obtain improvement in emotional functioning than in academic functioning. The program for the second group should be able to stimulate learning and elicit latent talents. Where an established curriculum does not reach certain children, leading to their failure, everyone should be alerted to a variety of possibilities which must include the teacher-child interaction.

The school at the center in general follows the public school curriculum which is modified and supplemented by courses to meet the changing individual interests of children. The special education programs, employing skilled educational staff, are generally individualized with curricula geared to the emotional limitations and therapeutic needs of the children.

The curriculum of the education program for children under psychiatric care provides for their social and emotional, as well as for intellectual, development. Every child is helped to develop optimally his capacities for communication, self-help, and management, social skills, the acquisition and adaptive utilization of knowledge, and other functions and skills necessary for independent living. Adequate organization and firm expectations in the classroom appear to be effective stimulations to the child's cognitive and social development.

Some doctrinaire gentlemen fear that attention to mental health promotes conformist ideas or will cause people to "adjust" to conditions of society which should be criticized and improved. I am aware, for example, that black teachers appear to be inhibited in disciplining the white children in the integrated classroom and are not aware of their reluctance. Their personalities in general tend toward being overly permissive with the children. However, black teachers may fail in their teaching goals with white children if they avoid the necessary firmness which they use with black children. The white teachers seem to maintain better discipline in the class, use incentive techniques for performance, show no favoritism, and their class shows good motivational responses to learning. However, white teachers may fail in their teaching goals with black children if they avoid the necessary firmness which they use with white children. The same issue applies to any teacher-child relationship, but where new arrangements occur the teacher must be alert to the unconscious inhibitions (1, 2).

Ekstein (3) emphasizes that

rather than looking at the curriculum as something external, an outline, a text to be followed, a course of study, a sequence of tasks to be covered, we should try to look behind its facade and into its psychological nature in order to gain a new perspective. The dictionary tells us that "curriculum" is to be understood as a course of study. This definition fails to emphasize that this entails more than a body of knowledge to be transmitted, more than a lecture outline, a textbook. The original root of the word goes back to the Roman chariot races over a predefined course. The Latin verb *curriculare* refers to running over a fixed course. However, we do not merely offer the student the structure of a fixed course, but an opportunity to function by moving forward in it. The concept of curriculum does not simply contain the thought of the goal to be reached at the end of the school term but also conveys the idea of a process leading to it. The means-and-end clinical discussions and the subject-versus-method controversies focus on but two inseparable sides of the same coin. However, the usual, and frequently violent, swings in teachers' colleges, boards of education, public sentiments and political action committees make it difficult for the educators, caught in the middle of these administrative and political storms, to synthesize these two aspects. All too often the teachers are forced to reach an unhappy compromise between "progressive" and "conservative" factions in this modern strife between faculties.

The curriculum builders, comparable to institutionalizers, stress the stable structure, the school, and the subject matter, while the latter emphasize method and teachers, the personal equation. The more sophisticated builders of curricula, of course, think not only in terms of subject matter to be taught but also process and method. . . .

The child needs both the school and the teacher, the subject and the process, and has but few ways to influence the struggle we engage in at his expense. . . . It is the school and the teacher who will decide to what degree the child will love to be educated or will be educated to love and be loved. Thus, education can be possible only within an interpersonal context in spite of the ever-increasing automation of the school industry which tries to disguise this as the work of teaching machines. For it is in this interpersonal context that intraphysic learning goes on. The core curriculum has to be understood as the external link which unites the child and the teacher at the common task, the common struggle. This mutuality of goal and conflict is what makes teaching possible as a process.

Teachers are not always aware of their teaching style or the role of the teacher-child-class interaction. Those who think they are firm in their technique are found to be quite permissive when observed in action. Only a few actually show sufficient firmness in their attitude to stimulate an alert response in the children. The majority convey a degree of acceptance that on the one hand allows the children to feel freer, but on the other hand does not stimulate the child who has difficulty in self-control toward more disciplined behavior. Excessive reliance on touching children as an expression of warmth in a relationship may merely be a repetition of the home situation. One need not assume that the children from a broken home or the underprivileged all come from homes which provide them with only rough physical contact.

A supportive, but balanced, controlling or firm teaching style may be more effective in teaching language. The teacher who in her permissive, warm, touching contacts appeals to the pleasure principle may overlook the role of the superego or ego in fostering the reality principle so essential for learning. The teacher who is less indulgent, firmer, but supportive does far better in achieving improvements, although he is a capable, warm and sensitive person. Children who are aggressive and responsive to the teacher's discipline show evidence of growth. When teachers use task-appropriate procedures and display calm acceptance of children, their pupils' self-concepts are higher.

In many psychiatric treatment centers for children, the curriculum is imposed on both teacher and child by the school principal in collaboration with the treatment team members. This curriculum claims that it initiates the process, the interchange, the struggle, the mutual satisfaction, the failures and successes of teaching and learning. In these centers, teachers and children alike stress only the end, the goal, the examination to be passed, the grade average for public school entrance after discharge from the center, rather than the process, the pleasure of functioning, of achieving.

In the school, the curriculum, the task, is given to children from the outside. The teacher's task is to identify himself with the goal of the treatment team and the learning problems of the child. He looks at his tasks in terms of goals and the processes toward that goal. The ways of teaching a curriculum and acquiring a curriculum have to be synthesized. The teacher's problem is also to identify with the curriculum, the external task which it imposes, as well as the internal situation which it brings about and which initiates the process of change. The same holds true for the child who opposes the external task as well as wants to meet it, as he struggles towards his own autonomy and against external controls which he still needs. In other words, I see a set of natural enemies, though, hopefully, enemies with an underlying wish of surviving and succeeding together.*

It has been said that there can be no teaching without at times creating natural hostility. The teacher cannot expect that the children will love him primarily. They may well love him dominantly, but in part they must also dislike or even hate him because he imposes structure on them. The child must meet these external requirements, the core curriculum, in order to get grades or equivalent forms of recognition and acceptance which he needs just as he needs acceptance, love and praise from his parents when he has done well. Teachers' experience indicates that there is a striking need for organization and discipline in the classroom when children come from homes which lack organization. Also, the emotionally immature child who was "babied" at home and is responded to on a personal basis by the teacher, tends to remain immature and even to lose ground on the reading achievement tests.

The grades or the equivalent forms of recognition and acceptance are not only the child's link to the teacher but to the other treatment team members and the parents as well. Thus, the child works for love, for reward. One might add that the teacher, too, teaches for rewards and for love. He is confronted not only with the child whom he is to help but with the school principal, the members of the treatment team, and the generation of parents whose praise, whose admiration and rewards he, too, needs, regardless how mature he may be.

Teachers residing in the behavior modification country describe the curriculum as a task imposed upon the child which he meets as he is confronted with methods of positive and negative

---

* Reprinted by permission.

reinforcement. Everyone is paid for what he does. Every positive solution is met with reward and every negative failure is met with punishment. A psychologist once suggested that the proverbial teaching machines are better than any available teacher. I believe that much more happens than such learning theorists consider and that human learners are more complex than pigeons; that the teaching and learning process around the core curriculum brings about more than the acquisition of mechanical skills; and that the curriculum is the guarantor, the link between the child and the teacher, the creator of an interpersonal situation and an interpersonal need.

Recent studies indicate that as early as second grade, children indicate concrete distrust of teaching machines and of computerized programmed learning (often based on commercials of an advertised product). By fourth grade, they have distrust for specific "booby traps" and "tricky" elements of audio-visual instruments. By sixth grade, they show global distrust of all educational "right ons" and "turns ons." Children between eleven and twelve exhibit a drop in attention when a mind-molder subject is shown, compared to prior attention to a teacher's teaching. Attention continues to decrease during later programming in a series. The children are far less tempted than we have thought by glowing pictures of goods and services. They seem to be resisting the role of acquisitive robots. Disinterest and mistrust simply increase with age until a picture emerges of older children jaded to programmed learning exposures, paying less attention to them, and making fewer comments about them, especially positive comments. The children feel they are being lied to, incessantly and systematically, by the most influential person in their lives, the teacher.

Some educators-romanticists still fear that the academic function of education may be jeopardized when teachers pay attention to emotional aspects of personality and character development. It has been held by some psychiatric instant analysts that the teachers' choice of a profession had been unconsciously determined by a need to reject the instinctual urges of childhood still present within themselves. Also, teachers' prejudices seem to represent either a repetition of childhood attitudes or a flight from these to the other extreme. Whether this is true or not, the frequency of personality disorders is very high among children in the classes of unstable teachers, and children who have a disturbance in their ability to establish a relationship with the teacher tend to foster a "giving up" by the teacher and the learning achievement is diminished.

Some school services in psychiatric treatment centers are confronted with many children who are not as yet ready for normal learning situations. Such services cannot make the fullest use of the core curriculum. For them, such structure becomes a straightjacket of conformity, and they fall victim to every mechanical shortcut that will get them through the next treatment and education modality.

As Ekstein again explains (3)

> the structure of the curriculum is often thought in terms of reality pressure—the demands of society—and the pressure from the instinctual need system of the child. According to the tripartite model of personality, the id is viewed in terms of its instinctual needs for gratification and the avoidance of danger and pain; the ego in terms of its executive functions, its capacities for delay, for mastery, for solutions, for defense and adaptation; and the superego as having incorporated the demands of parents, of society, or morality, and having brought about the creation of ideal goals. This complex intrapsychic system is in constant interchange with external reality, which alters with the demands of society that fluctuate and change, progress and regress, as are documented, for example, by the vicissitudes of curriculum demands on child and teacher.
>
> Our graphic model constitutes an analogue to Freud's tripartite model. The teaching function is related to the function of the ego in terms of mastery. The learning function, the struggle against learning and requirement, is related to the psychic organization characterized as id. The administration function which sets the task of the core curriculum is related to the superego formation. The school system is then a kind of social replica of the tripartite model and expresses an insight into the intrapsychic and interpsychic nature of learning and teaching. This functional division requires differing skills . . . from those engaged in the teaching field; a more sophisticated knowledge of what goes on in teachers when they teach; in children when they learn; in administrators when they administer systems within a given commu-

nity, which is never entirely free of social change and social pressure. The curriculum is the common task . . . which unites them and about which they struggle with each other just as they must work for each other. The teacher will identify with the task set by the administration just as he will from time to time rebel against it. Sometimes he will overidentify with the administration and victimize the child. The teacher must acquire the skill to maintain equal distance from administration and child, from child and parent, and he must be identified with the process of education rather than with any of the participants. That is his task. The way he teaches and enforces the requirements or adapts them for a special situation; the way he rewards and punishes; the way he loves his subject; the way that he, nevertheless, holds on to his purpose, his task, will sometimes influence the child as powerfully, even at times more powerfully, than what he is teaching and what he offers as reward or punishment.

The child, on the other hand, will identify not only with the teacher's love of knowledge, mastery of subject, but his way of searching, of allowing difference of opinion, of allowing insight learning in addition to repetition learning. Even his ways of examining will influence what the child will draw out of the school system. The child will sense the teacher's reactions to authority, to parents, to the school administration, to political pressure. He will absorb all these things just as much as, if not more than, the text prescribed by the curriculum. The passivity and activity of the learner; the struggle for autonomy of learning; the capacity for acceptance of outer controls when necessary; the whole issue of initiative in learning and trust in teachers will be influenced by the teacher's awareness of the psychological impact of the curriculum and his skill in making use of that awareness.

But what holds true for teacher and child is also true for the administrator of the school. Does he leave room for the autonomy and the initiative of the teacher? Does he see the teacher merely as the blind executive organ of external tasks for which he is responsible? Does he help the teacher with the task of teaching, or is supervision of him an authoritarian function merely instead of an authoritative privilege? Is the administrator used by the teacher solely as a kind of external superego agent, a police officer to whom to send the child when he, the teacher, cannot handle him? Or, can a relationship develop between the principal and the teacher which is an equivalent of learning and teaching on a higher level? How does the principal react to the outside pressures?

The child who enters the school works at first for love, identifies with the idealized teacher and his ways of teaching, and learns, thus, to love the work . . . to work for love . . . to love of work. Neither will be indispensable. There will be an ingredient of each aspect in the most adaptable person. But what holds true for the child is also true for the other participants in the process of education. There are mothers who do not feed primarily out of love for work but in order to get rid of the task as quickly as possible. In the same way, there are teachers and school administrators who have developed little in themselves which can be characterized as the love of educational work. Perhaps this has to do with the impossible tasks I mentioned in the beginning. Society's pressures and demands on educators have always been enormous while actual rewards and recognition have remained far behind.

The original overidealization of the teaching profession, so much a part of teachers' training and so much an inner expectation of the young teacher, leads to the confrontation with psychic and social reality. This process frequently ends with both disillusioned teachers and administrators and is often accompanied by outside ridicule. The teacher's professional skill is constantly beset by social unrest . . . , while it is to remain the steady link for an adult generation full of uncertainties. The world has not learned all it needs in its struggle for adaptation and cannot really teach all that it ought to teach the young in preparation for future, often unpredictable, tasks. The teachers get the impossible task of transmitting knowledge, skills, and attitudes of life to the young in such a way that the generation of children can be the fulfillment of the overt and covert hopes of the older generation.*

TYPOLOGY OF FOUR CONCEPTS OF TEACHER'S ROLE

In describing the teacher's role, some people fall into the trap of the girl or boy scout list of what a teacher must be or must have in the way of character traits and attitudes to be a good teacher (such lists always weary me): happy, patient, understanding, calm, sensitive, aware, all-seeing, able to ignore, humor-filled, attractive, personable, etc. I am sure that all of us have seen some of the best, most inspired, health-giving teachers who have "nutty aspects" and who may be total flops with adults at a cocktail party but who are artists with children; and we have seen some teachers who could pass with a near-perfect percent any questionnaire, rating scale or self-evaluating sheet that any Ed-Psych department could devise who are unstimulating, dull, boring and bored teachers (4).

The point really is that we are not going to get models of men-

---

* Reprinted by permission.

tal health in the teaching profession and that we must, by very real effort in depth contact and in-service training, make it possible for teachers to understand what they do and feel that gets in their way of being good teachers so that they may be helped to find alternate approaches that will not damage their charges and will aid in making for growth. Part of a child's opportunity for learning at school is to learn to deal with many varied personalities, including some nuts and some normals, so long as the nuttiness or normalness does not damage them or interfere with the task of learning.

Being a teacher has special problems. Relatively isolated by the four walls of her room, the teacher is bound by rules, regulations and limits which are imposed upon her from above. She is a person with relatively little autonomy or choice in what she teaches, and there are occasionally restrictions even on the methods she can use. While support, encouragement and rewards are extremely limited, the expectations are never-ending: teachers must be transmitters of knowledge, communicators of values and attitudes, administrators of institutional policies, and models of identification.

Working with teachers we get to know about the feelings and enthusiasm which motivate them as well as the guilt which they so often feel for not being all things to all children, for not "reaching" the difficult or isolated child, for failing to meet their own extremely high standards of achievement.

The nostrums of many "methods courses" seem overemphasized and unreal, and the techniques of managing, stimulating, controlling, leading and supporting simultaneously must be learned the hard way, on the job.

It appears as though teachers are pursuing along one route the same goals which clinicians are pursuing by another. There is much which each discipline could add to the breadth and depth of the other. It is clear that one long-range task of the center is some understanding of the points at which these parallel roads touch, trying to ascertain how the insights of clinical psychiatry and psychology can be used in the educational process, to enhance its effectiveness as well as enhancing child (and even teacher) mental health.

To me, formal and informal education is a mutual, cooperative endeavor. If a child gets a good education it is not only because he has gone through a good school system but also because he lives in an environment where education and learning are valued.

Mumford's studies (5) on the marked differences in teacher orientations to the work of the psychiatric treatment team and the ways teachers use to support or sabotage its efforts, led to a typology of four concepts of the teacher's role, each with its own consistent set of attitudes toward the team's work. The types have been designated as the "teacher-guide," the "teacher-authority," the "teacher-friend" and the "no-teacher." These types help to explain some remarkably different behaviors and attitudes of teachers toward the treatment team. The team, I believe, can work only with the three types effectively when it recognizes and respects the special framework of each.

As teachers are an integral part of the child's life, they do become involved with children's problems and can effectively support or subvert the treatment team's work with children. The team which is able to mobilize positive feelings of teachers can gain an extremely powerful and effective ally for its work with children. Indeed, if the treatment team members fail to meet expectations of the teachers who are potential supporters of its work, it may unwittingly set the stage for effective opposition.

Following are excerpts from Mumford's description of the different typology of concepts of the teacher's role.

"Teacher-Guide": A "Teacher-Guide" is described as the teacher who

> . . . feels that he is responsible for leading the child toward a greater development of his intellectual capacities.
> . . . accepts the fact that emotional problems might interfere with the child's academic performance so that teaching and guidance are necessarily related.
> . . . is alert to some potential difficulties that could follow should a teacher become very involved with the child.
> . . . differentiates between advising and guiding as a teacher on the one hand and on the other hand acting as friend of the child.
> . . . sees limits to his own knowledge and training in handling emotional problems of children.

. . . is the most likely to seek help from the psychiatrist as a technically competent expert.

. . . expects active help and exchange with the psychiatrist.

. . . sees student confidences in the context of patient-to-doctor, not friend-to-friend and is relatively comfortable in talking to the psychiatrist about a student.

. . . describes himself as a professional concerned with one aspect of the total development of the child.

. . . expresses impatience with lectures but can be enthusiastic about open discussion of individual student problems.

. . . is greatly disappointed in the psychiatrist who attempts to set up a program that would be the least offensive from the standpoint of the "teacher-authorities" and the "teacher-friends."

. . . prefers the treatment team to be closer to the school and sees any tendency toward isolation of the treatment team as most unfortunate and one that sets up an us-against-them situation.

. . . wants many teachers involved in treatment teamwork.

. . . is prone to spend time discussing students and teaching problems with fellow faculty members.

. . . resents anything like a small "elite" group—the guidance team.

. . . risks having turn his disappointment into a determined opposition if the psychiatrist fails to meet some of the more urgent expectations of the teacher-guide.

. . . accepts the psychiatric consultation which is consistent with the medical model of consultation between specialty colleagues as well as with the experience of professionals (social workers, psychologists, nurses, etc.). This pattern avoids one pitfall of psychiatric consultation in the schools, the trap of the consultant seeing the teacher as the patient.

"Teacher-Authority": A "Teacher-Authority" is described as the teacher who

. . . feels that lack of problems in the classroom and productivity before the class indicate the presence of a good teacher.

. . . raises the question of whether the school should have any guidance from the treatment team at all.

. . . is more concerned than other teachers with the performance of his students in competitive examinations.

. . . is concerned with the psychiatrist's concern which . . . might encourage the child and faculty to be too relaxed about demands.

. . . feels that all children have problems and that teachers should learn to stand on their own feet and solve them.

. . . is not apt to want more advice from the psychiatrist about how to handle a child.

. . . is mildly interested in seminars offered by psychiatrists. If he goes to them he wants general discussions and didactic material, especially if it includes material on group dynamics that can be translated to the teaching situation.

. . . feels he does not need to know so much about a student and expresses some concern over the "harm" such talk could do.

. . . prefers a totally separate guidance department, away from school.

"Teacher-Friend": A "Teacher-Friend" is described as the teacher who

. . . believes that classroom performance may be influenced by emotional and social factors.

. . . derives some of his feeling that he is a good teacher from having students seek him out, confide in him, and want him as an advisor.

. . . feels he has some special intuition about students and this conviction is important to him.

. . . goes out of his way and gives extra time for the individual student who is his.

. . . intercedes with the family and with the administration.

. . . is vulnerable to personal disappointment and frustration, as in a friendship, having "stuck his neck out" for the student.

. . . feels he "knows better" than the psychiatrist because he is a teacher who has known hundreds of students over a number of years and also because he knows the particular student personally, and the psychiatrist does not.

. . . is unlikely to seek professional help with emerging problems. He may struggle until he is forced to give up.

. . . feels that the psychiatrist is no resource for early consultation, but only for referral as a sort of last resort, justified only when the student is also a problem to other teachers who thus legitimize his "turning the student in."

. . . feels he already knows his own students better than the psychiatrist, and he does not want to be reminded of one he has had to "refer."

. . . feels that the referral to a psychiatrist may represent a personal defeat and one which he may want to forget about.

. . . raises more often the issue of confidentiality as he feels that a student has confided in him out of a personal relationship and mutual trust. In this context, relaying student confidences to the psychiatrist is more like betrayal of a personal exchange than the professional's move to help a student through consultation with a fellow professional.

. . . is annoyed by discussions of individual students because of his special concern about confidentiality.

. . . is reluctant to admit the presence of mental illness in the students.

. . . seldom seeks advice, possibly resenting it as an intrusion on his relationship and a challenge to his special mystique.

. . . feels competent to handle anything he defines as a "minor problem."

. . . may object to seminars as being "stuff we already know" or "a lot of theory that is just one group's opinion."

. . . prefers a totally separate guidance department . . . away from school.

. . . tends to move individually within the orbit of his own coterie of students, helping some measurably and occasionally "rejecting" one into guidance.

. . . indulges in unflattering asides to students about psychiatry or sabotages the individual student's approach to the psychiatrist.

. . . feels that he is possibly the least likely of the three types to join in effective concerted faculty action because he is oriented toward friendship and approval of students rather than faculty or administration.

The "No-Teacher": A "No-Teacher" is described as the teacher who

fills a teaching position for a while but never develops an acceptable concept of the professional role.

The importance of recognizing early the "no-teacher" is to save time. He does not last long. The psychiatrist in a school can expect little help, but much frustration from the "no-teacher."*

From what has been learned so far, it becomes obvious that "school mental health" must not be presented as another requirement to be added to the responsibilities of teachers. Rather, there must be an increased awareness that there are mental health aspects to all phases of school life, not only in the classroom, not only with the disturbed child, but with all children, and within the school and the center as organizations. Here there is much the teachers and mental health professionals can learn from their separate experiences which can be fruitfully shared and applied. The center, I am convinced, can serve as a bridge across which this sharing and collaboration can develop. Teachers and mental health professionals should continue the study of the literature current in the field, observing programs over the country, and in-

---

* Reprinted by permission.

viting experienced educators to give their views on how and at what points education of the child in the residential treatment center should be carried out.

POSITIVE AND NEGATIVE ASPECTS OF THE SCHOOL EXPERIENCE

An adequate educational program must be based on an adequate evaluation of the child and his total dynamics in relation to his problems, to whatever conflict-free areas of response he has, and to the every interest, desire or need which can motivate a positive, active response in the educational setting. Interests in food, radios, television, bugs, worms, kittens—whatever their dynamics—may be used as stepping-stones to satisfy reality and ego-building experiences. The school experience can play a major role in the total treatment process with an emotionally disturbed child.

According to Hirschberg (6), it is

an experience with great ego-building potentials since it is oriented to reality; it aims toward the development of skill and mastery; it can aid in the development of self-image and even of self-esteem; it can offer a source of gratification at varying levels of ability, of aspiration, and of interests; and it can utilize, in successive stages of development and improvement in the child, varying amounts of group participation and group identification, depending on the child's strengths and the needs at the time.

Unfortunately, it is also true that the school experience can be an ego-alien experience for the emotionally disturbed child unless certain factors in the school structure, in the teacher and in the child himself are carefully evaluated. . . . Since the rate of growth and development varies in each individual child, and even within the same child, the various aspects of the developmental process do not always proceed at the same rate, and are differently affected by the dynamics of the child. Moreover, since each developmental step is taken tentatively, an emotionally disturbed child may fluctuate even more than normal children do from one level of adjustment to another in the transitional stages and the educational program must be flexible enough to meet the changing individual needs of each child. In this sense, a positive school experience is one which not only meets the particular "educational" need of the child, but which serves to improve the child's total functional capacity. The teacher is thus required to teach in a manner that both imparts knowledge and skill, and also best meets the emotional needs of the child and his individual potentialities for growth in coping constructively with his problems.

Considering the school in an educational community first, we have three major possibilities: the ordinary classroom, the special class and the special school. The emotionally disturbed child will be able to use or will need one or the other of these possibilities depending on several factors: he can usually adjust to the ordinary classroom if (1) he is able to respond positively to group pressure and to the direction of an adult who is concerned with the group as a whole, and is not free for intensive attention to him alone; (2) his motivation for cooperation is high; (3) he is able to derive satisfactions from usual classroom activities; (4) his overt behavior is not disrupting to the group; (5) he requires no special supervision or observation.

A special classroom or special school will be necessary depending on the degree of deviation from these. . . . Special schools provide smaller groups, special motivation, and more attention for each child within the framework of a group situation.

. . . When the reality of the school experience is examined in terms of its therapeutic meanings in the planned ego development of an emotionally disturbed child, . . . the teacher-pupil relationship must offer dependable acceptance of the child and of his dependency strivings, and his need for security—while at the same time the teacher must have insight into her own needs as well as the child's in order to maintain her freedom to give, or to withhold, or to structure the relationship on the basis of the child and her understanding. Only in this kind of relationship can the child's ego expand and be strengthened, and hence the child gains greater capacity to adapt to life's stress. Furthermore, the more insight which the teacher has into the teacher-pupil relationship, the greater the relief of the child's anxiety about any such close relationship. . . .

. . . The teacher-pupil relationship allows the educational process to help the child learn and to help the child grow, but it always remains structured around the purpose of education and not treatment of the child. In both teaching and treatment there is the common goal of achieving sufficient emotional growth in the child so that more effective functioning will be possible from the child, but the method and the structure differ. . . .

. . . An important point regarding the therapeutic meanings of education is that the child's anxiety is dealt with in the educational process through the use of reality rather than through the interpretation of it. This can be seen in several ways: (1) the relationship between the teacher and the child is seldom if ever, interpreted, whereas in psychotherapy the therapist-child relationship is often interpreted; (2)

in teaching, the need is to know which defense patterns are healthy for the particular child in his conflicts and then to attempt to support and strengthen such defenses; whereas in therapy an attempt is made to give the child either verbal or experiential insight into the nature of his defenses, into the ways in which conflict is handled; (3) in teaching, we try to help the child with the reality pressures which have increased his need for the disturbed behavior and to offer tolerable or attractive reality stimulations at his level of capacity to respond; whereas in therapy the task is to free the child of his own internal needs for disturbed behavior; we are attempting to make certain unconscious material conscious; (4) the teacher is focused on the "situational present" and offers the child realistic help with difficult patterns of adaptation and learning; whereas the therapist focuses on the "historical present" by offering his help in relationship to the internalized as well as situational conflicts; (5) the teacher seeks generally to allay the child's anxiety through the educational process; whereas the therapist often intentionally arouses, for a therapeutic goal, amounts of anxiety which the child can tolerate in order to facilitate the treatment process. Although anxiety may be generated in the child by the teaching process, the teacher frequently uses her relationship with the child for the purpose of absorbing such anxieties; this ability to "feel oneself" into the child's attitudes and yet not lose one's identity is a valuable capacity for both teacher and therapist. Although anxiety may be part of the motivation toward learning, the teacher responds to such anxiety by realistic environmental modification rather than by the interpretive use of such anxiety, as a therapist might.

In regard to the specifically educational role of the school experience in planned ego development, the emotionally disturbed child is dependent upon the educator to a far greater degree than is the average child in the classroom, since he is frequently less able to endure the ordinary anxieties aroused in a classroom and is more sensitive to the teacher-pupil relationship.

The content and the process of the teaching may have particular significance for the emotionally disturbed child. We cannot neglect the "what" in our interest in the "how, when and why." . . . The more the content can be oriented to the reality of the child and his interests and needs, the greater the likelihood that the learning experience will be integrated into the personality with a decreasing need for maintaining defense patterns which prevent learning. Thus the pedagogical techniques of the teacher become a major tool and the need for the teacher to uncover conflict in order to teach emotionally disturbed children does not exist. This does not mean that feelings of the children about the realities of the learning process and the classroom are to be ignored. Emotionally disturbed children need to learn that, although certain actions can and should be controlled in the classroom, the feelings themselves are not forbidden and need not lead to guilt.

. . . When sufficient therapeutic progress has been made, and when the school experience has been sufficiently weighed on the side of successful experiences, then the readiness of the child for a broader educational approach will become apparent.*

THE EMOTIONALLY DISTURBED CHILD IN THE CLASSROOM

Fortunately, we know many things about children who are emotionally disturbed, and most of what we know suggests that classroom teachers can usually do a great deal not only to educate such children but to promote their acceptance and to foster their general welfare.

Emotionally disturbed or mentally ill children have a wide range of individual differences: They vary greatly in the nature, extent, and severity of their emotional and mental disturbances and related disabilities and handicaps. Their scholastic aptitude, intellectual ability, and learning characteristics range from superior to very inferior. Their personal-social characteristics range from excellent to poor. (Much of the variation in personal-social characteristics among children who are emotionally disturbed, as well as that between such children and their nondisturbed age, grade or ability peers, can be attributed to environmental factors rather than to the physical causes or to other stable characteristics, such as those which are genetic and/or physiological.)

Children with emotional or mental illness frequently have specific learning disabilities. Such disabilities may be related to cognitive, perceptual, motoric or environmental factors which complicate or prevent the children's development of skills in spoken or written language, reading, arithmetic, and other scholastic areas.

Because of their great heterogeneity, no universal characteristic of these children as a group provides a meaningful guide to understanding the individual child who is emotionally or mentally ill. Teachers should not rely on stereotypes as a guide to reacting to and working with the child who has emotional or mental handicaps.

---

* Reprinted by permission.

Even though educational retardation frequently accompanies emotional disturbance, the teacher must be aware that many children with severe emotional handicaps are quite able intellectually. The uncritical use or faulty interpretation of conventional psychological and educational tests and testing procedures can vastly complicate the assessment of intellectual ability. Many children with emotional handicaps have been misdiagnosed as retarded individuals because of motor and/or communication or learning problems which interfere with test performance.

An unnecessary amount of experiential deprivation may accompany emotional disturbance. Parents and teachers, by overprotecting, can contribute to such deprivation. Loss of mental stimulation prevents the acquisition of many valuable experiences. All the child's potential for intellect needs to be exploited so that the child is able to get to and be involved in important childhood learning experiences. While some experiences must be brought to the child, overdoing this can prevent him from developing the motivation, curiosity and mobility he needs to engage in significant experiences.

Educational retardation frequently accompanies emotional disturbance. Both intellectual retardation and experiential deprivation contribute to educational retardation, as do loss of school time for psychiatric treatment, absence for recuperation and rest, and inappropriate or inadequate school placement or programming. Cooperation on the part of the school, psychiatrist and child will keep such lost time at a minimum.

The children who suffer educational retardation are now called "socially disadvantaged," a term which has replaced the earlier term "culturally deprived." This replacement became necessary because the children of many poor families do not lack a culture; the culture of their families simply does not prepare them well for competent performance in school and in contemporary democratic commercial-industrial society.

Some writers are making a major, but unnecessary, controversy by seeking to assign blame for the educational retardation of socially disadvantaged children to some existing social situation or institution. The public school comes in for much of the blame. Books and articles are written saying that the public school as we know it cannot do the job; that "our children are dying" mentally; that the bureaucracy of the educational system in the big cities is solely responsible for the low school achievement of so many slum children.

Why do some writers who are trying to do the right thing about socially disadvantaged children ignore the manifest evidence of the importance and significance of the preschool years in the mental development of children? Most of them are nonscientists. They lack the discipline and frame of mind that would lead them to look for evidence and weigh it. The few who are scientists are caught in a political situation that forces them to overstress one element (the school) in a complex situation.

The reasons for the behavior of the critics appear to be the following four, in various selections and combinations for each individual.

—Some have a deep drive to criticize the institutions of our society, especially those maintained by the "establishment." For them, "any problem of the society is caused by the establishment, which imposes a rigid bureaucratic system on people who should be free." Since there is no such institution serving children below the age of five or six, they must blame the school as we now know it. If we had public nursery schools for three- and four-year-olds, these same critics would find something in these nursery schools to criticize. They do not criticize the institution of the family, because in their mystique it is a "natural" institution, not an artificial one like the school.

—Some suffer a compulsion to see the problem of educational retardation as a simple one with a simple solution. They cannot tolerate the ambiguity of a problem with complex causes and consequent complex solutions. They propose such simplistic solutions as smaller classes, teachers with more faith in the effectiveness of the schools, educational parks, local community control of the schools, and on and on.

—Some want to protect the lower-class culture from criticism. They fear that lower-class family structure will be made a scapegoat by people with such dubious motives as school budget economy and opposition to racial intergration. Consequently they "play down" the influence of the school.

—Some simply want to make a "quick buck." Some free-lance writers fall into this category. To prophesy the doom of the public school is currently fashionable, and if this kind of thing sells, they will write it.

It is not likely that one-sided criticism of the school factor, while ignoring the family factor, will help us to make the wise allocation of our resources and the wise investment in experimentation that we need to solve the basic problem of increasing educational opportunity for the disadvantaged child. More research and development work is what we need.

Setting realistic goals is one of the major problems in the educational management of children with emotional disturbance or mental illness. The tendency is to expect either too little or too much from such children. Evidence indicates that children learn to set unrealistic levels of aspiration for themselves as a result of inappropriate expectations by others. The best objective for the teacher would seem to be to arrange assignments of just manageable difficulty. The goal should be ever-increasing independence in functioning through success experiences.

Below are several suggestions for the classroom teacher with emotionally disturbed children.

—Be guided by behavioral and functional evidence of abilities and disabilities instead of making educational decisions solely in terms of psychiatric diagnoses or stereotyped thinking about categories of mental disorders.

—View the emotional disturbance as only one of many important attributes of the child rather than as if it were his most significant characteristic.

—Provide a setting for, and expect achievement of, the child in terms of his aptitudes, abilities and other attributes, not in terms of his emotional disturbance alone. Differentiate the effects of mental limitations from effects that have their source in other environmental causes, such as experiential deprivation, educational retardation and attitudes.

—Obtain assistance in the form of constructive consultation

and specialized equipment or materials from those who assume special responsibilities for children with mental illness. However, consider the child one of your students rather than "one of theirs" (the therapists').

—Remember that the child with emotional disturbance probably needs as many firsthand experiences as possible. Help the child to develop concepts meaningful to him and in line with his own reality. Do not impose upon him artificial concepts he cannot understand or appreciate because of his lack of intelligence or experience.

—Do not thoughtlessly exploit the child with mental illness by showing him off to other children, to teachers, or to visitors.

OBJECTIVES OF SCHOOL SERVICE

The school service consists of a nongraded school which provides educational experiences at levels ranging from preschool through junior high school to children of the residential and day treatment center. The school is fully integrated with the other clinical services and operates on a twelve-month-per-year basis. Its programs are designed not only to serve the child's academic needs but also to increase his overall-competence.

Education, as applied to emotionally disturbed children, requires that in any curriculum adjustment made for them emphasis be placed on education in keeping with the capacities, limitations and interests of each child; on education for wholesome social experiences; on education in keeping with the interests of all children; and on education to help children learn more about the dynamic force of their emotions and to come to accept their individual emotional strengths and weaknesses. The welfare and education of children demand the development not only of cognitive processes but also of the social skills and behavior which emerge from the school experience.

The application of these principles requires that for emotionally disturbed children, specific objectives be formulated of a simpler and more practical nature than those which may be utilized with normal children. Happy social relationships, physical efficiency, wise use of leisure time, and acceptance of responsibilities are of major importance.

While the center's primary function is treatment, through its school service it retains many features of a private school. When one examines the prescription-like way in which activities and education are used for individual children, however, one becomes aware that they are both used flexibly in the treatment program. Thus, the school differs from regular schools in that it takes into account not only the academic needs of its children but also their emotional needs. The school has the responsibility of setting the emotional scene so that there is a balance between protection and competition always with a view to emotional maturity. The school is designed to help develop creative patterns of behavior, to stimulate interest in learning, and, where indicated, to maintain scholastic achievement sufficient to allow the children to continue their own grade when they are discharged.

The school's basic aim is to create a dynamic teaching and learning situation adjusted to the capacity of the individual child, his needs and his skills. Education is, of course, emphasized because, regardless of the origin of the malfunction of these children, much of their current behavior is related to their inability to obtain self-esteem and gratification from school. The school, however, early in the program, does not try to force academic performance on all students. I believe that children are not all created equal in their abilities and that their talents and aptitudes differ. A child who is not a good book student but works well with his hands is encouraged to go in the direction of his strength. He is confronted with his disability but given hope that he can overcome it.

Teaching in the school has certain positive values. Interestingly enough it has been found that learning an academic subject produces less anxiety in some shy, withdrawn children than do some of the other center activities. The activity of the children with the teacher who is aware of the treatment needs provides for some children an introduction to therapy, for in some ways it represents an intermediate stage between the extremes of the formal classroom, on the one hand, and the therapy session on the other.

The school provides the appropriate emotional atmosphere in which socially undesirable attitudes or prejudices are at a minimum. It also provides a curricular differentiation and richness as part of its responsibility in mental health. Taking a course in the school does not call for the child to produce material relative to himself and his emotional problems. As a result of the teaching, the withdrawn, apathetic and inhibited child is gently prodded and led into communication with his peers. The indecisive child, with feelings of inadequacy and inferiority, is helped to develop a sense of achievement. For some children attempts are made to arouse an interest in and appreciation of the value of academic study, while the teaching itself is organized to provide group feeling, a sense of achievement, and assistance in making a social adjustment. In the school, the child is accepted at whatever educational level he may be functioning, is provided with opportunities to progress at a rate dictated by his own emotional and intellectual status, is given specific help when he is ready for it, is afforded success experiences in an atmosphere of kind firmness, and is helped to build a more robust personality, that is, to become more emotionally mature.

Another objective of the school is that children gradually raise their educational achievement to a level where they can compete in a public school and the school seeks to help them attain the emotional adjustment necessary to withstand the pressure of a large public school before returning to their own homes and community schools. Thus a child's school progress and school adjustment is set up as a goal for him by teachers and other members of the treatment team; a child recognizes going to public school as definite achievement.

Finally, an important objective of the school is to train the present teachers now rather than wait for Utopia, when all teachers will have understanding insights into behavior problems. Teachers with adequate knowledge of mental mechanisms and personality development can be of material assistance as members of the professional team which seeks a better understanding of the many facets of educational problems.

Even though the teacher who has been trained in our modern teachers' colleges has learned from many angles how wide the individual differences are among the children of the same grade, of the average classroom and has been saturated, verbally at least, with the principle of adapting the learning job of each child to his particular readiness and ability to succeed at that job, he tends still to have all these children do about the same thing at the same time.

In the ideal form of training for teachers, first preference should go to grounding in the subject that is taught, followed by familiarity with methods of teaching, a grasp of psychological principles concerning intellectual development and individual differences and aptitudes, understanding normal personality development and individual differences in motivation, acquaintance with mental hygiene and psychopathology of childhood and adolescence, and, finally, personal maturity in a teacher. The teachers should not use mental health material as a primary focus in teaching but they should be familiar with these principles in order that they may do a better job than otherwise of promoting intellectual capacity and skill in their students. Good teachers as noncontrolling, warm persons may not necessarily be the most effective for a learning achievement goal. Teaching style roles or behavior cannot be generalized as more or less effective except in terms of the various goals to be achieved. Goals in teaching must include the integration of cognitive, social and behavioral growth, not just an increase in cognitive skills. Our cooperative work with teachers can start right there. Whatever understanding fosters more effective teaching patterns will improve the teachers' self-image.

STAFF

The staff of the school service consists of the academic principal, the secretary, six academic teachers, one occupational therapist and one crafts instructor. In addition, a reading specialist supplements the reading program and one mental health technician serves as a teaching aide (reading, tutoring).

A high teacher-child ratio is maintained as well as the flexibility that makes it possible for teachers to give special attention to individual children at different stages in their treatment and progress.

Principal—Duties and Functions

The resources of the school service are managed by the principal, who is directly responsible to the director of the center. The principal supervises all staff assigned to the school service.

The principal is the vehicle through which the educational goals of the school are accomplished. His actions must always focus upon the welfare of the children.

The principal's formal job description charges him with planning, organizing and directing the education programs under the general supervision of the director of the center. He is responsible for creating an environment in which the best that is known about the education of emotionally disturbed children is consistently practiced.

Instructional leadership comprises the largest and most important area of the principal's work: organizing and supervising the instructional staff; planning and developing the curriculum to meet the changing needs of the school population; classifying, assigning and grouping pupils for instruction; promoting sound mental health practices in the classroom; establishing and maintaining therapeutic discipline measures; providing an effective in-service training program to stimulate and update teacher competencies; developing staff participation in decision-making; and evaluating the effectiveness of programs and staff.

In the amount of time required, the next major area of responsibility revolves about direct contact with children. Such contact may be represented by individual child conferences, both formal and informal; by classroom teaching, either on a regular basis, as a substitute for an absent teacher, or by individual educational testing; and by frequent visits to activities in progress. Contact and observation opportunities are necessary not only for knowing each individual child but are essential to meaningful participation in treatment team, diagnostic and appraisal functions and in making recommendations for the future educational management of the child.

In many areas of activity, such as administrative management, supplies and equipment, and plant supervision, the school principal's functions somewhat parallel those of his public school counterpart. The major difference lies in the area of school-community and school-parent relationships, where the center's principal may not be required to exercise the sophisticated public relations techniques needed by the public school principal. Nevertheless, it is important that avenues of communications be maintained with local public school officials on matters of common interest.

In general, the principal must know the characteristics, needs, and educational provisions appropriate for each emotionally disturbed child and must manage his resources in such a manner so as to fulfill those needs to the maximum degree possible.

Teacher—Duties and Functions

The teacher performs his educational duties and functions under the supervision of the principal. Each teacher holds a valid teacher's certificate.

The teacher of emotionally disturbed children must possess qualities and skills different in degree if not in kind from those of the "Dos and Don'ts" list of regular teachers. The teacher in the program is aware of a departure from certain trends employed in an elementary school or junior high school where the basic aim of instruction is to advance knowledge. In the school, in addition to the aim of advancing knowledge, equally important is the objective to increase the self-confidence of the child and to help his resocialization.

Children usually find desirable the following teachers' qualities: cooperative, democratic attitude; kindliness and consideration for the individual; patience; wide interests; personal appearance and pleasing manner; sense of humor; good disposition and consistent behavior; interest in pupil's problems and flexibility; use of recognition and praise and unusual proficiency in teaching.

Teaching, like any other profession involves a wide variety of activities. The responsibilities of the teacher in the psychiatric center differ from those of the teacher in a public school. The teacher's administrative, teaching and helping activities include:

—giving instruction (the primary responsibility);

—arranging the classroom in such a way as to provide a good environment for learning;

—adapting material to children's needs;

—providing social rewards (praise when the child learns something well);

—grading papers, keeping records and making reports;

—guiding extracurricular activities;

—conferring with members of the treatment team;

—attending teachers' meetings and participating in treatment team meetings and diagnostic and appraisal conferences;

—estimating the child's readiness to learn (growth, prior experience, desire to learn);

—estimating motivation to learn (arousing interest in the child in what is being taught and giving the child a desire to learn);

—emphasizing teaching instead of learning;

—adapting his teaching to the child's level;

—bringing education within the child's understanding;

—teaching the child to relate ideas, to analyze problems and evaluate the outcome of a course;

—helping the child to learn to achieve some goal that is important to him;

—directing the child to ways of learning outside the traditional classroom techniques;

—helping the child to set for himself progressively more difficult goals and keep at the task until he succeeds;

—counseling children on individual problems.

A successful teacher in a children's psychiatric treatment center

—remembers that teachers are not therapists in the psychiatric sense, nor are they expected to do psychotherapy. Teachers become more effective if they are not "part-time therapists." Effective teachers and effective psychotherapists probably possess a cluster of similar personal attributes which enable them to communicate with disturbed children. However, teachers do not consider themselves as therapists, although they regard the child's emotional well-being as primary.

—is well informed on the principles of child growth and development.

—has a thorough knowledge of the fields he is teaching and the best ways to teach.

—teaches because he loves and respects children, not only because "teaching is a respectable profession."

—distinguishes behavior that is significant of serious emotional disturbance from that which is momentary or passing (aggressive behavior that stems from exuberance, enterprise, ambition and initiative; aggressive behavior that manifests itself in hostility, resentment and hatred).

—is able to tolerate a high degree of disturbed behavior.

—tries to ascertain what among certain things is worth the child's learning and at what degree of difficulty in each the child can learn successfully.

—seeks to ascertain how each child in the classroom feels and why he feels as he does.

—is able to establish working relations with the students, gain their confidence and guide them into constructive activities.

—enjoys working with people and is interested in children as growing personalities.

—uses his knowledge as a means of encouraging others to learn.

—finds study a rewarding activity.

—has an aptitude for learning.

—is able to impart his knowledge to others.

—has a feeling of adequacy, a feeling of belonging.

—studies human nature and himself.

—sets the example in the ability to adjust to various problems of life.

—lives in the outside world in such a way that he is capable of encouraging a relaxed atmosphere in his class.

—emphasizes the importance of each day, and does not fret unduly about the future.

—keeps his lessons interesting.

—encourages in the children the action of thinking, to develop the capacity to think, and does not merely transmit to the children the product of his thoughts.

—revises his attitudes, and is not shocked or influenced by new ideas, by new principles of teaching, by the antics of his pupils, or by any confession which he hears from a disturbed child.

—refuses to resort to excuses, alibis and subterfuges.

—realizes that if he is frightened, the fear may express itself in aggressive behavior toward his pupils.

—does his best in spite of criticism and hardships.

—works off his feelings of hostility and stubbornness.

A good teacher, when following the curriculum, would not merely make the children absorb a body of knowledge, like pouring knowledge into an empty mind via a funnel. A good teacher would rather bring about an active progress of thinking, of learning and of mastering.

An efficient teacher must be an important person to his pupils, and they should be proud of his leadership. He should conduct himself with dignity, as befits a leader; dress, walk and talk as such; and should resist any challenge to displace him. One glance from his eyes is usually enough. The unconscious mind is very familiar with what the leader will do if challenged. The child has a bit of the wolf in him, and if the leader of the pack shows any weakness, the young ones will challenge his leadership and take great pleasure in pulling him down.

The teacher's role as a model for identification can enhance the child's self-esteem and foster the development of his personality. Basic ingredients in personality development such as trust in oneself and in others and an acceptance of their significance in engendering self-esteem and love are usually established before a child enters school. Nonetheless, there are many opportunities in the teacher-child relationship to foster these essential elements in the child's character and learning patterns. Personality factors are quite labile in young children and for many years thereafter. Thus, in addition to understanding group dynamics, teachers need an awareness of the child's psychic structure at each given phase because each child has his unique reactions to the teacher's behavior as well as to the learning process. The teacher-child relationship has often been compared in significance to the parent-child relationship as it relates to the personality with which the child must face the world. One who assumes the mantle of "teacher" thereby takes upon himself a profound responsibility for the future.

The teacher education colleges and universities impress their students with the fact that a teacher's behavior interacts with that of the individual child in a classroom as well as with the group as a whole. These interactions establish intricate patterns of social transaction. Yet, in general, teachers are not provided with the necessary feedback of information regarding their own behavior so that they can objectively appreciate how they participate in the teacher-child-group interactions with which they have to cope. Teachers need a thoughtful feedback in order to help them perceive their role and responsibility in the teacher-child interaction. This understanding can then be translated into behavior which will enable them to develop a balance between controls or limits and permissiveness or indulgence. Children will identify with the teacher who has achieved a balance of controls and thus can use the relationship for developing self-control (7).

EDUCATIONAL CHARACTERISTICS OF STUDENT POPULATION

a. Age range: six to twelve years. Appropriate programs are offered to children functioning from kindergarten to high school freshman levels.

b. Intellectual range: Mildly retarded to superior intelligence children as measured by standardized tests of intellectual functioning.

c. Psychiatric diagnosis: Behavioral disorders, severe psychoneuroses and psychoses.

d. Sex ratio: Boys-girls 4:1.

e. Educational deficit: Average educational deficit on admission exceeds two years with reading deficits ranging to four years.

f. School history: The typical emotionally disturbed child has a long history of school failure, suspension, truancy, placement in special classes, etc., too often with major learning disabilities.

g. Speech disorder: Functional speech disorders (lisping, stuttering, revenge speech) are prevalent handicaps.

GROUPING OF CHILDREN

A trap into which some centers fall is the conventional way they approach the grouping of children. Teachers are advised that groups and subgroups have an effect on the mental health and task performance of the class. They also point out the advantages and disadvantages in heterogeneous grouping—in other words, the same business that is in every education textbook.

The psychiatric treatment field, however, demands more than a textbook grouping, i.e. knowledge about the forces that operate to make a group a group; the forces that operate to block learning; to block the teacher; to form subgroups, hostile or cooperative, fighting, fleeing, dependent; what kind of group valence a teacher elicits; what kind of relations go on between groups within the class, with the school, among staff and children.

Each child's educational experience is strongly influenced by the other children with whom he interacts. For this reason, the grouping of children is always a vital consideration and is periodically re-evaluated. Some of the factors considered are the level of developmental maturation, chronological age, sex, special handicaps, and psychopathology and psychotherapeutic needs.

Although it is recognized that grouping requires careful selection of children and teachers, small groups of two to five children are formed. Children are grouped for instruction on the basis of achievement as demonstrated on a standardized achievement battery and on the basis of the child's therapeutic needs, considering such factors as chronological age, intellectual capacity, emotional status, past school performance, and the characteristics of the children already in the group. Modified schedules are provided for those children whose illness precludes full participation. Academic groups are limited to five students or less in order to provide maximum individual attention with minimum distractions.

An effort is made to structure class groups so that the differences among the individual students in any one class and by any one criterion are not too great. A child might have one class in a group of three or four children and other classes alone, depending on his ability to get along with individual children and on his grade placement. Severely psychotic children who cannot be graded, but who can in some measure respond to a routine educational approach, are attending a special class. The child's movement into, through and out of different programs or phases of a program are considered in terms of the timing of changes and the potentially disruptive effects changes may have upon the child, the family, the group, and the program.

ORGANIZATION OF INSTRUCTION

The standard requirements of the center's school are the same as those of the public schools. The teachers instruct only the subjects for which they are qualified; the children receive only the grades which they rightfully have earned. Punctuality and proper class decorum are expected of all children.

Instruction is organized on a departmentalization basis, with all children except the preschool group moving to another classroom or activity every forty minutes, for a total of six periods per day. The preschool or "Early Learning Experiences" group is housed in a self-contained classroom and is in session during the morning periods only. In the majority of schools, due to the inappropriate physical design of the school building and other factors, children are allowed a compulsive moving from classroom to classroom at the end of each period. This practice, I believe, keeps many a pupil too busy to think and educates him in progressive immaturity with the result of no formal personal relationship between child and teacher, of little opportunity to help children see the interrelationships between school subjects, and of encouraging the teacher to regard himself as a subject-matter specialist rather than as a generalist in working with children.

USE OF SPECIAL TEACHING MATERIAL

The program includes the provision of special education experiences for children whose emotional disturbances and academic retardation make it difficult for them to learn, the opportunity to remedy deficits in education for those who have fallen behind because of their illness, and the maintenance and progression of education and intellectual development for all children during their period of disability.

Due to the unusual educational deficits and unique learning styles encountered, teachers must be able to use a broader range of materials and equipment than does the ordinary classroom teacher. In addition to conventional materials and audio-visual aids, effective use is made of learning games and puzzles, multimedia kits, auditory and visual perception training programs, and manipulative devices and models. Teacher-produced materials and adaptations for specific children are often necessary.

The seating arrangement and general decor of the room must be aimed at reducing distractions. A structured program, a stimulating curriculum, and consistent limits provide further controls; the rest is up to the relationship the teacher is able to establish with each child.

MANAGEMENT AND CONTROL
Democracy in Treatment and Education

Many modern teachers feel that the application of mental hygiene principles to the classroom is associated with the emphasis upon what is being called "tolerance" and "democracy in education." They also feel that the spirit of democracy encourages careful vigilance to make certain that the emotionally disturbed child receives full share of any improvement in the field of education. Thus they choose to change from a frontal attack on behavior problems to an indirect approach (searching for causal factors, defining the misbehavior as calls for help, an attempt to satisfy some pressing emotional inner need, a search for security, or desire for attention), i.e. to cultivate democratic relationships and tolerant attitudes in the class, a feeling of friendliness, of good will. The teachers expect the same democratic spirit to be felt by the children themselves and thus perceive the classroom as a workshop in democratic living, i.e. the child is tolerated, is not forced to control himself, is allowed to feel that he has a choice in the management of affairs (in the name of relief from tension), is allowed excessive verbalism (in the name of individualistic competition). I believe that as there can be no democracy in the interpretation of a disease, the same is true in interpretation matters of education.

The prevailing psychological theory which guides the clinical and educational operations with children suggests that the major portion of the child's personality is established prior to the onset of school. It is, of course, common knowledge that preschool and school children are extremely impressionable and malleable. However, it is also true that what they have encountered in their early and later childhood in terms of attitudes and experiences often establishes lasting, and sometimes immutable, behavioral patterns.

In my efforts for management and control of the children I try to re-examine the usual broad diagnostic categories in order to achieve the educational philosophy that every child should have an opportunity to learn to the best of his ability. In working with the children, I found many whose symptomatology suggests the presence of a true emotional disorder or mental illness. The bulk of these children come from homes considered broken and underprivileged in a number of respects. It seems, therefore, that parental psychological and emotional pathogens are communicable. Their spread follows laws similar to those which govern the spread of biological pathogens. Psychiatry has accepted this principle with the general systems theory.

Mental diseases fail to fall into neat categories; the causes for them, according to current theories, are multiple and complex. Now psychiatrists have begun to suspect that mental illness in the form of transient mood disturbances, periods of decreased efficiency, times of irritability, and disinterest in the world around us happen to all of us. For most of us, these periods are transient because our inherent strengths, or the resources we draw on, help us to re-establish the vital balance. For children whose strengths are still developing the question then is: How can we help them grow into mature, mentally healthy adults?

Abdication of Parental Responsibility

The amount of knowledge accumulated in the last decade equals the amount gathered in all the years of written history. This proliferation of knowledge, along with the associated amplification of the complexity of the environment to which man now has to adjust, explodes many of the simplistic, and oftentimes comforting, beliefs once held regarding the functioning of our physical and human universe.

These changes produce feelings of inadequacy and incompetency in increasing numbers of parents, so much so that in many areas they abdicate their traditional responsibilities and insist that other public institutions assume some of the burden. The center and its school is often being asked to compensate for the parents' failures. Often these responsibilities have been willed to public institutions without thoughtful exploration of whether they are indeed the agencies best-suited for the task. I wonder if this transfer of responsibility does not at times result in repercussions beyond what the center and its school anticipated.

What I see is a variation and range from disorganization in the home to a lack of sensitivity to the child as an individual. A number of children present a picture of emotional immaturity. Many of them are indulged with permissiveness or they are ignored at home which creates a lack of self-discipline. The "tough" treatment presumed to be prevalent in such homes is not apparent in my interviews with parents, contradicting the idea that a punitive approach is the style of control to which they are accustomed and understand. If such children are indulged with overpermissiveness or in various ways babied in school, the classroom experience becomes a repetition of the situation encountered in their own family and deprives them of stimulation toward self-discipline necessary in the learning process.

Permissiveness versus Discipline

The two major sources for influencing development and behavior in the classroom are the teacher and the children, and these two areas present us with a large number of relevant variables in any systematic study of the educational process. Teachers need to be assured that too much permissiveness is perceived by children as a lack of interest. The child may withdraw from the relationship and become passive, with low self-esteem because he feels he cannot win love or approval and begins to daydream and become variously inattentive. On the other hand he may become angry and act out his hostility through varying means. Many teachers have low self-esteem, too, fostered in no small way by our culture. They feel their work is not appreciated, that others "intrude" when they recommend various methods of teaching and management.

The severely emotionally disturbed child poses challenging problems of classroom management. Most, if not all, such children have been unable to function in a public school setting. Therefore, primary emphasis throughout the school is devoted to increasing the child's tolerance for school by placing him in a nonthreatening learning environment. From the beginning, the atmosphere in the classroom is made as comfortable as possible by structure. Children cannot sit where they wish. Formality is the keynote of the teacher's attitude. Initially some children may appear quite apathetic. Yet when their interest can be aroused and their attention obtained, they become very active. It may be mentioned that even drills and repetition which are necessary for those who cannot concentrate are conducted in a lively but structured manner. Gaiety and earnestness are not at all exclusive, and both may be necessary to draw out an inhibited child.

The relationship the child has with his teacher still appears to be the most important single factor in stimulating and motivating the child to learn, especially in the earliest grades. Even those children with obviously limited skills or less than average intelligence, or internal pressures that push them into hyperactivity, will make significantly different academic progress if they encounter an understanding teacher.

The educational process is described as one that leads from learning for love (reward and punishment) to a love of learning (insight, identification). The school houses every child for six hours per day, five days a week, and fifty-two weeks per year. During his months or years of enrollment, the child experiences physical, mental and social growth ranging from nearly total dependence to nearly total independence. The center decides what quantity and quality of services the school should furnish in order to fulfill its role in the treatment of emotionally disturbed children through planned ego development.

The policy of the center in relation to disciplinary problems which may arise is to support the school in the need for obeying rules and regulations. No corporal punishment of any kind is permitted. No isolation rooms are used. No aides or crisis intervention personnel are assigned. No "comprehensive behavior modification" scheme is used, nor are staff allowed to give individual children gifts of candy or toys.

Discipline is effected ultimately through the skills and endurance of the classroom teachers. If a teacher cannot handle a situation she may ask for help from the principal or a group worker. The group worker can call the campus on-duty nurse or, in her absence, the director of nursing. The child with self-destructive activities might require a companion to hold him constantly in an attempt to prevent him from injuring himself.

Teachers try to familiarize themselves with some of the dynamics underlying each child's behavior in order to anticipate and to tolerate aberrant and disruptive conduct. In order to accomplish this, teachers try to achieve a balance between undue repression and the absence of restraint; that is, avoiding the extremes of instinct gratification or restriction. Thus, they set up minimal educational and behavioral goals for each child and reinforcements in the form of certificates, stars (never small prizes, candy, chips or tokens) are made available, never permitting these reinforcers to accumulate toward a longer range goal. Also, the children are helped to realize that they are working for the teacher's approval and love or for the sake of achievement itself. The veteran teachers are found to need these techniques less than the new, inexperienced teachers.

Unlike many fanatic operant conditioners who overlook dynamic factors and insist they have discovered a bright new cure-all when they propose that rewarding children is more efficacious than punishing them and that by consistently ignoring unacceptable behavior responses, these patterns tend to die out. I believe it is to the school's credit the acknowledgement that there is something of significance behind behavior: that dynamics of an individual personality make for personality differences, and I say, *Vive cette différence.* When we "shape" the dynamics out of existence, if we don't murder each other first, we will bore each other to death. Some teachers, like any good teachers, even before Pavlov, use the conditioning theory as a method to deal with specific behavior or learning responses in which rewards are carefully arrived at by finding what will indeed be rewarding for a given child, and avoidance measures are sought that will work for unwanted behavior. Of course, aside from the fact that even unsticky M&M® candies may not be as attractive as some unwanted behavior, there is the often overlooked fact that with all the attention paid to a child or group of children to determine appropriate rewards, there is a good bit of interpersonal relating going on that may have something to do with the results; besides, by such attention the teacher may observe and learn more about the child, whether for the sake of rewards or not, to make his teaching more effective.

TYPES OF SCHOOL SERVICES
Instruction in "Tool" Subjects

All children are enrolled in the basic educational necessities of reading, language arts, mathematics and social studies. In addition, science instruction is provided on a limited basis. Reading and mathematics are scheduled on a daily basis, while language arts and social studies are on a three-day-per-week or two-day-per-week basis. Children still struggling toward recovery are not allowed to enroll in more than one class a day. In no case are children permitted to take more than five subjects. Proper balance between the academic and emotional needs of the children is sought and maintained.

The school makes no arrangements for children to attend classes either on a part-time or a full-time basis in the city when they have progressed to the stage at which they can attend such classes.

I found that the stigma of mental illness which is often present in our society has not presented serious problems for children having attended school in a psychiatric treatment center. When they are ready for re-entry into a classroom in the public school, all credits earned in the center school are transferred to the school of their community.

Remedial and Corrective Reading

The most common educational characteristic of the emotionally disturbed child is a deficiency in communication skills, particularly in reading. As reading disability is a frequent cause in personality disturbance, a remedial reading program is available, goals are set up within the child's achievement range, and many devices are used to encourage and interest him in learning to read. Projects funded under federal or state loans can provide for a reading specialist and materials.

The reading specialist supplies intensive individual tutoring to those children whose reading problems are amenable to remedial or corrective procedures. Each child is seen individually and has his own materials for use in each session. The remedial reading teacher develops a close and meaningful relationship with the child, comparable to his relationships with the other education and treatment team members.

Extracurricular Individual Tutoring

The center recognizes that the child's educational needs cannot be viewed separately and apart from his total treatment needs. This awareness brings about the development of a supplementary tutoring program for children having difficulty in specific subjects.

In response to requests from students who wish to progress more rapidly or those who need assistance in grasping particular concepts, teachers often supply extra help after school on a time-available basis. The additional tutoring is especially beneficial to those children who desire to improve their scholastic achievement prior to discharge.

Preparatory Program

Children whose problems about school are so severe so as to rule out their school attendance (unable to attend and temporarily suspended) are taught in the preparatory program by guides recruited from the ranks of nursing staff interested in remedial education.

The program provides fundamental schoolwork, recreation, and various projects such as simple arts and crafts, spontaneous graphic art, gardening, etc. The school principal acts as consultant to the program.

Speech Therapy and Training

Whenever learning responses are examined in the light of interpersonal interaction, teachers keep in mind the child's capacity for language and speech function. If a child has a disability in these areas, it alters his self-perception, his ability to perceive others, and, of course, his interpersonal relationships. Therefore, I believe it is unwise to describe a disturbance in learning on the basis of the child's being nonverbal or as stuttering or lisping and in general a slow or lazy child, without having thoroughly examined the entire process of interaction in the school, the family, the child's personality structure, and his neurophysiology. When this is done and disordered language and/or speech is diagnosed, the child is referred for speech therapy.

In the center, the available part-time speech therapist provides only one or two brief speech therapy sessions per week. As a result, much of the responsibility for follow-up practice and reinforcement of the therapist's recommendations for helping children to overcome speech handicaps or to succeed in school rests with the classroom teacher. Children with speech problems are expected to do the classroom assignments and take the tests required of all children, although it may be necessary in some cases to modify assignments from oral to written. The child is helped to understand that speech is a tool and that his lack of proficiency with this one instrument does not minimize his value as a member of the group.

Articulation defects account for the majority of speech problems among children. It seems that these often result from a child's inability to listen to different sounds and distinguish between them.

The classroom teacher is not expected to become a speech therapist, but she can find many ways in which the daily classroom program can focus on specific articulation defects. Learning to listen and learning about listening can benefit the children with speech problems and at the same time improve the auditory discrimination skills of all children.

The teacher can develop many creative listening games based on words starting with sounds that are difficult for children to differentiate. Similarly, all will benefit from learning how to introduce and identify themselves, introduce others, express social amenities, answer the telephone, and give messages orally.

Many teachers and other staff members worry about how best to help the stutterer, the child whose speech is interrupted by pauses, blockings, repetitions, hesitations, and bodily contortions. Although speech correctionists, pathologists and psychologists disagree as to the causes of stuttering, they are in agreement that the child's environment and the attitude others show toward his manner of speech affect his stuttering. Following are some ways in which a classroom teacher and other staff members can help a child who stutters.

—Establish a favorable atmosphere for speaking in the classroom, office, residence, etc.

—Try to help the stuttering child maintain a calm and happy attitude toward school, other activities and himself.

—Try to speak in an unhurried manner with a pleasant, low-pitched voice.

—Learn to accept the way the stutterer speaks. Show patience and kindness but not pity. Look directly at the stutterer's eyes and do not turn away when he encounters speaking difficulties.

—Help the stutterer feel that he is a worthy member of his group.

—Give him opportunities to develop and express abilities in areas other than speech, so that he can experience success.

—Encourage him to participate in group activities like games, singing, dancing and discussions.

—Encourage the stutterer to speak; expect him to take part in recitations and fulfill all assignments, oral and written; help him to know that even though he may stutter, he can speak with no fear of ridicule.

—Do not compare the stutterer's speech or other skills with those of his peers.

—Do not tell him not to stutter; the harder he tries not to stutter, the greater will be the tensions and the worse the stuttering.

—Do not tell him to take a deep breath before speaking, to think before he starts, or to stop and start over.

—Do not praise the stutterer when he doesn't stutter. Praise his speech on the basis of adequate preparation, clearness, good expression, and calm manner.

—Do not tell the stutterer the word he is trying to say or cut his speech off unfinished.

—Encourage the stutterer to realize that it is not important for him to have fluent speech, but that it is very important for him to speak in all situations, regardless of stuttering.

In the school the teacher discusses with the speech therapist the step-by-step program for the child who has speech problems. The classroom teacher's greatest contribution in these cases, however, is a positive attitude. If classroom teachers believe in and express enthusiasm for the speech therapy program, the children are likely to share the enthusiasm.

Some children referred for speech therapy are apprehensive about going to the speech room for the first lesson. They may fear that something unpleasant or painful will occur or that they will miss important classroom, O.T. or R.T. work. They may feel ashamed because they do not speak as well as other children. These fears can be minimized or even banished by understanding teachers.

By following any or all of the suggestions below, the classroom teacher can help to create a positive, wholesome attitude about the speech program.

—Have a short class discussion on speech therapy in which children exchange ideas and ask questions.

—Invite the speech therapist to visit the room, tell about the program, and answer questions.

—Arrange for the children to visit the speech therapy room briefly, possibly to observe a lesson.

—Speak of a child's appointment for speech therapy as a fine opportunity and privilege, rather than as something unpleasant which he must do.

—Let children who are having therapy report to the class on the lessons.

—For children in the day treatment program, encourage parents to cooperate by assisting with assignments to be carried out at home.

Another way in which the teacher can help the therapy program is by following up the speech lessons in the classroom. When the therapist feels that a child has mastered a sound, he notifies the teacher, who can then encourage the child to make correct use of the sound in reading and speaking. In this way the child comes to integrate his newly learned sounds with his total speech pattern. Even more important this makes him realize that his classroom teacher appreciates him and his efforts to improve his speech.

Occupational Therapy

The occupational therapy program functions in two broad areas, attempting to meet the child's needs and also to make use of the therapeutic opportunities afforded by the group formation in and out of the shop. A wide variety of art and craft activities are used for appropriate therapeutic purposes, for improvement of perceptual motor functions, and for identifying areas of creativity and aptitude in the child.

The art and craft shop is small and compact. An average of four children use it at one time. When there are occasional outbursts of negative behavior, the therapist attempts to handle within the group. If this fails, the child is removed from the shop. In spite of the severe disturbance of many of the children, it often is not necessary to lock the tool cupboards which are kept open during the work period. However, the tools are closely watched by the therapist and none are allowed to be removed from the shop.

Children choose their own media, and numerous types of projects are underway in any period. Work in leather, plastic, copper, and dressmaking projects are all popular. Standards set for individual projects vary from child to child according to his developmental level. A spontaneous graphic art period is also held in the shop twice weekly.

Industrial Arts

Practical instruction in the use of common hand tools is provided, and the skills necessary to complete simple woodwork projects are developed. More capable children have opportunities to work with power tools under close supervision. Safety is stressed.

Educational Field Trips

Trips to museums, factories, public services or other points of interest are arranged from time to time in order to expand the therapeutic learning environment. Contact with the world outside the center is an essential element in a total treatment program.

Special Interest Groups

Teachers are encouraged to sponsor and conduct after school interest clubs or hobby groups which do not conflict with scheduled activities. The social and emotional benefits accruing to children from such volunteer participation may sometimes exceed the gains made under more formal auspices.

Holiday Program

Children are involved in producing, staging and presenting an annual holiday program in December, to which parents, "visiting friends," and staff are invited. The program provides an opportunity to observe the children in a different context, often with gratifying disclosures of unexpected talents and skills.

Library Services

A modestly stocked library is available to supplement the regular curriculum. In the absence of authorization for a librarian, teachers of the language arts specialty provide weekly postschool periods to facilitate library use by students.

Educational Evaluations

Objective evaluations of a child's educational achievement, using standardized tests, are administered by the principal or his assistant shortly after admission and before discharge.

Diagnostic and Appraisal Evaluations

Because the child's educational experiences are considered to have a therapeutic effect upon him, plans for his education are included into his total treatment program. Since the aim of teaching is essentially an academic one as well as therapeutic, the teachers meet with the center's psychiatrists, psychologists, social workers, adjunctive therapists, and nursing staff to keep informed of the problems and concerns of the children.

Thus, during the course of treatment, regularly scheduled diagnostic and appraisal conferences are held for each individual child to enable the teaching and treatment staffs to communicate and evaluate the effectiveness of the treatment and education programs, and to recognize the child's change of needs.

The observations of teachers are an important source of data about the progress of the child. However, because the learning problems of emotionally disturbed children have the disconcerting quality of fluctuating widely in response to emotional factors, extensive and time-consuming educational testing, diagnosis, prescription and remediation of every interfering symptom is not attempted. When I ask a teacher about her detailed observations in a classroom, it is well-nigh impossible to expect to come away with a behavioral analysis of every happening. Instead, the child's basic educational needs are ascertained through a combination of achievement testing and general teacher observation.

During the conference, the education staff also have the opportunity to hear and discuss dynamic understanding of the child's problems in relation to educational concepts and remedial procedures. By gaining better understanding of a child's illness and treatment progress, the teachers become better equipped to discourage his weaknesses and to develop his strengths as these become evident in the classroom. Similarly, feedback from the education staff is used constructively in the child's total treatment program. Also, a curriculum of individualized instruction appropriate for that child at that time is evolved, and modifications and refinements are made as treatment progresses and deficiencies are clarified.

Group Achievement Testing

Group achievement testing of the entire student population is conducted annually in May. Specialized evaluation of specific disabilities is conducted when indicated.

School Administrative Procedures

HOURS OF WORK. Working hours for school personnel are from 8 AM to 4:30 PM, Monday through Friday with the exception of official state holidays. Members of the school staff are expected to remain at their normal place of duty during working hours unless authorized by the principal to be elsewhere. If a member is unable to report for work for any reason, the school secretary is notified as soon after 8:00 AM as possible. (Telephone , Extension). In the event of sickness or injury during work, notify the school secretary or principal.

STANDARDS OF WORK. School personnel are expected to comply fully with the provisions of this manual. Staff having problems which cannot be resolved within the school consult with the principal for possible referral to higher authority. Every employee's job performance is officially evaluated by his immediate supervisor at least annually.

SCHOOL OFFICE. The school secretary's duties are assigned by the principal. Typing or secretarial service for the faculty may be furnished when it does not interfere with her primary duties. The privacy of work in progress is to be respected, and her desk and equipment used only with her permission. The working file of educational information maintained on each student is available for examination by faculty members; information contained therein is treated as confidential. Personal telephone calls, unless of an emergency nature, are not made from office phones.

FACULTY LOUNGE, ROOM # .... Individual mail boxes in the faculty lounge are checked twice a day for messages. Personal mail is not to be received through the center. A bulletin board is provided in the lounge for official memorandums, schedules and notices. Smoking by staff in the school is restricted to Room # ... and the adjacent school office. Inasmuch as the lounge must also be used as a work room, tutoring room, and testing room, all personnel are expected to assist in maintaining the room in presentable condition at all times.

KEYS. Keys required by the individual in the performance of his duties are issued on hand receipt; any other key needed temporarily may be checked out with the school secretary and returned immediately after use. Keys are *not* to be given to students or left in unsecured places. Lost keys must be reported.

MEETINGS. Faculty meetings are held each Monday afternoon at 2:30 PM in the faculty lounge unless otherwise announced. A staff education meeting is held the first Wednesday of each month at 2:30 PM in the administrative building classroom. Diagnostic and appraisal meetings are held on Tuesday and Thursday at 2:30 PM in the psychiatric conference room or as announced in the daily bulletin; teachers attend those meetings involving their students unless other duties intervene.

RECURRING REPORTS.

a. *School Progress Notes:* These are to be completed on each student by each of his teachers in each subject. The report consists of a numerical rating of academic and behavioral progress together with a brief statement describing typical performance of level of functioning. The report is due at nine-week intervals on the dates listed in the school calendar. The original copy is filed in the medical records, with a copy to the child's psychiatrist.

b. *Monthly Activity Report:* Prepared by the principal for submission to the director at the end of each month, containing relevant statistical data as well as information concerning plans and recommendations.

c. *Visitors and Community Visits Report:* A list of visitors to the school, and official participation by school personnel in community events, compiled by the school secretary for submission at the end of the month to the assistant director.

d. *Volunteer Services Report:* A list of donations and contributions of volunteer time, compiled by the school secretary for submission at the end of the month to the administrative assistant.

e. *Personnel Report:* A report of employment interviews and personnel gains and losses, prepared by the principal for submission to the administrative assistant at the end of the month.

f. *Educational Summary:* When the treatment team determines that a child's discharge is imminent, the principal will prepare an educational summary indicating the subjects taught, the materials used, objective test results, subjective comments of teachers, and recommendations for the child's future educational management. A copy is placed in the child's medical records and two copies are provided to the social worker coordinating the case.

SPECIAL EVENTS. During the school year, the school will sponsor one event, normally, a year-end holiday production, to which outside staff and visitors may be invited. Responsibility for producing this program will be apportioned among teachers for presentation on the date published in the school calendar.

DISPLAY CASE. Examples of student work or subject area materials may be exhibited in the display case in the school's hallway. Opportunity to prepare displays is apportioned to subject area teachers in accordance with a schedule published in the school calendar.

VISITORS. Visitors to the school are directed to the receptionist in the administration building for clearance. Visitors are not ordinarily admitted to classes in progress. Limited one-way observation facilities are available to authorized persons by prior arrangement with the principal.

SUNSHINE FUND. School personnel contribute twenty-five cents per month to a "Sunshine Fund" to be used for greeting cards, postage, or such other unofficial needs as the group may determine. Membership is voluntary and may be discontinued at any time. The school secretary, as custodian, collects and accounts for the fund.

INSECT CONTROL. Any food brought into the school for consumption by staff members is properly stored and disposed of to prevent insect infestations. No food, coffee or other edibles are permitted in classrooms. Cups and utensils used in other parts of the building are washed and the room is left in sanitary condition by the users.

IN-SERVICE EDUCATION. A schedule of in-service education focusing on a topic of major interest is planned on an annual basis. Instructional personnel are afforded opportunities to visit and observe programs dealing with emotionally disturbed children in nearby counties, as well as to hear visiting speakers, see appropriate films and study pertinent papers and reports.

Instructional Equipment, Materials and Supplies

CONSERVATION. The proper care and use of the center's property is a responsibility of each employee; persons handling such property are expected to be alert at all times to prevent excessive and wasteful consumption or depreciation of equipment, materials and supplies. Damaged or inoperable equipment is reported to the principal. Teachers may secure ordinary supplies from the stockroom as needed; however, the school secretary is notified when the last item of a kind is taken. Removal of materials and supplies for private use is prohibited. Electrically operated machines are turned off immediately after use and are unplugged during extended breaks.

REQUESTS FOR INSTRUCTIONAL MATERIALS. An essential condition for individualized instruction is the availability of a broad spectrum of materials, supplies and other resources. Teachers are afforded the opportunity to request additional instructional materials at three-month intervals. These requests, consolidated by departments, must include quantity desired, description and catalog page number, price and vendor's name. The principal will review all requests and make a determination concerning the types and quantities to be forwarded on purchase requisitions.

INDUSTRIAL ARTS TOOLS. Power tools in the industrial arts shop may be used by other staff members only by arrangement with the industrial arts instructor, and only during such times as will not interfere with regular classes. Users will clean up debris and return materials to their proper places after use. Hand tools may be obtained by arrangement with the industrial arts instructor; such tools must be returned to the industrial arts shop the same day.

AUDIO-VISUAL EQUIPMENT. Except for certain equipment assigned to specific classrooms, all audio-visual equipment is located in Room # ... in order to be available to all teachers. When removing a piece of equipment from Room # ..., the teacher signs for it in the checkout book located therein. Reservations of equipment may be made not more than one week in advance. All equipment is returned to Room # ... by the end of the school day. Damaged or malfunctioning equipment is reported to the principal.

Instructional Procedures and Policies

CLASSROOM HOUSEKEEPING. Teachers are encouraged to take pride in the appearance of their rooms. Scotch tape, glue or paste is not used on walls or chalkboards. Materials and equipment are returned to their proper place at the end of the school day. Classroom doors are kept closed during class periods to minimize distractions to students within the room as well as to prevent disturbances to adjacent classrooms. When the classroom is not in use, the teacher will close and lock the door.

STUDENT MOVEMENT. Change of class is announced at forty-minute intervals by three short rings of the bell. Students are released promptly so that they are not late to the following activity. Teachers are expected to be at their classrooms when the students arrive and to assist students in reaching their assigned rooms. Any absentee for whom a reason is not known is reported to the school secretary immediately. Any student outside his classroom on a legitimate errand during class must carry a hall pass signed by the instructor. Students are not permitted in the office or faculty lounge unless escorted by a teacher. Students are not left unattended by teachers except when absolutely necessary. All student appointments for individual therapy are written on an appointment slip and given to the appropriate teacher, who sees that the child is sent to therapy at the proper time.

STUDENT DISCIPLINE AND CONTROL. Teachers make every effort to anticipate and counteract disturbed behavior within the classroom. No gifts of toys, candy or other edibles are used as behavior modifiers. Corporal punishment is not permitted. In the event assistance is needed for student control, the teacher may use the emergency key to signal the school secretary, who immediately ascertains what help is needed. If it becomes necessary to remove a student from the classroom, he may be sent to the center hallway for a cooling off period or conference with the principal, if available. If the child is completely out of control the school secretary may notify the appropriate on-duty nurse for assistance.

CONTRABAND ARTICLES. Children are not permitted to bring toys, radios, athletic equipment or other distracting items to school. Such articles are held by the teacher or turned in to the school office for return to the child at the end of the child's school day. Chewing gum is also prohibited. Harmful or potentially dangerous items (such as knives, matches, cigarettes, lighters, etc.) will be confiscated by the teacher, labeled with the date, child's name and name of staff member who confiscated the item, and the item turned in to the school office for transmittal to the child's psychiatrist.

STUDENT APPEARANCE. Students are expected to be adequately dressed upon arrival at school. By "adequate" is meant shoes and reasonably clean outer garments in good condition. Shirttails will be tucked in. Students deemed improperly dressed are reported to the principal, who coordinates the problem with the appropriate service.

FIRST AID. School personnel do not dispense bandages or otherwise attempt to treat minor scratches, bruises, etc. In the event of any injury to a child which requires more than cleansing with cold water, the school secretary is requested to notify the appropriate residence or day treatment nurse.

STUDENT APPOINTMENTS DURING NON-SCHOOL HOURS. In order to minimize conflict with child care procedures of the nursing service, teachers who require children for tutoring, testing or other activities during non-school hours are requested to notify the school secretary as early in the day as possible. The school secretary then notifies the nursing service secretary (Ext.) of the names of the children and appointment times. The nursing service secretary effects coordination of all requests with the proper residence.

EDUCATIONAL FIELD TRIPS. Field trips as planned educational

experiences are encouraged. The teacher planning the trip is requested to inform the principal in writing two weeks prior to the proposed trip and, upon receiving clearance from the principal, proceeds to make the necessary arrangements with the facility to be visited. The principal makes arrangements to reserve transportation and arrange for additional escorts. A maximum of six children may be scheduled per trip; escort is on the ratio of one adult to two children. Trips are planned so that the children will be returned in time for regular meals.

INTEREST GROUPS, CLUBS AND SPECIAL PROJECTS. Teachers are encouraged to sponsor after-school interest clubs or hobby groups for which they have time and qualifications. However, in order to prevent conflict and duplication of activities, only those clubs, newspapers or extracurricular projects which have received the prior approval of the principal are conducted.

FIRE ALARM PROCEDURE. The fire alarm is five short rings of the school bell repeated three times. Upon the sounding of the alarm teachers escort their classes to a safe distance outside the building via the exit route posted near the light switch in each room. Teachers are required to become familiar with the exit procedure for their classrooms. The "all clear" signal is one long ring on the school bell. Unannounced fire drills are held from time to time.

PERSONAL RELATIONS. Teachers are expected to maintain professional objectivity at all times in their contacts with students and to refrain from use of inappropriate gestures or language. Teachers require students to address them as "Mr. . . . . . . ," or "Mrs. . . . . . . ," etc. Staff members also use the formal address in the presence or hearing of children.

LESSON PLANS. In view of the unpredictable progress of the emotionally disturbed child, detailed lesson plans are not required. However, each teacher maintains a folder, workbook or similar guide relating to each student, indicating the current status of the child, the materials he is using, and any special individualized programs being used.

HOMEWORK. Unless prescribed as a treatment measure for a certain child or children, homework is not approved for routine instructional purposes. Teachers do not make requests that nursing personnel assist children with academic problems. Normally, children are not permitted to take curriculum textbooks from the school; however, teachers may at their discretion check out supplementary classroom books to students on a voluntary basis. Completed workbooks and papers may be given to the student.

GENERAL RESPONSIBILITIES. In addition to assigned teaching duties, each member of the instructional staff is expected to carry his or her fair share of the total concerns of the school, including clinical meetings, in-service training, policy making, administrative meetings, committee assignments, testing and evaluations, and any other professional duties and responsibilities necessary to making the school function as an effective element in the treatment milieu.

REFERENCES

1. Berman, G., and Eisenberg, M.: Psychosocial aspects of academic achievement. *Am J Orthopsychiatry, 41:3*, 406-414, 1971.
2. Marcus, I. M.: The influence of teacher-child interaction on the learning process. *J Child Psychiatry, 10:3*, 481-500, 1971.
3. Ekstein, R.: Psychoanalytic notes on the function of the curriculum. *Reiss-Davis Clin Bull, 3:1*, 36-46, 1966.
4. Rossman, W. B.: Helping teachers appreciate emotional problems in children. *Am J Psychiatry, 108:5*, 374-380, 1951.
5. Mumford, E.: Teacher response to school mental health programs. *Am J Psychiatry, 125:1*, 75-81, 1968.
6. Hirschberg, J. Cotter: The role of education in the treatment of emotionally disturbed children through planned ego development. *Am J Orthopsychiatry, 23:4*, 1953.
7. Bullis, H. E.: An educational program for development of the "normal" personality. *Am J Psychiatry, 109:5*, 375-377, 1952.

PARAPROFESSIONAL SERVICE

MENTAL HEALTH TECHNICIAN
Introduction

FOR SEVERAL YEARS NOW the different new career programs have tried to develop a specialist in the mental health field who does not have the usual academic credentials obtained after many years of special studies and training. In an effort to find an identity for this specialist, many names were used, e.g. "rehabilitation technician, indigenous helper, paraprofessional, rehabilitator, sociopsychiatric specialist, care giver, resource person, socioeducational, and mental health technologist." The effort has been romanticized and woefully misconceived, misapplied and, at times, misunderstood and inappropriately handled.

It has been claimed that the creation of the mental health technician was due to a reaction against the maldistribution of psychiatric care and waiting lists, or no care at all, as well as to a movement towards the recognition of social problems as a causative factor in mental illness.

Whether there are motives behind such a concept, in recent years the pressures of manpower shortage in the mental health field have crept up on us and have grasped us to the point that we finally realized that as members of the mental health field with many years of special studies and training, we are spending many long and wasted hours in taking care of matters which other persons could take care of if only properly taught how to do them. Recent attempts of redistribution of functions among present staff members have tried to do just that. The redistribution made it possible for professional staff members to focus on special tasks and become more effective.

The center, therefore, accepts members of the mental health technicians group and makes use of their services in a manner that has proven beneficial to all concerned.

185

Center's Objectives in Relation to Technicians

The center's professional staff learn to perceive the presence of a co-worker with limited training and experience as not infringing upon their respected professional terrain. It provides a climate in which the mental health technician can develop an identity, a positive self-image and dignity; can realize his or her own resources more fully; can develop observation, sensitivity and communication skills; can achieve potential for both upward and sideward movement; and can branch into a variety of other related disciplines in the area of child or adult psychiatric patient care in the various clinical psychiatric services.

The center makes use of the services of such a technician who is employed in entry-level position and performs for compensation commensurate with duties and with commitment and adherence to the policies, rules and regulations of the center.

Requirements and Qualifications of the Technician

As a minimum requirement, the technician
—must be a graduate of an approved two-year junior college and have the degree of "Associate of Arts" with a speciality in mental health.
—must be able to live and communicate with children.
—must be able to work, cooperate and communicate with his or her co-workers.
—must be willing and able to accept and utilize professional supervision.
—must fulfill his or her assigned function in a manner that is satisfactory to the supervisors.
—must be well-adjusted and have an acceptable appearance.

Utilization of the Technician at the Center

The technician can be utilized in both the residential and day treatment programs as a group worker, special teacher, adjunctive therapist, social worker and group psychotherapist.

The technician can function as a group worker a rank above the present nursing charge aide and below nurse classification. In this capacity, he or she is in charge of a group of six to eight children. A group approach combined with attention to the individual child is one way of hastening the process of rehabilitation of the child with an acute emotional or mental disturbance. It helps to mobilize the child's strengths, to increase his participation and to help him accept as much responsibility as possible for himself. The group methods tend to dilute the tendency that everybody has when in the psychiatric setting—the tendency to become dependent upon others for care.

Group work in the center is not like a typical group therapy situation in which an effort is made over a long period of time to work through a child's complex of problems. It is aimed at dealing with a specific problem, the crisis which caused the child's breakdown in good functioning.

The technician can function as a teacher for a group of children in need of "early learning experience." These are children mostly five to six years of age who are not able to attend regular classes of first grade level in the school. The technician can also function as a recreational therapy aide.

The technician should serve professional staff members of all disciplines in every level of activity and facilitate their mobility as a whole, not one part at the expense of another. An example of this is the coordinated effort with the social work service for home-extension service by helping parents learn how to carry through with day treatment program at home. The technician can make follow-up visits, give social reinforcement to the parents afterwards, and respond to other needs as they are found.

The mental health technician can be assigned as a co-therapist in group psychotherapy and, after several months of experience and upon approval of the psychotherapy board, can serve as a group psychotherapist. He should participate in psychotherapy and literature seminars.

Anticipated Problems in the Management of the Technician

1. Because of his relatively limited training and experience, a mental health technician might
   —find himself at cross purposes and may have a more difficult time than usual in coming to a discovering of his identity.
   —fail to utilize data supplied by other team members.

—attempt to dominate team decisions.

—feel unsafe from criticism and antagonism of others.

—respond out of fear of being left out of treatment process.

—take too conservative a position in pointing out the child's illness and progress.

2. Because of their familiarity with their professional role definition structuring, staff members might

—consider the technician as a mere aide to an over-burdened professional.

—consider the technician as a nonprofessional doing the unattractive, low status tasks that professionals avoid.

—magnify his negative rather than positive impact on the center.

—use the technician to reinforce their own feelings and thoughts.

In order to prevent and/or manage these anticipated problems the director of the center

—provides supervision to the technicians.

—appoints an advisory committee which meets regularly and evaluates the technician's performance and his impact on the total staff and treatment and education programs of the center.

EDUCATION AND RESEARCH DEPARTMENT

THE EDUCATION AND RESEARCH DEPARTMENT within a psychiatric setting is considered a valuable adjunct to the treatment of patients. I believe that the better the educational and research functions of the treatment setting the higher are its standards of treatment and care and the more efficient its results.

In the center, education and research are authorized only when certain standards are met and when practiced under specifically defined conditions.

The staff at the center strives to collect, disseminate and exchange scientific knowledge and information important for progress in the mental health field. It exerts whatever effort is necessary to maintain a balance between the creation of new knowledge and the practical application of such knowledge to the delivery of services. It is the responsibility of the center to develop an in-service training program for its staff and a program of education for the community by inviting groups from schools, agencies and other institutions specializing in children's mental health matters. The center serves as a demonstration teaching facility to the community at large. Observations by the public of the center's functions become an accepted part of the center's environment.

EDUCATION AND RESEACH COMMITTEE

To insure that efficient and reliable administrative procedures be developed and adhered to in implementing the education and research programs in the center, the director, in agreement with and the support of the clinical staff, appoints a committee which is known as the Education and Research Committee. It is composed of the Director of Education and Research (chairman), the Director of Psychology, the Director of Social Work Service, the School Principal, the Director of Nursing Service and the Coordinator of In-service Nursing Training, and the Director of Adjunctive Therapies Service. Committee members meet each second week of the month.

By definition, the Director of Education and Research is responsible for coordinating and supervising research and training activities in the center. He is the person who is consulted about the legitimacy of a new education, training or research program. It is his responsibility to evaluate if the person who desires to do research or to start an education or training program is qualified to carry it out. He is also responsible for the maintenance and standards of educational training and research programs in the center. Any changes, additions or deletions in the education, training and research are cleared through the office of the director of education and research.

The director of education and research submits to the director of the center a written monthly report and at the end of the year the "Annual Report on the Education and Research Activities."

OBJECTIVES

The objectives of the Education and Research Department are:

1. To plan, develop and maintain sound educational training and research programs, and to coordinate such programs with the treatment and education goals of the center.

2. To provide the resources necessary to conduct sound education, training and research

by supporting and acting as consultant to supervisory and management personnel who desire or need such assistance,

by making available to employees the latest and best methods of educational techniques in the learning processes at the center,

by making use of local, state and national educational resources, thus maintaining an up-to-date and informed department.

3. To plan and implement in-service training programs for staff members of the center

by establishing schedules for training programs which permit the widest possible participation,

by encouraging participation in planning and conducting educational programs at all levels of the organizational structure at the center,

by insuring that responsibilities for training are delineated to each working unit of the center.

4. To evaluate specific staff development programs and the total educational endeavor at the center

by assisting individuals and working units to accomplish for themselves and their units appropriate functions of continuing education,

by establishing appropriate criteria for evaluating programs which couple programs and desirable educational goals.

5. To serve as liaison for educational institutions, other hospitals, libraries and other appropriate agencies

by cooperating with these various agencies in the promotion and development of careers in human service fields,

by stimulating interest in programs which prepare both professional and auxiliary personnel in the delivery of human services,

by participating in those programs which may, in time, provide additional strength to the training and staff development at the center.

STUDENTS—SUBJECTS—METHODS

All members of the staff of the center are involved in the educational and training programs. This enables a wide range of personnel from those with no training to those with much training and experience to benefit from this program.

The subject matters taught are adjusted to the needs of the various levels of functioning of the staff. This enables the specific individual to better understand his special function and also stimulate through knowledge his increased participation with the patients and staff. This, in turn, promotes better communication, better team participation, and an increased awareness of his importance as a staff member.

Subject matters taught include etiology, psychopathology, symptomatology of children's psychiatric disorders and their treatment modalities and procedures. Emphasis on interpersonal relationships between peers and adults in various areas of living (family, friends, school, etc.) is stressed.

Within the center, the roles of each service and their relationships are defined both objectively and subjectively. These include administration, teaching, in-service training, supervision, etc.

Methods of teaching and training for all different groups depend on the personal needs of the members of the group and the basic philosophy of the teacher. Teaching takes place with flexibility. Thus, in addition to the individual atmosphere of the center from the standpoint of the child and his treatment, there is a teaching and training atmosphere. Without question, the selection of the personnel who do the teaching and training is of the greatest importance.

In training, example is more important than precept. If the teaching persons in the center exemplify the highest ideals in child psychiatry and its affiliated services, the student will commonly seek to imitate the conduct he sees in these individuals. He will often acquire a great deal by a process of absorption. Humanitarian attitudes, kindness, and tolerance of others can be copied by a great number of those under a teacher who possesses these qualities.

Several ways of teaching are utilized: perceptors, formal didactic lectures, the use of reading material, varying types of seminars and conferences, the observation of others carrying out special procedures, and the performing by the student himself. All these ways are important and all are used in the training program. Today the formal didactic lectures are being used less and less in teaching. They are being replaced gradually by more seminars, conferences and small group discussions. Learning by doing is emphasized, thus giving the student some degree of independence with flexibility and better ego support.

The type of training is also individualized by paying attention to the personality of the student and by adopting the teaching of him as individual, rather than setting up a rigid program and insisting upon conformity.

PROCEDURES

Persons coming into a teaching and training program receive orientation to the center's setup and the place their training program occupies in the overall plan of the center. What is expected of them is clearly defined. This is accomplished through orientation by their respective Director of Service. They know what their rights and privileges are and their relationships with other persons. Lines of authority are explained to them. There is specific assignment of work. It is made clear that the purpose of the center is to help children get well, by doing something to them, for them, with them and about them.

The procedures followed at the center regarding the beginning of an activity in the education and research field are as follows.

Any staff member who wishes to become involved in teaching, training or research activities clears it with his supervisor. He then submits the proposal or the prospectus to the Director of Education and Research, who brings it up for discussion with the E & R (Education and Research) Committee. If the committee considers it of value, the applicant is invited to participate in the next meeting of the committee. Here he has an opportunity to give more details about his project.

It is also made clear that the ultimate decision is made by the Director of Education and Research who has consulted with the respective members. Each service director, through his regularly scheduled meetings, keeps the Director of Education and Research informed on the progress of the approved project. At his discretion, the Director of Education and Research can directly contact the person responsible for a certain project and discuss with him its progress.

It is the policy of the center that no education or research grant application be submitted prior to the approval of the Director of Education and Research. As the Director of Education and Research and the E & R Committee need to determine which education or research project the center is able to support, no equipment, books, etc. which is to be used for the project is purchased without prior approval of the Director of Education and Research and the director of the center.

PSYCHOTHERAPY SERVICE

I N THE CENTER THE MAJORITY of the treatment team members
are psychodynamically oriented. However, it is realized that
formal or direct psychotherapy is not the only treatment that
will make children well. Treatment at the center is organized
with the philosophy that psychotherapy is only one aspect of total treatment. I believe that, regardless of what happens in the
direct treatment experience with the psychotherapist, disturbed
children require an accepting and gratifying living experience
oriented to meet individual needs. Therefore an effort is made
so that much valuable time not be taken away from the other
treatment and education activities.

The goal of psychotherapy is similar to the total treatment
goal, that of helping the children return to their homes and their
community as quickly as possible and to relieve those symptoms
which made it impossible for them to adjust before admission.

PSYCHOTHERAPY BOARD

The importance of the function and place of psychotherapy
in the center's psychiatric treatment program is recognized by its
staff. As a specialized approach in the psychiatric treatment of
children, it is imperative that psychotherapy must meet certain
standards of operation and must be practiced only under conditions which insure that maximum benefits for the patients may
be derived from it. Thus psychotherapy is authorized only when
such standards are met and when practiced under specifically defined conditions.

To insure efficient and reliable procedures and to implement
the psychotherapy program, a committee is formed and is known
as the Psychotherapy Board. Its members include a child psychiatrist-chairman, the Director of Social Work Service, and the
Director of Psychology. The board members meet each second

week of the month to discuss and decide on matters pertaining to the

a) integration and coordination of all psychotherapeutic activities.

b) minimal standards expected in the conduct of formal psychotherapy.

c) adequate record system of all psychotherapeutic activity.

d) proper supervision for staff members doing psychotherapy.

e) periodic survey to determine the nature and amount of psychotherapy.

f) facilitation of revision and improvement in the psychotherapeutic program.

g) regular psychotherapy seminars for the psychotherapists and co-therapists.

The board has the authority to enforce conformity to the procedures it establishes to carry out its mandate with regard to the psychotherapy program at the center.

By "psychotherapy" the board refers to individual and group psychotherapy as well as to family therapy. The board considers as psychotherapists the child psychiatrists, psychologists and social workers. Also included are residents in adult and child psychiatry interns and trainees in psychology and social work, with the approval of the Psychotherapy Board.

INDIVIDUAL PSYCHOTHERAPY

Children in general receive a supportive type of psychotherapy in accordance with the recommendation of their psychiatrist. Sometimes this is proposed in the belief that they are not ready for interpretation or they are so suspicious that they need more time before they can be expected to relate to the psychotherapist.

For some children, however, an early relationship with the psychotherapist and interpretative therapy may be the focus of treatment. Within the security of the dependent relationship with the more emotionally mature psychotherapist whom they would gradually trust and imitate, the children will be able to lose their unconscious conflicts with help in learning new and more realistic solutions. The children will be encouraged to feel responsible for trying to understand more thoroughly their motives and feelings, and through this "corrective emotional experience" they would gradually gain self-confidence and develop some insight into the nature and origins of their conflicts and their illogical, unsatisfactory defenses.

Psychotherapists are not hesitant about discussing with the children the practical aspects of their behavior, for children are fully aware that their psychotherapists have knowledge about their behavior in the residence or in the school and with their parents during visits. Such reality situations are frequently utilized in treatment sessions.

Usually the psychotherapists wait for children to mention any anxieties about their behavior or their feelings about the nursing staff, teachers or the other children. If the children do not bring up difficulties in which they have become involved, the psychotherapists will suggest discussing them. Thus, children are made aware of the meaning of their symptoms and behavior and the reasons for treatment interviews to enable them to recognize the purposes of the treatment and to gain their conscious cooperation in it.

In psychotherapy sessions considerable use is made of story-telling by the children, of drawings and of play materials.

Throughout every phase of treatment a premium is placed on continuous relationship for the children and parents with their psychotherapists.

PLAY THERAPY

Play therapy to children is usually what verbalization is to the adult. Children are less able to recognize their anxieties. Children have a rich fantasy life which is often expressed in play. As one grows older, however, reality takes over. It is well-known that younger children express themselves through play rather than verbally. Play gives the child a neutral and appropriate milieu to express his inner and outer conflicts. The child acts out many of his unspoken conflicts. How and what he does are the clues which aid the psychotherapist in helping the child to solve some of his problems.

Use of Toys

Toys must be selected to meet the age and emotional levels of the children and have meaning to the child allowing him to express his feelings. It is less threatening to express oneself indirectly (pounding the pegboard) than by directly attacking the therapist. A younger child may make use of puppets to express family relations and feelings and reveal life styles and family conflicts. There are two major ways to use toys.

1. *Controlled-play:* The psychotherapist controls the available toys and sets the ground rules. This way he may be able to find a clue as to what is going on inside the child.

2. *Free-play:* An array of equipment relevant to the child's emotional age is available and the child determines what he will play with.

PREPARATION OF PLAYROOM. The psychotherapist goes into the playroom ahead of time to select the toys to be available to the child. It is essential that the psychotherapist selects media with which the child is comfortable and familiar, in order to avoid losing awareness of his own role.

Each psychotherapist takes responsibility for leaving the playroom in the same condition he found it. The psychotherapist is not to remove equipment without notifying the other psychotherapists.

COMMITTEE ON PLAYROOMS AND TOYS. The Committee on Playrooms and Toys examines the playrooms frequently. Inappropriate and broken material is discarded. The committee prepares a list of basic appropriate equipment to meet the criteria for play therapy. The Director of Nursing Service or her designate secures the equipment the committee deems appropriate and prepares and maintains an inventory of what is left.

PROCEDURES
Referral of Patients

In the center, the staff do not wait for a child to request individual or group psychotherapy. As the child does not understand what psychotherapy involves, the idea that he would be more receptive if he requests psychotherapy himself is considered at least ridiculous. It is true that most of the children who have an individual therapist often talk a great deal about their interviews, but according to my experience children request a therapist only after a long time in residence. This waiting period is not considered advisable, thus emphasis is being placed on assigning a child within the first month after admission.

The decision as to the need for psychotherapy for a child is determined by the dynamics of each individual case and is usually made at the time of the Initial Diagnostic and Appraisal Conference which takes place in the third week of his placement. For some children it may be decided that an intensive psychotherapeutic relationship should be developed early in placement.

The child's psychiatrist, as the leader of the treatment team, is responsible for the diagnosis of the child, for planning treatment, and defining therapeutic and educational goals.

Psychotherapy referrals are initiated by the child's psychiatrist and sent to the chairman of the psychotherapy board who maintains a list of referred children.

Assignment of Psychotherapy Case

A psychotherapist is designated by the board from a list of qualified and available staff members of the medical, psychology, and social work services.

The choice of psychotherapist is primarily made on the basis of personality, native ability and interest in psychotherapy. Emphasis is given on the personality of the psychotherapist and not on his years of education and training. On some occasions the child's problem, his age, his level of emotional development, and whether he needs a man or woman are taken under consideration since women therapists seem to like to treat smaller children and girls, and men prefer to be assigned to boys. In practice, however, many adolescent boys have women therapists and some girls have had men therapists. The latter is more exceptional.

The Psychotherapy Board notifies the psychotherapists who have treatment time available, and when possible the psychotherapists are given several referrals which fit the cases with which they choose to work. The Psychotherapy Board is available to consult with supervisors and psychotherapists in regard to any problems.

Transfer of Patient

Once a child is assigned to a psychotherapist, every effort is made to avoid a change. Exceptions are made, however, when experience shows that the child would benefit more from a different psychotherapist. Transfer is also considered when it is thought, for example, that an older boy needs a male psychotherapist or when it is found that he has not progressed in treatment and that his relationship with the psychotherapist is meaningless to him. Such transfer requests are granted after a review of the case by the psychotherapist's supervisor and the child's psychiatrist. When the decision is made for the patient to be transferred to another psychotherapist, notification is given to the board prior to the transfer date. The child's psychotherapist writes the transfer note in order to have the information available for the psychotherapist who takes over the patient. Suggestions as to the successor are welcomed by the board.

Supervision

By "supervisors" I refer to experienced staff members from the medical, psychology and social work service, who are approved by the Psychotherapy Board to supervise staff members in the conduct of individual, group psychotherapy and family therapy. Supervisors meet monthly to discuss problems of supervision and to follow the clinical growth of the psychotherapists they supervise.

Each psychotherapist is initially assigned one supervisor who assists him in the treatment of the patient or patients assigned to him. He has at least one weekly supervisory conference with his supervisor. He may refer to the process notes for supervisory meetings. The primary focus of such conferences is supervision of psychotherapy and not use of the supervisory hours for personal therapy. The psychotherapists are given opportunities to understand their reactions to the child's disturbance, and emphasis is placed on teaching psychotherapy techniques or giving detailed direction.

When needed, the psychotherapist receives additional information from the child's psychiatrist responsible for the total treatment of the child. This information is usually related with the treatment team's new recommendations and problems of countertransference which occur in other treatment areas. The child's psychiatrist may call for a Diagnostic and Appraisal Conference to discuss the course of therapy or to meet individual problems encountered in certain areas of treatment. He interprets both the dynamics of the child's behavior and the staff's reactions and then outlines the treatment direction and explains any alterations in the treatment plans.

The psychotherapist, after discussion with his supervisor, may also request that the child be put on the agenda for a Progress Diagnostic and Appraisal Conference. This usually occurs when a better understanding of the dynamics of the situation or more expert direction in treatment is needed.

Psychotherapy Seminar

Under the guidance of a child psychiatrist, all psychotherapists and group co-therapists meet every week to discuss general matters on the psychotherapy program and specific psychotherapeutic techniques and issues that arise during treatment.

Structural Arrangements

A child receives a pass from his nurse for each interview. He shows this to the schoolteacher or adjunctive therapist for permission to go to his psychotherapist. Some children are expected to keep track of the appointment without reminder, while for others the psychotherapist may ask the nursing staff or teachers to take this responsibility. Thus, these children are reminded of their special passes and when it is time for their appointments. In case a child is unable to use his pass for his appointment, arrangements are made for either the nursing staff or another adult to take the child to the psychotherapist.

Children are expected to keep appointments with their psychotherapists even if they do not wish to do so. However, if a child strongly resists going for his appointment, he is permitted to cancel it. His psychotherapist will try to work through with him his reasons for not wanting the appointment.

Most children are seen in individual psychotherapy at the administration building. This practice is preferable because of the difficulty in finding a place for sessions in the various residence units, and because in these units younger children resist staying alone with a psychotherapist when the nurse and other children are nearby. Also in such units it is difficult to prevent other children from interrupting psychotherapy sessions.

Children are seen either in the psychotherapist's office or in a playroom where there is a large assortment of toys and a wide variety of other play materials. Some older children, however, prefer to have their interviews in the psychotherapist's office and this is permitted.

The frequency of interviews is determined initially by information received before admission and later through the diagnostic and appraisal conferences. It is also determined by the time a psychotherapist has available and the child's willingness to keep his appointments.

Each child is seen a minimum of two times weekly. Appointments usually begin and terminate within the confines of the allotted hour. Fifty minutes is reserved for each appointment; however some children cannot remain that long and the session is terminated after forty minutes or sooner if the child is too upset to remain. His full time, however, is available to him when he can use it. A child who needs more intensive help during a period of treatment is seen a minimum of three times weekly. Arrangements are also made for children undergoing a particularly difficult time to see their psychotherapist more often than their scheduled appointments. If, for example, a child wants to see his psychotherapist at an unscheduled time he is given the appointment.

Psychotherapists who sometimes have to cancel appointments due to emergencies, illnesses or similar reasons telephone the residence nurse. Appointments that are missed are made up whenever possible. These precautions are taken because of the many painful separations and losses these children have suffered which have resulted in intensive fears of further similar experiences.

Deficiencies in Structural Arrangements

a) Frequent and often unnecessary changes in psychotherapy sessions create inconsistency in the staff's and the children's functions.

b) Sessions scheduled during times that are inconsistent with school class and adjunctive therapy hours cause disruption of ongoing activities.

c) Children being seen at inappropriate times result in their being removed from school classes and adjunctive therapy hours which they need most.

d) Psychotherapists who are late in keeping the exact time of their appointment with the children cause disruption of staff's and children's functions.

e) Psychotherapists who do not supervise the departure of their patients after psychotherapy sessions cause disruption of staff's and children's functions.

Recommendations for Correction of Deficiencies in Structural Arrangements

a) Make as few changes as possible in psychotherapy hours. If make-up time is necessary and you do not know what to do, discuss it with the supervisor.

b) Schedule sessions on the same time schedule as classes, thus only one class will be disrupted.

c) Schedule sessions at such a time that the child will not miss a class or another activity which he needs most—check with school principal or coordinator of adjunctive therapy.

d) Schedule sessions at Recreational Therapy time. (Adjunctive Therapy Service provides R.T. program also after 3:00 PM). Check with A.T. Coordinator.

e) Be on time for your appointments.

f) Accompany the child to the reception room and see to it that he returns to his school class or other activity. At times you may have to accompany him to the school or another activity.

Remember: Inconsistency in psychotherapy hours, lateness on the part of the psychotherapist, and disrupted classes are *not* therapeutic for the child and oftentimes result in the arousal of negative feelings in the child, other children and staff.

Psychotherapist's Role in Relation to Other Staff Members

The psychotherapist is not asked to take part in a child's management or to become involved in the discipline of a child. He enters into the daily activities of a child when it is indicated. Occasionally the residence nurse, without the child's knowledge, may call the child's psychotherapist when the child is in major difficulty in the residence and has been placed on restriction. The psychotherapist may use this opportunity to visit with the child and to talk with him about his problems, allowing for "on-the-spot" interviews which are considered of importance in the psychiatric treatment setting. However, this is not done routinely but only when the residence nurse feels that it is indicated. It is up to the child's psychotherapist to decide whether he will visit with the child or not. At times it is advisable to check with the child's psychiatrist. If the decision is made for the psychotherapist to visit the child, he asks the nurse to notify the child about the visit.

Through the frequent staff conferences, the psychotherapist is kept up-to-date on what happens in the residence, school and other activities. If the psychotherapist so desires he keeps in close touch with the child's daily routine through additional visits and conferences with the staff. He is strongly advised to take part in all conferences concerning the child's progress and review of treatment and to participate in all decisions as to whether visits with the family or relatives should be encouraged or curtailed, whether the child is able to handle additional privileges and freedom, or whether the child is ready for discharge.

In case the child's psychotherapist does not agree with the way certain staff handles discipline or other matters of management, he communicates this to the child's psychiatrist who discusses the psychotherapist's concern with the staff involved or decides to bring it up in an open staff conference or in an individual supervisory conference if that is indicated. Through this type of communication the psychiatrist is enabled to understand and discuss the concern of the psychotherapist as well as the authority on limits generally set by the various staff (relaxing or tightening of discipline) and particularly of the nursing staff who are equally responsible for the child's total treatment and the actual carrying out of proposed changes which are left to their discretion and authority, always under the psychiatrist's responsible supervision. Only on special occasions (e.g. when complete restriction is necessary) direct orders from the child's psychiatrist are required.

The child's occasional attempts to use his psychotherapist to circumvent other team members are also discussed in staff conferences, and treatment team members are made aware of the relation of the child's behavior in residence and other activities to the psychotherapy sessions and the importance of coordinating the total management of the child.

INDIVIDUAL PSYCHOTHERAPY REPORTS

Monthly Report by Psychotherapist to the Psychotherapy Board

A monthly report is forwarded by the psychotherapist to the chairman of the psychotherapy board by the seventh day of each month. This includes the names of all children receiving individual, group psychotherapy, and family therapy the preceding month, along with the name of the psychotherapist and the hours of individual, group psychotherapy and/or family therapy. A special form is used and is available at the chairman's office. The chairman of the board prepares a summary of all monthly reports.

Submitting Reports on Psychotherapy

Psychotherapists are responsible for the Initial, Progress and Final Reports on their psychotherapy children. These are sent to the child's psychiatrist after being signed by the psychotherapist. The child's psychiatrist initials and forwards them to the medical records office.

All reports are submitted in original and one copy. The original is filed in the child's Medical Master Chart. The copy is kept by the psychotherapist until the child's discharge, and then is filed in the Master Chart.

Types of Reports

These are: *Initial, Progress, Transfer* and *Final* Psychotherapy Notes. These types of individual psychotherapy notes are *not* meant to replace Psychotherapy Process Notes, that is, the recordings of each treatment session the psychotherapist may decide to keep for the purpose of supervision, *or* to replace the physician's, nurse's, etc. Progress Notes.

In writing notes on psychotherapy it should be remembered that the "success" of psychotherapy is a relative concept indicating to what extent the original treatment goals have been reached. It is not synonymous with the degree of recovery. Also that emphasis is put on the child's behavior in psychotherapy, as well as the psychotherapist's attitude and mode of action, while content material is almost absent or of a rather general nature. It is left up to the discretion of the psychotherapist how much of the content material can be revealed without violating the ethics and laws of confidentiality.

Furthermore, emphasis should be on the descriptions of what has been observed rather than on vague dynamic speculations. It is hoped that the writing of psychotherapy notes will help the psychotherapist, particularly the newcomer in the field, to review his work and to help him organize his thinking about what he is doing. It is also hoped that he will improve the quality of his psychotherapy notes and particularly secure continuity and adequate information about a child who might be transferred to another psychotherapist.

Initial Psychotherapy Note

This note is written *one month after the first psychotherapy session.* It gives the psychotherapist's initial impression of the treatment progress. The following outline form is suggested for the Initial Psychotherapy Note.

TABLE I

INITIAL PSYCHOTHERAPY NOTE

	Child's Name
Residential and Day Treatment Center	*Psychotherapist's Name*
Residence A (or B or Day Treat. Program)	*Date*

INITIAL PSYCHOTHERAPY NOTE

Period covered: Month-Day-Year to Month-Day-Year   *No. sessions:*

Identification: First name, age (years-months), legal status (voluntary, etc.) admission date, diagnosis after Initial D&A, date individual psychotherapy started.

Psychotherapist's comments: Reason for the selection of the child. Whatever the psychotherapist feels may be pertinent information to illustrate his pretherapeutic impression of the child.

Type of Treatment, Aims and Goals: (a) *Supportive-suppressive:* deals predominantly with conscious material and centers chiefly on support of child's strengths and assets.

(b) *Expressive-Uncovering* (insight psychotherapy): deals with uncovering unconscious conflicts and helping the child to endure the anxieties by reorganization of the ego defense mechanisms and support of ego functions.

(c) *Modified dynamically oriented psychotherapy:* uses supportive-suppressive methods as well as expressive ones with emphasis on free expression and better understanding of feelings and behavior for a clearer picture of external realities. Structure is more flexible.

Structural Arrangements: Time, place, frequency of sessions, agreements (cancellation of session, holidays, etc.).

Initial Impression: A brief description of the child's initial moves, general behavior during sessions, views of psychotherapy, use of the hour, major themes or conflicts, how they are presented, main defenses used, how child relates himself to therapist, any resistance, transference pattern, psychotherapist's attitude, feelings of improvement or aggravation of the illness, gains from psychotherapy.

Present Situation: A brief summary of the latest developments in the treatment situation.

Progress Psychotherapy Note

This note is written on a *three-month basis,* starting three months following the Initial Psychotherapy Note. The total hours of treatment to the date of Progress Psychotherapy Note will be noted in the identifying data at the beginning of each note. It is expected that the recordings of psychotherapy with children who show little movement may result in only slight changes in the content of these notes. The notes may, therefore, be shorter, but pertinent references to the areas in which the child is not changing are made. The following outline form is suggested for the Progress Psychotherapy Note.

TABLE II
PROGRESS PSYCHOTHERAPY NOTE

	Child's Name
Residential and Day Treatment Center	*Psychotherapist's Name*
Residence A (or B or Day Treat. Program)	*Date*

PROGRESS PSYCHOTHERAPY NOTE

Period covered: Month to Month—Year   *No. sessions:*   *Total:*

Type of treatment: Supportive-suppressive, modified dynamically oriented, etc.

Under which set of circumstances: As a residential or day treatment child, etc.

General behavior during sessions

Child's views of psychotherapy, subjective feelings of improvement or aggravation of his illness, gains from psychotherapy.

How does he make use of the hour—contents, theme. How are they presented? How does he relate to the psychotherapist?

Transference pattern: In what way does the psychotherapist frustrate the child's needs, in what respect are they gratified?

Main defense mechanisms used. List the classical defenses used. If possible, list what the defenses are used against and under which circumstances they are brought to action.

Resistance: Describe how the defenses show up in the therapeutic process. An example of their combination and sequence in form of "maneuver" during psychotherapy may be illustrative.

Psychotherapist's attitude: The psychotherapist's handling of the child's maneuvers. Describe what psychotherapist tried to accomplish, and why. Whether he succeeded or not.

Changes: Objective-subjective. Expectations of further changes.

Present situation: A brief summary of the latest developments in the treatment situation.

Transfer Psychotherapy Note

Follow the outline for the Initial Psychotherapy Note—PLUS

Review of the entire psychotherapy process and evaluation of the effect of the psychotherapy. Emphasis should be on recommendations and particularly what arrangements have been made to secure another psychotherapist for the child.

Present situation should include the preparations made for the transfer of the child to another psychotherapist; whether or not he has been informed; how it was done; how he reacted; any change in the psychotherapy situation since his notification; his fears and expectations about a new psychotherapist. If possible,

TABLE III

FINAL PSYCHOTHERAPY NOTE

	Child's Name
Residential and Day Treatment Center	*Psychotherapist's Name*
Residence A (or B or Day Treat. Program)	*Date*

FINAL PSYCHOTHERAPY NOTE

Period covered: Month-Year (started) to Month-Year (ended) *Total No. Sessions*
Identification, type of treatment, goals, structural arrangement.

Early phase of treatment, middle phase of treatment, changes in the defense patterning, which symptoms disappeared, which symptoms took their place, changes in the degree of anxiety tolerance, amount of insight gained into the problems, any emotional understanding of the problems, prediction of circumstances under which the child may be able to do well, of situations considered still traumatic. Review of original and later goals.

Tapering off the interviews, set termination date or abrupt termination—reasons. Separation anxiety. Child's readiness to leave.

Any regressive activity, temporary relapse, return of symptoms, doubts of stopping, anger of abandonment, of rejection, sadness, loss of relationship, nature and degree of decathexis (child's increased participation in outside activities).

Parent's feelings—their comfortableness. Child's expectations, understanding of present reality, acceptance of self.

Extent of original treatment goals reached.

Child's level of adjustment reached.

Prognosis—Circumstances under which the child will do well. Situations considered traumatic.

Recommendations: Return to home, continue psychotherapy or not, etc.

predictions as to how he will handle the new psychotherapist; what difficulties the new psychotherapist can expect.

Final Psychotherapy Note

This note is to be written the day following the termination of psychotherapy. It should describe what has been observed, not only vague dynamic speculations.

GROUP PSYCHOTHERAPY

Group psychotherapy at the center is aimed at improving relationships between children and staff, as well as relationships among the children themselves. An attempt is also made in providing some insight.

Structural arrangements include:

1. Number of children in each group: four to six;
2. Quarters for psychotherapy group sessions: school;

3. Frequency: one or twice a week;

4. Time: 11:00 AM and 1:40 PM;

5. Psychotherapists: child psychiatrists, psychologists, social workers;

6. Co-psychotherapists: psychologists, social workers, nurses, group workers, charge aides, mental health technicians.

At the center the information and suggestions described below (observed by Averill and his co-workers) (1), proved to be useful in conducting group psychotherapy with latency and early adolescence children.

Some of the *insights* that one hopes the children might gain over a period of time are the following:

1. All behavior has meaning.

2. Most of the child's behavior is self-defeating and compulsive in nature.

3. The children act towards adults and authority in a stereotyped manner as though all adults are the same and all are bad.

4. The children are angry at their parents, but are afraid to express this because they need them very badly.

5. The children are dependent on other people; this is possible without fear if they can distinguish adults one from the other.

6. The children are not as bad as they think they are, but they will never be as perfect as they wish to be.

7. Change and progress come from constructive effort.

8. To become aware of and tolerate anxiety, sadness and hopeless feelings without acting on them.

The group psychotherapist during the early period of psychotherapy should *remember the following* and pass them onto the group early in the beginning.

1. The group is to talk and not act.

2. No more limits will be set than are absolutely necessary for the safety of the children.

3. Whenever possible, remarks of the group psychotherapist are to be directed to the group of children rather than to individuals.

4. The children are free to talk about whatever is important to them.

5. All action, particularly of a negative or hostile nature is to

be commented upon by the psychotherapist and an effort made to bring out its verbal equivalent.

6. Create a warm, accepting atmosphere in the group.

7. Do not allow the children to scapegoat a member or project too much hostility outside the immediate situation. Invite them to direct their hostility towards the psychotherapist.

The group psychotherapist can expect the following *resistances* to develop.

1. Acting out in the group (poking, fighting, leave the room, absences).

2. Acting up outside the group (running away, fighting).

3. Exclusion of the psychotherapist by talking only to themselves.

4. Intense sexual preoccupation.

5. Breaking up into subgroups.

6. Numerous reality interferences which are hard for the psychotherapist to evaluate.

The group psychotherapist can expect the following *general themes* to develop, but not necessarily in this order.

1. Tell us what to say and do. You must control us.

2. Everybody is always telling us what to do. Nobody ever gives us any freedom.

3. We don't trust you. What are you up to? What are you going to do to us, for us, with us?

4. We are very bad kids. You are wasting your time. We are hopeless cases. Don't trust us.

5. We are hungry. Feed us. Give us something to show us you care.

6. You are like the rest. We are very angry at you. We don't need anything from anybody.

Group Psychotherapy Note

The regulations governing the conduct of group psychotherapy are the same as for the conduct of individual psychotherapy. Also, supervision of group psychotherapy is arranged through the Psychotherapy Board. A difference exists in the writing of psychotherapy notes.

TABLE IV
GROUP PSYCHOTHERAPY NOTE

	Child's Name
Residential and Day Treatment Center	*Psychotherapist's Name*
Residence A (or B or Day Treat. Program)	*Date*

GROUP PSYCHOTHERAPY NOTE

Period Covered: Month to Month-Year   *No. of Sessions:*

Type of Group Psychotherapy—Aims—Goals:

a) *Didactic* (Educational material presented for guided discussion) .

b) *Family Oriented* (Interpretations as if the group were a recreated family) .

c) *Group Dynamics* (Emphasis on group process) .

d) *Modified Didactic-Family Oriented-Group Dynamics*—Allows establishment of a social group climate, group cohesiveness, a setting for reality testing and trying out acceptable ways of relating, free expression and understanding of group feelings and behavior. For younger children and for psychotic children, there is more stress on structuring and on activities for the group rather than on interpersonal relations or problems.

Structural Arrangements: Setting (time, place) , frequency of sessions, group composition (homogeneity-heterogeneity) , agreements (cancellation of session or cotherapist as temporarily replacing leader, rules (type and degree of limits, holding-time, removal of child from session, holidays) etc.

Impressions on Changes in the Group Situation: Children's moves, general behavior, views of group during sessions, use of hour, major themes or conflicts, intrapersonal relationships and those towards psychotherapist and co-therapist. Children are observed in the group as a whole. Their interaction, feelings of participation, views of their problem are always described in relation to the other members of the group including the psychotherapist and co-therapist.

Group Psychotherapist's—Co-therapist's Attitudes: Creating warm, accepting atmosphere within the group. Listening, reeducating, pointing out, encouraging. Co-therapist passive-observer or active. Facilitating group interaction, allowing initiative, or bringing about group discussion leading to awareness. Focusing on daily events, group's current concerns.

Reminding group of agreements and responsibilities. Setting limits on regressive urges. Directing remarks to the group rather than to individuals. Commenting on physical negative or aggressive behavior and making effort to bring out its verbal equivalent. Maintaining a focus on the group as a whole, prohibiting the group to scapegoat a member.

Inviting the group to direct the hostility towards the therapist. Introducing displacement and sublimation opportunities.

Summarizing the hour by interpretation of the total group behavior (not the behavior of an individual member) .

Present Group Situation: Brief summary of latest developments in the group situation as well as changes in structural arrangements, new psychotherapist or co-therapist, transfers, discharges, new members, etc.

Recommendation on Changes in Group Situation: Structural arrangements, transfer, discharge, new members, group composition, psychotherapist's attitudes, goals, agreements, etc.

After the formation of the group, a note is written by the group psychotherapist and includes the names of all partipating children. This note is submitted to the chairman of the Psychotherapy Board.

A brief Progress Group Psychotherapy Note is prepared and is presented at the Initial and at each Progress and Final Diagnostic and Appraisal Conference for each child member of the group. The note is filed in the child's Medical Master Chart.

If a Diagnostic and Appraisal Conference does not take place within a period of three months, a Group Psychotherapy Note on the child is written at the end of the third month.

Group Psychotherapist and Co-therapist

Role of Co-therapist

The co-therapist in group psychotherapy serves as a receptor of verbal and nonverbal affect-laden expressions and communications between the group members and the psychotherapist. Although his function is primarily to provide an objective appraisal of a situation, the imposed passivity lessens his attention toward his own cognitive processes and leads to a propensity to become overly involved. Thus, unless he can exercise great control, it is difficult for him to be objective. However, his increased vulnerability and maximum receptivity to unconscious messages permit him to complement the therapeutic partnership. As he becomes involved with and identifies with group members as well as with the psychotherapist, he becomes more attuned to conflicts and reactions that may be disguised or are not clearly verbalized.

Review of Session

Immediately after the group session, the group psychotherapist and co-therapist review the session and the co-therapist has the chance to become active and report his observations. Through the additional material supplied by him, emotional responses or wishes that became prominent or fantasies that came to his mind at any particular time of the session are discussed and evaluated.

While some of these reactions of the co-therapist may be shared by the psychotherapist, others may be set aside because they are considered criticisms usually caused by personal rivalry or differences of status, temperament or techniques. These reactions need to be examined thoroughly because they may offer a substantial clue to unexplicit or unperceived parallel conflicts in the group. Thus, a suggestion by the co-therapist that the psychotherapist should have been more active during the session may reflect what the group felt but could not verbalize. The co-therapist is unwittingly the carrier of such a wish.

Strong Conflicts

Conflicts between the psychotherapist and co-therapist must be discussed by both in terms of the group situation at each given time. Because they both have different and complementary functions, their conflicts are closely connected with problems of transference and countertransference that have not been picked up, elucidated and worked through in the hourly session with the group.

The psychotherapist-co-therapist relationship reproduces in its midst those dormant or unverbalized conflicts in the group. When they both work as a unit, they can utilize the co-therapist's feelings and fantasies during the session to learn more about the group process and gauge transference and countertransference reactions.

A psychotherapist who is unable to work with the co-therapist to settle and understand the conflict may miss an invaluable opportunity to further the understanding of the group phenomena; the group may perceive the friction and utilize it to increase their resistance.

Strong Agreements

While disagreements and conflicts between psychotherapist and co-therapist are a sign of conflict within the group, strong agreements and enthusiastic identifications between these two partners can at times be just as representative of unspoken and unclarified problems within the group.

Such agreements may indicate that the co-therapist has identified so strongly with the psychotherapist and his countertransference that he shares the same blind spots and allies himself with and reinforces the unconscious defenses of the psychotherapist. Psychotherapist and co-therapist must learn to differentiate between agreement based on a realistic understanding and correct assessment of the group interaction and the kind of defensive enthusiasm that often hides hostile feelings towards the group and an unconscious wish to defeat it.

If the co-therapist is given a chance to contribute actively and not be relegated to a secondary position, much of the envy and resentment which he experiences and his role vis-à-vis the psychotherapist would clearly diminish. Both co-therapist and psychotherapist must work together to understand and solve any conflicts and problems in transference and countertransference if they are to understand and help their patients. If they cannot resolve their own problems, it may be necessary for a supervisor to intervene as a detached moderator.

FAMILY APPRAISAL

Health and illness are functions of the interrelations of organism and environment. The family is the basic unit of human experience; it is the primary group into which the functions of personality are integrated. The study of psychosocial pathology of everyday family life is a responsibility of the first priority if we are to meet the mental health challenge of our time.

In the center, the potential detriment to the younger family members resulting from the presence of an actively or inactively psychotic person in their midst receives the meticulous scrutiny it deserves. As the traffic of children between home and the center increases, a point may well be reached when the mental health needs of the family as a whole come into sharp conflict with those of the individual child.

Therapy cannot be primary; it must always be secondary to the precise assessment of pathology. Even though it is difficult to separate arbitrarily the diagnostic from the therapeutic efforts, the therapist has to secure pertinent information before deciding on the therapeutic work with the family. Thus during the initial period of family therapy the therapist adopts an active, investigative approach to the family with the purpose of understanding the major structural and functional operations within the family.

Relevant to the task of achieving family diagnosis are basic concepts, dynamic principles and behavioral criteria. Foci of pathogenic disturbance are evaluated within the framework of the psychodynamics of the family per se, conflict between family and community, interpersonal conflict in family pairs, and finally, intrapsychic conflict and symptoms within individual family members. Thus it is important to appraise

—The extent to which family conflict is controlled, compensated or decompensated.

—How far family conflict induces progressive damage to salient relationships, impairs complementarity in role relations, and therefore predisposes to breakdown of the child's adaptation.

—Can family integration be preserved despite conflict?

—Does conflict tend to destroy the link of child and family identity and thus magnify the malignancy of the child's pathology?

—Within the frame of family conflict, what are the vicissitudes of the child's opportunities to resolve or at least mitigate the destructive effects of intrapsychic conflict?

—What chance is there to discover a new and improved level of family role complementarity and with this, a better level of child's adaptation?

—How the family identifies and solves its problems.

—The effective expression and involvement of members within the family.

—The type of communication within the family and how well this communication is fostered and proceeds.

—The investigation of roles.

—Who controls the behavior of the family and how this is done.

—What measure and how the autonomy of individuals within the family is established.

—Common pathology among members of the family.

The diagnosis of the ill parent is initially made by the admitting team's analysis of the various components of psychotic attitude and behavior, and in addition, by impressions of how the predominant response of the parent might be perceived by the child in terms of avoidance, suspicion, etc. A psychiatric diagnosis is also made on the nonpsychotic parent who is also evaluated for helpfulness or harmfulness.

A number of children whose parents are seriously disturbed are admitted to the center. As Newman and San Martino (1) put it "Some of these parents have never been hospitalized and are maintained in the community with the help of tranquilizing drugs; others, once hospitalized, have been discharged quickly as part of an institution's early release program. Many parents, compensated psychotics, chronic paranoids and borderline personalities have never been identified as patients." Anthony (3) says that "they live in a relatively encapsulated microculture that manifests a high degree of tolerance for unusual or eccentric attitudes and behavior; . . . these families are often hypersensitive and suspicious of outsiders and regard their helpful intentions and interventions as intrusive and threatening. . . . The parents get by undetected because of the subtle and surreptitious nature of their disturbances."

Most of these parents are loosely rooted people and show less concern for the social consequences of their behavior. With their rootless life-style, they have less sense that anyone cares how one acts. Also, they are more susceptible to malaise and in some situations to physical or emotional disorders. They strive for value judgments, permissiveness rules their home, they are confused by the growing complexity of human institutions and take refuge in simplistic solutions, e.g. they seek the influence of the church or transcendental meditation or the juvenile judge who waggles his finger, and waggles and waggles. With increasing frequency, they form parents' associations and committees, hold a meeting to approve the minutes, to commercialize their religious views, discuss whether they should hold a conference or not; and the consensus is that they should hold off on the conference until they meet again. In the meantime, they just sit around and twiddle their thumbs.

Their children are resilient enough so that their schoolwork is not seriously affected if they are above average students. The average and below average students do have trouble.

The children have learned to adapt themselves to a double standard of reality, conforming to realistic expectations at school and elsewhere while maintaining an irrational orientation within the home, or the children are often assiduously coached by the nonpsychotic parent in the concealment of bizarre happenings and conspire in the preservation of secrecy.

According to Newman and San Martino (1)

> While their children may have symptoms apparently no more disabling than those of the majority of children admitted for treatment, the underlying pathology in both the child and his family is severe and chronic and presents a formidable challenge to therapeutic intervention. . . .
>
> Severely disturbed mothers, those who are psychotic or borderline, are different from neurotic mothers in ways which significantly affect their children. They are, as a group, angrier, needier, more frightened, fundamentally depressed, less able to see their children as individuals separate from themselves, and consequently less able to respond to their children's changing developmental needs. Their behavior is more rigid and stereotyped; their defenses are used more intensively and extensively and are less capable of modification. . . .
>
> Disturbed parents frequently both overstimulate and overly frustrate their children. The child's symptoms and character traits, his weaknesses and his strengths, are, in part, a response to the pressure of parental influence. His behavior is partly expressive of excessively stimulated and frustrated drives, partly defensive and fundamentally adaptive. Viewed broadly, the behavior of children who have a seriously disturbed parent manifests not only the child's attempted solution to internal conflict but also his adaptive response to external stress. The child may be withdrawn or gregarious, phobic or aggressive, intellectually precocious or academically underachieving. Each symptom or behavioral response is, in part, the child's attempt to cope with a reality of which a seriously disturbed parent is a significant component. . . .
>
> The oral, anal, phallic, and oedipal issues, inherent in every child, rooted in biology and in the family structure, manifest themselves in typical ways and set the stage for inevitable and unavoidable internal conflicts. Every child passes through these developmental progressions to latency and adolescence and inevitably experiences tensions, anxieties, and disappointments. . . .
>
> In any family in which there is a severely disturbed parent, a pat-

tern of adaptive interaction develops, involving all family members, to which each ultimately makes his own contribution. In many cases, the more overtly sick member becomes the scapegoat onto whom the others project their own disturbed and provocative wishes, feelings and thoughts. . . .

Parental beliefs about what constitutes treatment reflect their fantasies and the conflict solutions upon which these are based. Some of these beliefs are compatible with a problem-solving approach to therapy, while others clearly are not and challenge the therapist's judgement, intuition and skill.

The stage for traditional psychotherapy and casework is set if an introjecting, rationalizing, defensive style, linked to character traits of introspection, intellectuality and relative inaction and associated with the family's belief system emphasizing that evil and its cure are within oneself. . . .

Problem-solving as a method of treatment is impossible when the defenses are projection, denial, and intellectualization, the character traits suspiciousness and blaming, and the predominant belief system one proclaiming that evil and its correction are without. In cases of this type, the only possible, and necessarily limited, approach to therapy is for the therapist to ally himself partially with the parental paranoia and assume an authoritative, directive role, while at the same time supporting parental narcissism. . . .

These families require tremendous investment of time and energy, often with limited and uncertain therapeutic results. Understanding, ideally, should be backed up by a range of concrete services both for continuous professional care and for intensive intervention at times of crisis. These should include night and day treatment facilities for acute exacerbation of parental illness, reliable foster home care for their children, housekeeping and recreational services to ease daily living.

After a careful clinical evaluation of the child dealing with both specific and general factors, a global rating of his adjustment is made ranging from normal and better than normal adjustments to varying degrees of maladjustment requiring counseling, day treatment or residential treatment.

Anthony (3) explains that

a closer clinical look at the child in an open-ended, semistandardized interview attempts to get at: (1) his basic tendency to internalize or externalize his conflicts; (2) his degree of self-awareness and body-awareness as manifested through a low threshold for subjective experiences; (3) his proclivity to withdrawal, regression, suspicion, diversion, negativism, or hostility with stressful questioning; (4) his compliance to suggestibility or authority; and (5) his over-identification and involvement with the sick parent and his sickness. The last item is assessed by the child's knowledge of the development of the psychosis, his concerns with causation, diagnosis, prognosis, and treatment, and his reactions, in terms of his own inner convictions to the delusions and hallucinations to which he is exposed.

There are three groups of clinical disturbances which have been observed, two related specifically and one nonspecifically to the psychotic illness in the parent: (a) a group of children whose disturbances appear to represent precursors of the later psychosis in the adult (precursive group); (b) a group whose disturbances are apparently directly attributed to a symbiotic type of relationship between child and sick parent (symbiotic group); and (c) a group that is disturbed by the vagaries of the peculiar environment engendered by the presence of psychosis, i.e. reactions to the parental psychosis which may take the form of transient situational maladjustments, antisocial behavior or neurotic reactions.

Our data would support the view that the preschool phase is especially sensitive to the disturbing experiences of psychotic management, especially on the part of a chaotically reactive mother. This can result in an acute primitivization with a massive loss of developing ego skills. In the case of the older child, it may lead to transient situational disorders, acting out behavior, or to the development of such neurotic disturbances as nightmares, obsessions and phobias. . . . They respond to separation from the parent. In this sense, we speak of the neurosis of the child as the loudspeaker of the family trouble, often of several generations of trouble.

The precursive episodes stem from the parental psychosis and last from three days to three months and then dissipate even without treatment. Separation from the sick parent seems to have little value in the prevention of further episodes.

The microschizoid episode can be confused with sulkiness, except for the absence of antagonistic affect and the presence of a large number of strange subjective experiences. The child may appear unusually abstracted and unresponsive to his interests.

The microparanoidal episode is associated with an upsurge of suspiciousness and a sense of persecution that may develop loose systematization, especially in the older children. . . .

The hebephrenic episode is altogether less strikingly differentiated from the usual mode of behavior. The children appear "odd and peculiar" with vaguely demarcated episodes of silly, inappropriate and clownish behavior—usually under the stimulus of some minor stress. . . .

Induced or parapsychotic disturbances are associated with the parental psychosis and result from its impact on over-influenceable children. In this condition delusions, hallucinations, and other psychotic symptoms are imposed by the psychotic parent on one or other of the children. They may take form of *folie a deux,* Ganser syndrome, or a succession of twilight states. The conditions favoring such developments include a symbiotic relationship between mother and child, a lower than average intelligence in the child, a close identification with the sick parent, a high degree of suggestibility, especially in relation to bodily feelings, an almost abject passivity and submissiveness, and a marked involvement in the psychotic manifestations of the parent.

The parapsychosis seems most prone to develop in the case of a mother and a daughter who is over the age of five. The sick parent may overtly make the acceptance of her delusional beliefs a precondition for object relations, so that it becomes a case of "love me, love my delusion."

In general, the parapsychotic reactions mirror the parent's illness fairly closely, but unlike the prepsychotic reactions, they tend to disappear altogether when the child is permanently separated from the parent.

In addition to viewing the individual child as a separate person, he needs to be viewed also within the frame of the total life of his family. It is axiomatic that an integrated therapeutic approach to the family entity, if it is to aspire to psychological specificity, must rest on the foundation of comprehensive diagnosis of the family.

Again according to Anthony (3)

There are three main types of disorganization in the home environment or subculture of psychosis; in their fully developed forms they tend to reflect the type of psychotic disintegration of the parent as they do, to some extent, the type of disequilibrium in the child: (1) In the *process* environment, where the parent is hebephrenic or catatonic, the household suffers from neglect as a result of extreme degrees of *laissez-faire.* This is especially true when the sick parent is the mother. The children begin to lead separate lives of their own, unsupervised and undisciplined, and there is a high incidence of behavior problems and delinquency. (2) In the *paranoid* environment or "psuedo-community," there is "organized disorganization" in the sense that family life is incorporated into the workings of the delusional system, to the great bewilderment of the children. (3) The *reactive* environment is characterized by its inconsistency, chaotic management, contradictory communications, highly ambivalent but powerful affects, incoherent intentions and motives, and its disturbing degree of intrusiveness into the lives of the children. This "environment of irrationality" envelopes the family and makes for unpredictable storms and crises that hover over the lives of the children. At one moment they are pulled into intimate closeness, and at the next, they are thrust far away with bitter and unjustified accusations. The pulls of reality and unreality can set up peculiar conflicts of loyalty.*

FAMILY THERAPY

During the last decade, enthusiasm for "family therapy" has been reflected in a series of publications describing its history, techniques and theory. In some quarters, it has become the method of treatment although there are as yet no systematic studies of its comparative efficacy.

Those of us in child psychiatry who probe the changing trends of American family life and who work in a practical way to help families with their problems are becoming increasingly aware of the importance of family life in the world arena. Family psychology is a clue to world psychology. World changes not only influence family change, but family changes affect world change. In a sense, a family is a barometer indicating not only what is going on in the world today, but what will be going on tomorrow. This is partly because the family is sensitive to trends that have not yet become generally visible.

In the process of social transformation, the family changes its shape. It not only reflects these changes, but it absorbs and adapts them and thus changes the world. This role of the family in social change is understood by the example of the violence with which totalitarian cultures have developed their anti-family message to a point where the child must not only denounce his father and mother and all obligations to his ancestors, but must learn to deride and vilify his parents as narrow, bigoted, petty, cheap, mean and coarse exponents of a vicious tradition. It is through the breaking of the traditional family, say the totalitarians, that a new pattern of human interdependence must be created. If this is so, we may well take note of the ways in which our own alteration of family structure may change our life at

---

* Reprinted by permission.

large, and what it may portend for the world as a whole. Those of us who work with children and parents view the family in terms of a value system which is part of our culture as a whole. Our discussions of the family have often implied an ideal, a standard for the mother. She is expected to be warm, strong, direct, to enjoy her femininity and her motherhood, to give affection and support, to protect her children, to be firm but not overbearing, tender but not mawkish; to provide stimulus and support for the child's growth and his ultimate achievement of independence.

We have recently begun to learn, however, that in this picture some basic realities are missing, for one, the factor of individual differences. What is simple and natural for the mother to give may not completely meet the needs of every child. Family relationships are very individualized and the mother who is equally good for all the children cannot always be found in every home. What we do with this mother and with families in general will not only reflect the world trends of the twentieth century but will in some measure give direction to these trends. If humanity, democracy and the spirit of science can be combined in working with families, this ancient institution may be strengthened in the world area.

Potential Value

The center recognizes the potential value of family therapy and this recognition is supported by several relevant considerations:

1. In child psychiatry and individual psychotherapy certain problems continue to balk solution due to our inability to formulate the psychodynamics of the family group and thereby make possible reliable correlations of child and family behavior.

2. The role of the family in the stabilization of the mental health of the child has been widely discussed but practically neglected. Because of this, traditional standards of diagnosis, therapy and prognosis of emotional disturbances in children remain deficient in certain respects. The interrelations of child and family contribute to the determinants of mental health at every stage of maturation, infancy, childhood and adolescence. Such rela-

tions influence the precipitation of illness, its course, the likelihood of recovery, and the risk of relapse. Receptivity or resistance to therapy is partly the product of emotional interaction with other family members. Prediction of changes in behavior is accurate only to the extent that family processes are taken into account.

3. Disorders in children have undergone progressive transformation related to socio-cultural change and corresponding shifts in family strucure and function. Individual psychotherapy has not caught up with this challenge. The core of the problem is a shift in personality organization, particularly in defense operations which favor externalization of conflict and "acting out." The "symptoms" exhibited today are more moderate, credible and generally less fanciful and fantastic. There is a new breed of patient who seems to be the result of more openness and permissiveness in society at large. Eccentricity and expressions of hostility are more accepted these days and the contemporary patient's behavior is often no more "odd" than the behavior displayed by many of today's militant and youthful subcultures. Perhaps openness acts as a safety valve and makes it less likely that a person will effect a complete flight from reality.

The term "family therapy" means joint treatment sessions with all family members. Such therapeutic work is done most commonly in psychiatric clinics for children. The lessons learned through such work indicate that the parents are not merely interested responsibly in the child's emotional health and welfare; they are also asking more or less frankly for help for themselves as well. Also that treatment of the child alone, except when adolescence is reached, is usually inadequate and often justifiable.

There are many controversies of family therapy that are of interest, e.g.

—the theoretical question of the etiology of the child's disorder and the often practical question of who is the patient.

—the question of the advantages and disadvantages of family therapy work as against individual psychotherapy with the child.

—the question about which professional members can, may or

should be encouraged to learn to work with which member of the family.

—the question about the thoroughness of personality change versus mere symptomatic improvement that any psychotherapeutic method may hope to achieve and

—in which member of the family. In other words, will the child's disorder be less likely to receive adequate attention if clinical attention is "diffused" through the entire family?

Family therapy implies solution of the questions of what to treat, whom to treat, when to treat. It requires a formulation of intrapsychic conflict within the broader frame of salient patterns of family conflict, a correlation of disturbed homeostasis of individual personality with disturbed homeostasis of the family group.

It also requires that the corrective approach to pathogenic foci be made within the context of an explicit judgement regarding a set of appropriate goals and values for a healthy family in our society.

A therapeutic approach to the emotional disturbance of family life is conceived in the following steps:

1. A psychosocial evaluation of the family as a whole.

2. The application of appropriate levels of social support and educational guidance.

3. A psychotherapeutic approach to conflicted family relationships.

4. Individual psychotherapy for selected family members oriented initially to the specific dynamic relations of personality and family role, and to the balance between intrapsychic conflict and family conflict.

Conceptualizing the family as a unit is difficult. Working with individual children and parents is tempting because we are most accustomed to that method. It is easy to talk individually with the mother or the father or the child and hard to stay focused on the interaction of all the participants.

As psychiatric illness is a process, it is neither static nor is it ever an exclusively endogenous disorder. In the emotionally disturbed child, the interpersonal relations with his family are an integral part of his illness. In child psychiatry we are accustomed to evaluating the pathology of the family environment. We think of the behavior of the child as a kind of mirror of the psychological core of family and we believe effective emotional integration into family roles is necessary for the stabilization of the mental health of the child.

In troubled families, many conflicts may be reflected in one symptom. How each person reacts to these symptoms may give the therapist an indication of the family constellation, as well as insight into how family members relate. The symptom is the destructive interaction taking place around this single incident, as well as many other similar incidents, upon which are projected deeper family misunderstandings and conflicts.

These seemingly superficial problems express the misunderstandings, the positive and negative feelings, and the conflicts in relationships, and often bring to light destructive behavior in more significant areas of family interaction.

In this regard, children are an important part of family therapy because, through their natural honesty and through their actions, they often depict problems the family is afraid to discuss. Also it is the children who are most likely to develop symptoms indicating family malfunctions.

Because of the group nature of family therapy, some therapists maintain there is little or no difference between family therapy and group therapy. However, family therapy is, in a sense, a therapy of its own, or technique not like others in existence. For only in family therapy are the issues of dependency and independence, of parent and child relationships, of authority and power dealt with in the original structure in which these values are developed and these conflicts are experienced, the primary family unit.

In group therapy and in family therapy, the goal is to help each member develop his personality to its fullest capacity. To solve the apparent problems of the family, to help the family work together in a more constructive way is a realistic and important goal. The achievement of this goal may help each member become a more sincere and better integrated individual, thereby enabling him to function more comfortably; not only with his own family, but with outsiders as well.

Certain common clinical observations often document the social psychopathology of family life and the need for a corresponding program of therapeutic intervention. In a particular family, the person referred for psychiatric care may be the most sick or the least sick member of the group. The primary patient, in our case the child, often proves to be an emissary in disguise of an emotionally warped family. The child is brought to a psychiatrist by his family. He never comes on his own. The tendency is always to bring first to the psychiatrist the weakest and most defenseless member of the family, a child or the more docile of the marital partners. Thus the person referred may be viewed as a symptom of disturbed family homeostasis.

Psychiatric illness as a single or isolated instance in family life hardly occurs. Almost always other members of the family are also ill. The sick behaviors of these family members are often closely interwoven and mutually reinforcing. A critical focus of conflict and anxiety may move from one member of the family to another or from one family pair to another. In this sense the family group serves as a carrier of emotional disturbance. Sometimes two members share the same illness or one illness is the complement of the other or they may clash. In the latter instance the continuity of the family may be thrown into jeopardy. It is by no means rare that the core of family life is dominated by these reciprocal patterns of psychiatric disturbance.

It is also significant clinically that the main spur for psychiatric referral comes frequently from the suffering caused by family conflict rather than from the existence of mental symptoms per se. In many families there is no thought of psychiatric referral as long as the neurotic tendencies of the family members are tolerably well compensated within the pattern of reciprocal family role relations. The timing of the demand for professional help tends very much to coincide with acute decompensation of the balance of family relations, bringing in its wake a distressing family conflict. Critical upsets of the homeostasis of a family group thus become a significant mental health challenge.

Due to the fundamental interdependency and reciprocity of behavior in family relations, frequently if one member is treated, others must be treated too. If a disturbed child is treated, so must the mother be. If the mother is treated, the father needs attention too. This concern with the maintenance of a certain desired emotional balance in family relations is nowhere so convincingly reflected as in the family life of a child. In a certain sense, this trend reflects a need for a kind of vaccination procedure, a quest for immunity against the toxic effects of neurosis so that the unity of the family group may be preserved.

Goals

The goal of family therapy is to join the child and his family environment rather than to dichotomize them. It signifies the assessment of adaptation and mental health in the wider context of the child's organic involvement in his whole human community. It links child, family, community and culture.

The family shares common problems. In learning to work therapeutically with the parents is not equivalent to blaming them either for the child's conflicts and difficulties or for any of their feelings or behavior. This may sound elementary, but much experience shows it to be a primary lesson that one learns and relearns almost with every parent.

Family therapy affords the clinician direct observation of family transactions in place of his customary reliance upon the patient and informants for accounts of what occurs in the family. Congruent to this virtue, it provides the opportunity for immediate intervention on the therapist to manipulate pathologic interactions.

The key to achieving change within the family is to work with the family's strengths, not merely with its weaknesses. The family has some drive to stay together, to work out the problems, or the members would not continue to come to therapy sessions.

Family therapy can be of help for its members because it helps each member understand how he works within the family structure, what role he plays, whether his role is constructive or destructive, and how he can change it.

The family is helped to see that they are enmeshed in a collusion in which they all are working to perpetuate an unhappy situation. At best, the family has mixed feelings about wanting to break the pattern and almost always they need help to do so.

The reluctance to change is a common characteristic of many families in trouble. No one in the family wants to change the way the family operates, but they do want to lighten the pressure and the difficulty. The family is afraid of risking change because they cannot predict how this might upset the balance of power and interaction.

Conflict often is first presented in terms of externals. The family focuses mainly on the children and then, finally, on the marital conflict. But families are reluctant to discuss feelings; they prefer presenting their problems in external terms.

Problem-solving often is the key to the family's internal world. Most frequently one, two, or a few problems are sifted out for discussion as symbols of the full range of problems. They are concrete representations of the areas of tension, ambiguity, indecision and breakdown of solidarity in the group.

Therapist's Attitudes

Family therapy is not equivalent to casework, which usually aims at the modification of the parental attitudes through guidance designed to enlarge the understanding and the child's needs; neither is it merely an opportunity to instruct, advise or educate parents who appear to be "ignorant of modern psychology"; or to preach to those who appear to be "unworthy" of having children entrusted to them. Nor is it an opportunity to exhort them to be more loving, more patient, more tolerant, or more firm toward their children than they can be toward themselves.

The "abstract" therapist tends to take a patient's communications as symbolic of other hidden (unconscious?) thoughts and to interpret from this point of view. The "direct" therapist is more prone to accept the patient on the terms in which he expresses himself and to respond in a more interpersonal feeling fashion. Most therapists tend to be emotionally expressive on some occasions and more interpretive and "abstract" on other occasions, depending upon the patient and the patient's need at the time.

Some therapists assume, incorrectly, that they are manipulating the families or running their lives for them. Others in family therapy have distorted notions about psychodynamics and have said, in effect, "Forget everything you ever learned about people through the psychodynamic approach and start over again with a new concept about families." Of course, I do not agree with that. Instead, I suggest that the psychodynamic approach takes an "inside" look at people, while family therapy takes an "outside" look. They are both viewing the same phenomena, so it is possible to put observations into words that are understandable to both. The family therapist uses both sources of information, the details and the overall patterns.

The family therapist

—represents, in part, a parent figure to all the family members, supplementing the role and strengths of the parent. He is a catalyst, focusing the discussion, stimulating each member of the family to talk and to think, pointing out to the family obvious, but often overlooked, patterns.

—takes a stance which is primarily focused upon group or subgroup transactions within the family rather than the operations of any one individual in the family. This does not imply that he may not focus upon any one individual in the family at any particular time, but he must always bring the encounter with the individual back into the context of the family as a group.

—focuses upon strengths and utilizes these in order to modify the elements which are pathological.

—emphasizes on agreements instead of debating on differences of opinion.

—deals with the natural resistance of family members to openly discuss the real problem; once he has accomplished this, he then can deal with the patterns and styles which hinder understanding.

—points out misinterpretations, poor patterns of communication, the resistance to understand or to change, and other destructive behavior which prevents the family from constructing effective methods of handling anger, fear, dependency and other issues.

—orients his efforts towards the interpretation and consequent change of maladaptive transactions within the family to more adaptive ones because it is within this context that individuals in the family can derive greater satisfactions for the greater number of individuals therein.

—mobilizes the family to produce significant material. Often he can pinpoint the precise interaction that changes the interview from a dull session to one that becomes lively and meaningful. (*Critical event:* that part of an interview which appears most important from the viewpoint of producing movement in the therapy process.)

—encourages family members to talk to each other and to seek their own solutions rather than use the therapist as an expert who provides all the answers.

Structural Arrangements

Within the frame of a family therapy approach, individual psychotherapy is auxiliary to and dependent upon an integrated therapeutic program for the family as a social unit. Crucial to such a program is the consideration of appropriate levels of entry, and timing of such entry to affect in sequential stages specific components of the family disturbance. As an aid in the determination of such judgements, home visits by the social worker and careful recording of observations of family interactions in its natural setting are of the first importance.

Interpretation of the relevant data is of material help in reaching judgements as to the need and suitable timing of interventions with family therapy, educational guidance, psychiatric first aid, psychotherapy for conflicted family pairs, and individual psychotherapy for selected family members.

Whenever possible, our practice is to engage both parents as well as the child in psychotherapeutic work with professional members of the center's staff.

Family therapy is conducted in a separate family therapy room which usually has the comfort, ease, furniture and decorations associated with a family living room. It is into this setting that the entire family is ushered and the work of treatment unfolds. Members are asked to take any seats they wish.

There are three major approaches to family therapy. In *collaborative treatment* one or more members of the primary patient's family is also in treatment, usually each person with a different therapist. This is the team approach that one encounters in child guidance clinics where one professional sees the child and another treats the mother. Therapists meet in order to conjointly discuss the case.

A second type of family therapy is the *concomitant approach* which is used in marriage counseling where one therapist treats at least two members of the family, e.g. the marriage partners, but usually separate. They are seen jointly in treatment only on occasion.

A third type of family therapy, which is being used more and more, is the *conjoint* situation in which all members of the family are seen simultaneously by the therapist once a week, one and one-half hours per session. This type of family therapy is practiced in the center.

There are times during which the therapist may decide to plan office interviews in the following order:

an interview with the child (primary patient) and mother together,

an interview with the child alone,

an interview with child and father and finally,

an interview with the two parents without the child.

Or it might entail at an appropriate point an interview of the child and both parents, or the child and sibling together with one or both parents. At certain stages it may be appropriate to work concentratedly with mother and child together; husband and wife together; or even mother, father and child together.

Since the child is viewed both as an individual in distress and as a symptomatic expression of family pathology, the disturbance of this child becomes the fulcrum or entering wedge for the appropriate levels of intervention into the disorder of the family relations. The sequence of office interviews is arranged with a view to further elucidation of the interrelations of the child's affliction with the psychopathology of the family, and the corresponding interplay between his intrapsychic conflict and family conflict. The aid is to define the conflicts in which the child is locked with other family members, to assay the disturbances in the bond of individual and family identity, and the interdependence of homeostasis of individual personality with the homeostatic balance of the role relations in family pains and the family as a whole. It is possible, then, to mark out the patterns of family interaction which are potentially available for solution of conflict or for restitution.

Family Therapy Seminar

Each week professional staff—social workers, psychologists, psychiatrists, nurses—meet to further their knowledge of this technique and to present cases and exchange ideas about the families with which they are working. These seminars are used not only to add professional expertise in dealing with families but also used as a method of training staff and developing a core group of teachers and supervisors.

Because many approaches exist and many theories are used, the staff study group draws from a variety of professional opinions in putting together their own theoretical framework for working

TABLE V

FAMILY THERAPY NOTE

	Child's Name
Residential and Day Treatment Center	*Therapist's Name*
Residence A (or B or Day Treat. Program)	*Date*

FAMILY THERAPY NOTE (INITIAL, PROGRESS, FINAL)

Period covered: Month-Day-Year to Month-Day-Year   No. Sessions:

Family Members Participating: (father, mother, child, siblings)

Identification: First name, age (years-months), admission date, diagnosis after Initial D&A, date family therapy started.

Type of family: Natural parents, adoptive, divorced, one parent, others.

Structural Arrangements: Time, place, frequency, agreements, rules.

Present Situation: Family's major themes, defense mechanisms, patterns of communication, role of each family member, who attends, how often, who sits where.

Therapist's comments: Initial impression.

Aims and goals: Short and long term goals.

with families. The group is chaired by a child psychiatrist (psychotherapy and family therapy supervisor) who stresses that although psychodynamic understandings are important, the family therapy approach differs from individual therapy by dealing with the family in its operations as a group.

Family Therapy Note

This note is to be written one month after the first family therapy session and every third month thereafter.

REFERENCES

1. Averill, S. C., *et al.:* Group psychotherapy with young delinquents. *Bull Menninger Clinic, 37:*1, 1973.
2. Newman, M. B., and San Martino, M. R.: The child and the seriously disturbed parent. *J Child Psychiatry, 10(2):*358-374, 1971.
3. Anthony, J.: A clinical evaluation of children with psychotic parents. *Am J Psychiatry, 126:*177-184, 1969.

NURSING SERVICE

TREATMENT IN RESIDENCE

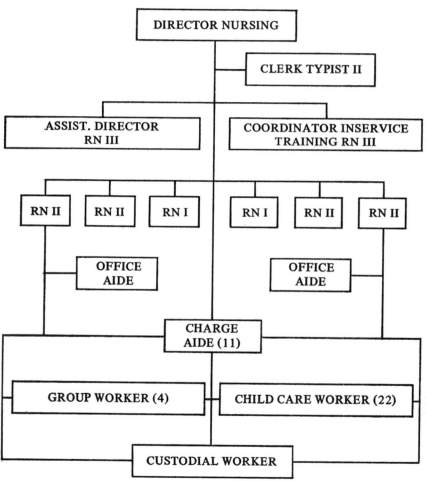

234

NURSING STAFF
General Orientation

THE RESIDENTIAL EXPERIENCE does more than afford parents and child an opportunity to progress in their individual therapy by temporarily relieving the tensions between them. It is also therapeutic in the positive sense through the interpersonal relationships that create a therapeutic atmosphere. For such relationships the most important component in residential treatment is the nursing staff, the immediate part of the child's daily living who augments the professional staff.

The nursing staff is an integral part of the total treatment plan if medical, psychiatric, remedial education and group work are to help the child. The titles supplied to the nursing staff positions by the center are generally descriptive of a child care role: child care worker, social group worker, charge aide, office aide, nurse. The nursing staff members are mature adults, genuinely fond of children and capable of understanding their emotional needs and of feeling with them. For the children's own gratification rather than primarily for their own satisfaction, the nursing staff members establish security, first for the children's dependent needs and then for the needs of striving for growth and mastery. Being the personnel most closely involved with the children on an ongoing basis, they help them begin the day and they see them to bed at night. They are also involved, to varying degrees, with their recreation, mealtimes and other aspects of their daily life. They do not avoid frequent intimate physical contacts with the children. They tuck younger children into bed, and may kiss them goodnight, and allow the very young child to sit on their laps.

Even though nursing staff members vary in their age, the majority are young. This variety of nursing staff provides the child who is not able or ready to form a close tie the chance to relate on a more superficial basis to someone closer to him in age. While in contact with several different individuals, the child is free to form his closest ties with the nursing staff member whom he can accept at the moment.

Living in the residence is intended to provide children who have experienced severe conflict with their parents and other adults an experience where nursing staff combines tolerance, firmness, patience and understanding with confidence in the child's eventual ability to develop greater adequacy. The nursing staff are chosen on the basis of their warm feeling, their firmness and their ability to identify themselves with the children. Such people are indeed hard to find, and it is my pleasure that I have been able to select a number of them.

Both male and female nursing staff wear white uniforms and white shoes while on duty, with the exception of field trips.

The philosophy often expressed by psychiatrists, social workers, psychologists and others professionally trained to understand and treat the problems of emotionally disturbed children is that residential nursing staffs are fully fitted to be substitute parents for such children. The center does not subscribe to this philosophy. The role of the nursing staff at the center is not that of a substitute parent. The real parent retains his parental role in the child's life, even though the child is placed; and the residence does not have foster value for the child. It is believed that if the child were to relate to the nursing staff as parental figures, there might be further conflict in his familial relationships. The chief job of the nursing staff is seen to be the physical care and supervision of the child. It is true that the nursing staff members contribute to the general tone of the living setting. They are constantly asking to make judicious use of their authoritative role, affording a medium in which the child can find a place according to his own interests and tendencies. They can, to a degree, provide a strong and secure quality for the overaggressive, disorganized children. They can encourage participation of the fearful, uncertain ones and help them find status in the group according to their own tendencies.

The nursing staff members' relationship to a child is formed around the child's actual behavior in a living setting. They represent authority insofar as the center takes over responsibility for control in the life of a child. They try, however, not to mold the child's actions, but rather to help him become aware of the manner in which he tends to direct his own actions. In the center the nursing staff's response to a child does not differ from that of the therapist in that their concern is primarily to help the child express and examine his feelings and to help him to act in relation to living requirements.

The residence nurse, who is not actually a substitute mother but is seen as such by the whole group, spends a great deal of time working directly with children, as well as in supervision of the charge aide, group workers and child care workers. In collaboration with the psychiatrist, she selects children whose personality problems will not clash to engage in activities together. She plans some activities, but free choice by the children and group workers is also possible. The philosophy of the staff is that through creative and satisfying activities, therapy does take place. Emphasis is also placed on re-education of poor habit patterns by establishing routines that are tolerable to the children and yet have re-educational value.

The nursing staff maintains a warm and individual relationship with each child. They bring to the attention of the other treatment team members observations which lead one to feel that the child is seeking the relationship of a child to a parent. Such observations frequently call for a consideration of what the child needs additionally from his parents that might lead to an increase in the frequency of parental visits or more prolonged visits home.

In spite of the fact that sufficient direct psychiatric help for the children can be secured, the nursing staff have to carry much of the responsibility for child care and management under psychiatric direction and supervision. Even though they are viewed in part as group leaders who must understand the dynamics of group relationships, they must understand and be able to work with the individual child.

The nursing staff's function is conceived as primarily involving ego training within an affectional relationship. The development of this relationship is geared to the child's readiness for it since his capacity to accept such a relationship is often one of the most serious areas of his problem. The nursing staff's efforts are focused toward habit training, guidance, incentive, discipline and reward, as they are equated to ego-development. Nursing staff also affords security through dependency satisfaction to the child, through providing for his personal care, attention to his appearance, and concern for him when he is ill or upset. Nursing staff are encouraged to join in spontaneous recreation activities, while delegating leadership for organized and scheduled activities to the appropriate personnel.

I believe the residential nursing staff members are key personnel because they provide the environment in which the child is enabled to work through all the conflicts for which he is being helped by the psychiatrist and his individual psychotherapist. It is in residence that he must find the opportunity to test out new strengths. He can also be helped to form positive emotional relationships by accepting residential nursing staff to supplement his relationships with his therapists. This may provide a bridge to more healthy relationships with his own parents.

There is much evidence in the nursing records of the children's use of the nursing staff to test acceptance of new feelings and new ideas. For example, if a child has been receiving sex information from his psychotherapist he may repeat the information to the nursing staff member to see if it is acceptable to her or he may ask the same questions of the staff that he has asked the psychotherapist to make sure he receives the same answers. If he is being helped by the psychotherapist to act out aggressive feelings, he may act his out with the nursing staff member to see if it is acceptable to her. The residence seems to become a place in which it is safe to behave in a new way, and the residential people are safe adults with whom to try out new ways of relating before the ultimate test of home and parents.

Because many of the children have regressed to infantile behavior level or have a great need to do so, the nursing staff members report that they accept and sometimes encourage infantile behavior when indicated, especially to establish a therapeutic relationship which is later used to foster growth. At the same time the nursing staffs are expected to be alert to every time a child is ready to give up infantile patterns and progress to more mature ways. More mature behavior is encouraged by staff at that point and acknowledgement made when observed.

While the nursing staff members encourage meaningful individual relationships with children, they are aware of the possibility that the child may attempt to utilize them vicariously to channel off feelings which are more directly related to his psychotherapist. There is constant communication between the nursing staff and the child's psychotherapist, and the latter always knows what the child is discussing with the nursing staff and can use it in the psychotherapy sessions. Some children deliberately use the nursing staff to communicate with their psychotherapist when they find it too difficult to talk directly to him. Thus, nursing staff are in a position where they may respond according to the external implications of the behavior allowing the child's feelings to be considered in a primary manner. Accordingly, some incidents may have less intensely moving significance for the child at the moment but the nursing staff is asked to always bring into relief the apparent basic motivation behind an act. Such motivation is encouraged to be discussed in a selective manner either at the time the act occurs or later. In any event, the nursing staff informs the psychotherapist about such episodes.

When children attempt to introduce issues into psychotherapy sessions which call for decisions related to their practical living, these issues are not referred to the nursing staff for settlement, but are discussed among all treatment team members. The nursing staff, through their biweekly held Residence Team Meetings, as well as daily informal meetings, carefully follow the reports of the psychotherapist, teacher, recreational therapist, as well as the social worker's work which is being carried on with the parents. They are also helped to understand the manner in which a child's behavior in residence may be a reflection of his trends in psychotherapy. For example, projections of hostility or uncooperativeness towards nursing staff may simply reflect the child's feelings as they are aroused in individual or group psychotherapy or family therapy.

DUTIES AND FUNCTIONS

The nursing service personnel consists of fifty members: nine registered nurses (Director of Nursing, coordinators of nursing shifts and in-service training), six nurses, secretary, two office aides, custodial worker, eleven charge aides and twenty-six child care workers. Their duties and functions are as follows.

Director of Nursing Service

The Director of Nursing Service is administratively responsible to the director of the center. She is delegated authority with accompanying responsibility to carry out her duties and to develop administrative and clinical abilities in the nursing staff for the benefit of the entire center.

She is charged with nursing policy-making recommendations, and together with the nursing staff she actively participates in the formulation and revision of the *Manual of Nursing Policies and Procedures.* Her responsibilities embrace nursing services, in-service nursing training, and the preparatory program.

She is a member of the Advisory Council and Education and Research Committee.

She works closely and assures the cooperation of the members of nursing staff with the director of the center, all psychiatrists, Director of Psychology, Social Work, Adjunctive Therapies, School Principal and Administrative Assistant, all acting in an advisory capacity to her.

She submits her weekly report during the administrative conference, at which time she discusses problems with the other members, giving them details on the daily problems she faces. She also submits to the director of the center a written monthly report and at the end of the year the "Annual Report on Nursing Activities."

She may delegate certain of her administrative duties to her secretary, coordinator of shifts (assistant director of nursing services), coordinator of in-service nursing training, but she continues to assume the ultimate responsibility.

Any infractions that involve both the nursing staff and staff from other services are discussed with her, the director of the center, and the director of the involved service.

Because she is responsible for staffing the nursing service, she interviews, employs, trains, assigns, supervises and disciplines all the nursing personnel. She shares certain of these duties with the administrative assistant and the director of the center.

She is also given free access to such documents as the budget and payroll information for the nursing personnel and takes an active part in the preparation of the budget for the nursing service.

She is responsible for the professional conduct of the nurses, group workers, charge aides and child care workers and assumes responsibility for all aspects of the nursing programs for the children assigned to them.

She builds up a good administrative organization through which the entire nursing staff can function at optimum capacity. By appropriate counsel, fair dealing, and efficient management she fosters professional growth, efficiency and satisfaction among the nursing personnel.

She is always available for discussion with her employees of both personal and professional problems; however, she maintains lines of authority so that only those problems that require her personal attention are brought to her. Her employees know that their problems are important to her and they can depend upon her and her assistants to advise them when necessary.

Through her nursing staff she is responsible for providing a clean, attractive and wholesome environment for the children. This implies not only good housekeeping principles and physical hygiene but also good mental hygiene, since the environment is not only physical but also emotional. She interprets the nursing needs for adequate supplies and equipment to the administrative assistant whose responsibility it is to order, stock and dispense those supplies.

She is charged with the responsibility for the direction and supervision of in-service education and training programs for the nursing personnel and assigns a full-time coordinator to plan, supervise and execute the educational program. She actively participates in an advisory capacity, as well as doing some of the teaching.

As steward of the largest group of personnel in the center, it is also her responsibility to supervise a positive physical health program for all nursing personnel. Toward that end she may delegate specific duties to certain members of her staff to see that nursing personnel do not expose children or co-workers to communicable disease; that they have routine physical and chest X-ray examinations on time; and that they receive prompt and adequate medical attention when necessary.

While the center is maintained for the emotionally disturbed children rather than the employees, it also accepts the responsibility for the mental well-being of the personnel it employs. Because the emotional problems of employees influence their relation to their co-workers and children, it is the responsibility of their employer to see that their own mental conflicts are not reflected in their daily contacts with the children. She, therefore, accepts this challenge as part of her responsibility for providing a wholesome environment for the children by keeping the nursing personnel emotionally and mentally fit. She may act as counselor in advising an individual to seek help.

By example and precept she encourages active participation by her nurses in the activities of professional nursing organizations, so as to help them to assume their rightful place in the affairs of their profession and to project the center into the community.

She also acts as one of the center's most valuable assets in the promotion of good publicity and good community relationships. By her active participation in club work in the community, she interprets the needs of the center in performing the services it renders to the public and serves to prevent misrepresentation of incidents that may occur at the center and could be erroneously reported by the press. Through her efforts, the community can serve the center to great advantage and can become aware of the services the center can render the community.

Nursing Service Secretary

General Typing, Filing, Reservations, Schedules, Lists

MONDAY through FRIDAY
Nursing Director's schedule
Filing of reports
Type dictated memos pertinent to nursing
Report pertinent information (Daily Bulletin)
Census Preparatory Program
Reserve vehicles for off-ground trips
In addition:
WEDNESDAY
Type weekend work schedule, seven copies
Route schedule via courier
THURSDAY
Housekeeping supplies for residences
Weekend work schedule (eight copies)
Field trips (Signature Director of Nursing)
FRIDAY
Past list
Route schedule via courier
Redirect schedule after residence psychiatrist approves it
Preparatory program schedule to residence (twelve copies)

Specific Typing-Filing

1. New employees
2. Resignations and terminations
3. Employee performance evaluations
4. Incident reports (employee)
5. Field trips
6. Weekend work schedule
7. Miscellaneous filing-dittos
    (a) Cash requisitions to administrative assistant
    (b) Clinical 24-hour reports
    (c) Daily bulletin
    (d) Donated clothing requisition

(e) Monthly drug count
(f) Count sheets
(g) Pass list
(h) Housekeeping (once per month)
(i) Time sheets
(j) Work orders
(k) Supplies requisition to administrative assistant
(l) Birthday monies
(m) Memos

Assistant Director of Nursing Service and Coordinator of Shifts

The Assistant Director of Nursing Service assumes the responsibility for the nursing service in the absence of the director.

She is also the coordinator of shifts (day, evening and night shift); however, she is not assigned to any specific shift. Instead, she is in close liaison with the Director of Nursing Service, all residence chiefs and the Chief of Day Treatment Program, as well as with all nurses and the coordinator of in-service training.

As the coordinator of shifts, she

a) provides better communication among all shifts.

b) assists the nurses in charge of shifts in administrative and clinical matters.

c) discusses with the nursing staff of all shifts any changes in policies, organization and procedures in general; and changes of treatment approaches to individual children in particular.

d) reports directly to the Director of Nursing Service any observations made on the twenty-four-hour period, including recommendations for better integration among different functions of the nursing service and between nursing and other services.

Coordinator of In-Service Nursing Training

In-service education and training is one of the essential features of the center's therapeutic milieu. Since the staff is expected to participate in policy-making, organization and procedures in carrying out the treatment programs, their educational needs must be considered.

To varying degrees, in-service training is both intra- and inter-disciplinary. Although everyone at the center is a potential force in the treatment of children, the nursing staff, the people who have the most direct contact with the children, must have specialized training. Therefore, they must be taught to approach their work diagnostically and therapeutically and to review and evaluate the children's progress periodically.

Involved in their training is more than an orientation to the center's operations or a formalized educational approach to the functions and methodology of residential psychiatric treatment. A continuous learning experience that permeates the day-to-day work of the staff must be provided so that each staff member will broaden his knowledge and develop skills, attitudes and values so that he may function as a productive member of the psychiatric team. This will be of direct benefit to the children in that it assures a maximum amount of consistent knowledgeable care throughout their residence.

To achieve this, in-service nursing training is coordinated by a registered nurse who is responsible for carrying out all in-service nursing education and training duties. She is administratively responsible to the Director of Nursing Service and cooperates with the Director of Education of the center. She plans, supervises and executes the nursing education and training program through active teaching and utilization of teaching and training resources at the center. She instructs all nursing staff on a regular basis through both formal and informal individual and group contacts, through supervision, and by participating in diagnostic and appraisal conferences and other staff meetings. Educational seminars are also conducted to further the professional and non-professional education of the staff and to keep them informed about the current literature and development in the field.

The Coordinator of In-service Training continuously strives to upgrade contributions and the effectiveness of the staff by maintaining good interpersonal relations, by providing opportunities for the staff to learn, and by emphasizing to them the importance of their roles.

In addition to her in-service nursing training duties, the coordinator, as a registered nurse performs clinical duties such as residence coverage, supervision of the preparatory program, and co-ordination of the immunization program.

Residence Psychiatric Nurse

The residence nurse is under the immediate direction of the residence psychiatrist. She is the direct line of communication from residence staff to the residence psychiatrist and responsible for the supervision of the eight-hour shift and the care and treatment of children.

General Nursing

As the center is in itself a small therapeutic community, inevitably it poses all the problems of a general medical practice. There are medical and surgical emergencies to contend with, and a variety of preventive measures to be carried out (epidemics, infectious diseases, poisoning, etc.). These call for a knowledge of public health techniques, the use of preventive inoculations, and the maintenance of a high level of general health in the center.

Psychiatrist's Immediate Assistant

In the absence of the psychiatrist, she is responsible for the management of the residence. Her observations and records concerning children's health have special weight because of her more exacting scientific background. She is an important member of the treatment team as far as understanding the children's problems and carrying out the plan of treatment. Since she must enforce the management and control of children and the daily routine of the residence, she is responsible for most privileges as well as restrictions for children when she deems it necessary for their welfare and the proper conduct of the center.

Residence Supervisor

She is responsible for developing and maintaining therapeutically effective relationships among the children and the nursing staff. It is part of her duties to create a secure and wholesome atmosphere in the specialized environment of the residence. She, along with the charge aide, office aide, group workers and child care workers, assists children individually and in groups to meet the ordinary demands of their everyday living. She supervises the charge aides, office aide, group workers, volunteers, student nurses and other personnel in the residence, scheduling and coordinating their activities for maximal therapeutic effect. In some instances she supplements adjunctive therapy activities.

Treatment

She is responsible for carrying out the nursing instructions of the treatment team, for providing emergency support for children in psychological crisis, and assisting in the administration of many forms of medical treatment. She administers parenteral medications.

Under the direction of the psychiatrist she may be a group cotherapist. She attends the weekly scheduled psychotherapy seminars. She also attends the weekly-held group workers' meeting under the direction of the Director of Nursing Service.

In an effort to improve the quality of treatment and provide continuous nursing authority and responsibility on the center's campus, the day shift nurses alternate weekly as campus on-duty (O.D.) nurse.

Education-Training

She has a major educational function and assists in the teaching and training of all personnel who are to have any contact with the residence environment. The child care worker, the psychotherapist, the psychiatric social worker, the psychologist, the volunteer, and the student nurse all gain part of their clinical experiences from the assistance of the psychiatric nurse.

Responsibilities of the Campus O.D. Nurse

1. *Routine*

Obtain assignment from the Director of Nursing.

Make rounds on both residences, giving assistance if needed and check children who are disturbed, on restriction, physically ill, etc.

Remain on one residence unless called to assist charge aide.

Inform charge aides of your whereabouts.

Give your report to the nurse in charge of the oncoming shift.

2. *Information to obtain before calling the Director of Nursing Service or the psychiatrist.*

See the child. It is your responsibility to determine if it is necessary to call the Director of Nursing Service or the psychiatrist. In case of illness or injury, take T.P.R. and blood pressure (B/P), observe *vital* signs (color, condition of skin, respiration) and general physical condition. Note a child's specific complaint. Note any previous history which may have a bearing on present illness or injury.

3. *Information to give when the Director of Nursing or the psychiatrist is called.*

Child's name, residence, specific complaint. Apparent physical condition.

Note and report of T.P.R. and B/P.

Previous history which might have some bearing on injury or illness.

Accompany the psychiatrist to see the child.

Office Aide

The office aide is responsible to the residence nurse (in her absence, to the charge aide) for carrying the following duties:

1. Telephone and other messages—relay pertinent information.
2. Requisitioning—supply orders.
3. Typing—pertinent information related to residence.
4. Preparation—Admission-Discharge Chart.
5. Recording—mail—packages (incoming and outgoing)—laboratory appointments and dates.
6. Tallying—"Doctor's Progress Notes"—Drug Tally Sheet.
7. Transcribing "doctor's orders" (after being reviewed by R.N.).
8. Key—sharp count (sharp objects)—roll call—staff.
9. Charting—patient's weight-height.
10. Charts—proper order.
11. Routing—pertinent residence data and articles.
12. Filing.

13. Maintaining nursing station—physical order and cleanliness.

14. Maintain balance of children's money.

15. Prepare and administer passes and update school schedule.

16. Courier.

Charge Aide

An employee in a position allocated to this class is responsible for supervision of the group workers and child care workers in the care and observation of children. In the absence of the residence nurse, she is also responsible for the supervision of the office aide.

She remains in the residence during the periods the children are in scheduled activities. Work follows well-established rules and procedures and is performed under the general supervision of the residence nurse. Reports unusual incidents to residence nurse or residence psychiatrist. Assists children in their personal care and spends time with children. Gives medication and administers treatment as directed by the nurse. Supervises and participates in the general housekeeping duties. Performs related work as required (counts sharps, keys, charting, safety precautions).

(NOTE: These examples are intended only as illustrations of the various types of work performed in positions allocated to this class. The omission of specific statements of duties does not exclude them from the position if the work is similar, related, or a logical assignment to the position.)

GROUP WORKER—GROUP WORK PROGRAM

A child's everyday residential living experiences are the most important measures of his ultimate ability to adapt to the outside community. Thus, many noteworthy and commendable efforts are being made to provide for a careful structuring of his physical, emotional, mental and social environment of the psychiatric treatment program so every interaction and activity is therapeutic for the child. All these efforts constitute the milieu therapy, the method and philosophy of treatment that is accepted a priori being of value in the treatment of children. In the center, the therapeutic milieu is involved with three areas: emotional, intellectual and social. Most of the child's everyday experiences take place within the various services (school, adjunctive therapies, residence, etc.) and his reactions to everyday reality find their most conspicuous expression within these groups.

Teaching, lecturing or giving advice to children falls far short in providing the kind of insight that comes out of life's encounters and the emotional reactions that occur. Learning that concerns itself only with the intellectual and emotional development of children does not consistently produce well-adjusted children. In the daily life activities, school curriculum, etc., the children pass from one individual to another, on a scheduled basis, and have no real opportunity to develop consistent relationships with adults. For example, in scheduled classes which change from hour to hour, it is impossible to furnish childen with a person who could maintain a consistent relationship and help the child to discuss, learn and understand social living and stable relationships. Therefore, the need for a program utilizing an agent to promote social living is evidently necessary to help the children progress toward a social maturity through the use of social relationship experiences and activities.

The center's role as a resource for promotion of social living is expressed by its established social group work program which embraces all social living activities and is integrated with the total treatment program of the center. The program's agent is the social group worker who is recruited from the ranks of the nursing service personnel which by its nature is usually more familiar with the child's social living in the center.

Objectives

With regard to its intent, the program aspires to

—bring improved social living attitudes to the residence, school, recreational and other activities; that is, to help the children to learn how to get along better with themselves and with others.

—develop desirable personality traits in children by setting proper examples for them, by encouraging them to practice desirable personality traits in place of undesirable traits, by helping them build more robust personalities; that is, become more emotionally and socially mature.

—provide positive values of group experience as well as an outlet for creative abilities.

—help the children in their freedom of expression and give them adequate opportunities to discuss social experiences (particularly children who feel threatened in the group situation, and those who tend to isolate themselves or remain in the periphery of the group, clinging and demanding).

—bring more nursing personnel into the treatment team and policy-making council of the center to facilitate changes necessary for its most favorable operation and expand innovations originated by the entire staff.

Consideration

The group work concept is carefully explained to those connected with it.

The group worker, by definition, is a person who has more frequent and more continuous contact with the children to which he or she is assigned than any other professional or nonprofessional staff member.

Early and continued consideration is given to the group worker's orientation, participation, reaction and progress.

Another consideration is the steady attention paid to the children's acceptance of the group workers. In order to accomplish such an acceptance by the children, demonstration of acceptance of the group worker by the other staff members is important.

Qualities of the Group Worker

The group worker must

have a genuine interest in children.

have a good appearance and a pleasant personality.

fulfill many of the roles of the parents, but at the same time realize that she cannot and must not take the place of the parent.

be able to set a proper example in social graces that the child may emulate.

possess clear concepts about the children's individual differences and fundamental needs.

obtain, improve and maintain general orientation and background about the emotional attitudes of each child. Collateral reading to improve her understanding is necessary.

be aware that psychological growth in children comes from within and that social growth comes through appropriate relationships.

be aware that coercion used to "improve the personality" often fails to meet the individual child's needs.

be agreeable and eager to contribute to the overall planning of the center, which aspires to provide the child with a unified and harmonious treatment program. Avoid the role of psychotherapist disguised as a group worker, because psychotherapy from the standpoint of the psychiatrist is a discipline too technical for the group worker and her job does not require that she develop these technical skills.

maintain constant communication and liaison between professional and nonprofessional staff.

be able and willing to accept professional supervision and properly oriented guidance.

Duties—Procedures

The group workers are assigned to the units of the Residence A (Units I and II) and Residence B (Units I and II) as well as to units of the day treatment program.

The group workers are responsible to their charge aide and nurse for the children of the unit to which they are assigned. Through the nurse they are responsible to the Director of Nursing Service.

The group workers work from 6:45 AM to 3:00 PM Monday through Friday. The work week includes one weekend day. Arriving 6:45 AM they report to the nurse and are present in the assigned unit listening and relating to the children. After the morning daily routine is over and upon the nurse's instructions, the group workers, in an orderly fashion, accompany their children to the assembly area.

The group workers are charged with the overall performance of their unit and are responsible for the general management of their children. They inform the nurse of the child's needs (new clothing, the child's requests for visit home or with relatives, etc.). They are also the ones who inform their child about staff decisions as to special privileges or his participation in activities outside the residence such as recreation, field trips, etc. They pay the attention necessary for the children's physical care and share in general supervision. Permissions or restrictions imposed by the nurse or charge aide are handled by the group workers who have the most meaningful relationship to the child. At times they find it necessary to prevent their group of children from ganging up on individual children who embarrass them in the residence or the campus.

A number of group workers are assigned duties in the preparatory program. They work directly with their charge aides, nurse and children in teaching specific skills or in putting on a particular program which requires skills the other nursing personnel may not possess.

All group workers are assigned as co-therapists in the Group Psychotherapy Services.

An effort is made to focus on the residence living group with each unit's group worker as the leader. The group workers are available to all the residence personnel and the psychiatrist for suggestions as to activities. The activities of groups vary with the interests of the children and are planned, as far as possible, on the basis of the group workers' knowledge of their needs. Thus, one group might use their time for woodworking or work with clay. Other groups might be more interested in record playing and similar activities. Some small children use their group period to "play house" with dolls.

Observation of group activities is carefully recorded by the group workers and shared with the nursing staff and other treatment team members. Many interrelated problems of the children are brought into focus and worked through as a result of these group contacts.

The group workers are always aware of their children's scheduled activities and their attendance. Thus, they are able to provide their children any help they need and evaluate at firsthand their children's interaction with adults or other children. They do not interfere, praise or criticize the functions of other staff members. They move in only at a time of crisis and always with the permission, verbal or nonverbal, of the other staff member (teacher, adjunctive therapist, etc.). They share with the other staff members' responsibilities in carrying out the psychiatrist's orders as pertaining to the children's treatment.

The group workers are encouraged to participate in all clinical meetings (residence, school, adjunctive therapies, psychology, social work, nursing, etc.) which are taking place during the day. They are also responsible for the preparation and presentation of the nursing report on their child during all diagnostic and appraisal conferences.

The group workers are supervised as a group by the Director of Nursing in regularly scheduled weekly conferences. As children in units belong to groups of different developmental maturation, their specific physical, emotional and social needs are discussed and questions and suggestions regarding the programs available to meet these needs are seriously weighed.

Child Care Worker

A child care worker is a nonprofessional employee who has the primary responsibility of performing selected functions of nursing in the care of emotionally disturbed children. The child care worker must be willing and able to develop an understanding of desirable interpersonal relationships and children's needs in order to help establish an atmosphere that will promote a child's recovery.

It is mandatory that the child care worker be in constant attendance of the children under his care. Observing and reporting symptoms of physical illness and significant changes in behavior are also responsibilities of the child care worker.

The child care worker should be a good listener and companion in the same manner as a good parent is; always seeking to develop his observational skills of a child's interaction with his total environment.

The child care worker must be willing to assist the children in developing self-care skills, coordination, socialization, acceptable behavior patterns, acquiring social skills, and acceptance of peers; and to motivate a child to maintain a neat environment and good personal hygiene. The basic principle characterizing a successful child care worker is the warm, mature and secure relationship he offers to each of the children. A child care worker is not a substitute parent or a babysitter or a mere friend, or a therapist.

A child care worker works in an integral part of the therapeutic team, communication with other shifts and with his superiors being open and complete.

A child care worker should be well-educated, well-adjusted, have a good appearance, be able to communicate with the children and members of the staff, and have a real affection for children. He is being encouraged to develop his skills, to regard his work as a profession, to exchange ideas with others in the same field, and to develop potential in working with children.

A child care worker should exhibit normal behavior, thought, mood, appearance and conduct. He is an educator and teacher guide. He must recognize the social significance of the child within the framework of the family from which he comes; he must build bridges for the child, teaching him to create meaningful relationships. Therefore, the worker must have genuine, positive feelings and the capacity to demonstrate those feelings through affection for, and pleasure from, being with children. In addition, he must be able to relate well to authority figures.

All children, disturbed children included, are fascinated by new things and a variety of things. Experienced child care workers insist that a child care worker should have what Switzer calls "handles" and know how to apply them and get the most out of them. It does not really matter whether a particular handle is the capacity to pole vault, the ability to classify sea shells, or the skill to build and fly a kite.

The child care worker assists the children in getting up in the morning, puts them to bed at night, takes care of their everyday needs, cares for them when they are ill, provides them with a time and place and help for homework, helps them with their hobbies, and organizes and participates in their activities in their residence and in the community.

Secondary responsibilities include those necessary functions of housekeeping and clerical chores which maintain the unit in smooth operation.

One of the biggest jobs of a child care worker is just being a good listener. Disturbed children are verbally destructive, attacking with words the people around them. Four-letter words are most common. To them it is the most effective way of communicating their despair. These children are running from reality. They just cannot face life. They fight back with everything possible. Some are physically destructive, breaking windows and chairs, tearing up anything close. A child care worker uses himself to provide structure, control, limits, healthy expectations, support, praise for achievement, and solace in defeat.

Custodial Worker

8:00- 9:00 AM Infirmary— (Monday-Wednesday-Friday) Sweep, mop and buff and empty trash and dust. Clean and sanitize lavatory, including bathtub.

8:00- 9:00 AM (Tuesday and Thursday) Clean windows *interior and exterior* of residences and hobby room. Clean *exterior* of bedroom windows.

9:00-10:00 AM Residence B—Bedrooms and day rooms—sweep and empty trash daily. Mop and buff (Monday-Wednesday-Friday).

10:00-10:15 AM Break

10:30-11:30 AM Residence B—Bedrooms and day rooms—sweep and empty trash daily. Unit II Mop and buff (Monday-Wednesday-Friday).

11:30-12:00 Lunch

12:30- 1:30 PM Residence A—Bedrooms and day rooms—sweep and empty trash daily. Unit II Mop and buff (Monday-Wednesday-Friday).

1:30- 2:30 PM Residence A—Bedrooms and day rooms—sweep and empty trash daily. Unit II Mop and buff (Monday-Wednesday-Friday).

2:30- 2:45 PM Break

3:00- 4:00 PM Any additional similar assignment as required by Director of Nursing.

Strip Schedule

1st Tuesday —Strip 6 bedrooms in Unit I—Residence B

1st Thursday—Strip day room and game room in Unit I— Residence B

2nd Tuesday —Strip 6 bedrooms in Unit II—Residence B

2nd Thursday—Strip day room in Unit II—Residence B

3rd Tuesday —Strip 6 bedrooms in Unit I—Residence A

3rd Thursday—Strip day room and game room in Unit I— Residence A

4th Tuesday —Strip 6 bedrooms in Unit II—Residence A

4th Thursday—Strip day room in Unit II—Residence A

5th Tuesday —Strip infirmary

5th Thursday—Inventory supplies and equipment and make out supply order and pick up.

PHYSICAL PLANT—UNITS—BED CAPACITY

The residential treatment center is the inpatient service. Its forty-eight children (three-fourths boys and one-fourth girls) range in age from six to twelve years.

The policy of having groups of children in residence representative of both sexes and of ages six to twelve years is based on the fact that this is what children in a normal community encounter.

The residential complex of buildings consists of:

1. Residence A for boys (twenty-four beds), Unit I: open unit (privilege unit) ages ten to twelve; Unit II: closed unit (admission unit) ages eight to ten.

2. Residence B for boys and girls (twenty-four beds), Unit I: girls ages six to twelve; Unit II: boys ages six to eight.

3. Nursing building which contains the

   a) Infirmary: with two beds and necessary facilities for children in need of isolation because of a contagious disease

   b) Medical examination room and nursing staff room

   c) Preparatory program classrooms

4. Dining rooms, separate for Residence A and Residence B, and kitchen.

The atmosphere in the residences is that of a typical hospital.

The residences are tastefully furnished in styles appropriate to the children's socioeconomic backgrounds: simple, contemporary, but not "arty," designs and colors are employed. Posters are not allowed in the children's bedrooms. Magazines are kept in the hobby room.

The number of children per room varies from one to three.

Grouping of Children

Even though the staff is less in a position to group children flexibly in terms of either homogeneous age groups or in terms of carefully selected groups based on symptom patterns or diagnoses, the groups of children are divided on the basis of sex and age.

Age grouping takes into consideration the interests, size, personality and emotional problems of the children in assigning them to units. Thus, a few older boys remain with the younger group because their emotional development is below their chronological age level and they cannot compete with older boys. Although the various age groups do not mingle freely, separation is not adhered to consistently because only a few difficulties rise in spite of their different physical, recreational and other needs.

PREPARATORY PROGRAM

PURPOSE: To provide

a) evaluatory, therapeutic and educational services for children who do not, cannot, or should not attend prescribed activiies.

b) opportunities for more efficient management and control of children on prescribed activities.

TYPE OF CHILD

a) *Newly admitted:* This child is usually undergoing a three-week diagnostic evaluation. Therefore, he may not yet be ready during this period for any prescribed activity, except at the discretion of his admitting child psychiatrist.

b) *Unable to attend prescribed activities:* This child usually is
—severely acting-out, overly impulsive, overdemanding, too disturbed for any type of prescribed activity.

—not able to attempt prescribed activity.

—completely bizarre and/or undisciplined.

c) *Temporarily suspended from prescribed activities:* This child is the one who presents with severe reactions (regression, overanxiety, hyperactivity, destructiveness) for a brief period as a result of treatment efforts, parents' visits, etc.

CAPACITY: Maximum ten children

PLANT: Nursing building and campus grounds

TIME SCHEDULE: On a five-day week basis, from 9:00 AM to 11:30 AM and from 1:00 PM to 2:30 PM.

STAFF

Coordinator: Director of Nursing Services in close liaison with the child's psychiatrist.

Group Workers: The group workers, as part of their group work program, and in consultation with the child's psychiatrist, Residence or DTP Nurse, work out each child's schedule for class, recreation, project and work assignment. They also help in the child's management and control.

Consultants: Directors of services or their designates.

Guides: Nursing staff.

PROGRAM: Provide *schoolwork* (fundamentals), *recreation* (groups of playing games, singing, listening to radio, watching TV, etc.) and *projects* (simple arts-crafts, small compact shop, spontaneous graphic art, gardening, etc.).

INTAKE-RELEASE

Admission: The concerned director of the service (School Principal, Adjunctive Therapist, etc.) notifies the child's psychiatrist who then holds a conference with the Director of Nursing Service and the child's psychiatrist. On some occasions, a child may be excluded from a prescribed activity (e.g. school) but continue to attend another prescribed activity (e.g. recreational therapy).

Re-admission to Prescribed Activity: Preparatory program staff (child's psychiatrist and Director of Nursing) hold a conference with the concerned director of the service. Again, a child may return on a part-time or full-time basis to a prescribed activity but not to another. Group workers are charged with the smooth scheduling of such cases.

DAILY ROUTINE

The daily routine at the center is much like that of a private hospital; all children have an individualized treatment and education program. Thus, within the overall schedule each child has a somewhat different routine. I consider the assessment of the potential impact on the treatment process of a given group of children to be basically a clinical matter and to remain the clinician's task. It should not be given to the so-called "modern" and "social science conscious" professional.

Minor Variations in Daily Routine

The schedules for the two residences differ according to the age and needs of each child with respect to the morning time, personal hygiene time, quiet time and bedtime and are coordinated with other elements in the treatment program. There is much direct supervision and special attention for the younger children's daily routine.

Acceptable Manners and Habits

It is considered an important part of the nursing staff's job that children be encouraged to behave in an acceptable manner, to be clean, to dress neatly and attractively, and to develop socially acceptable manners and habits. They are discouraged from loud talk and bad language. An effort is made by the staff to develop and maintain an informal, friendly atmosphere which permits the children to express themselves as needed but which at the same time establishes limits. Thus, too much closeness, interest or devotion is not encouraged on the part of the staff. They are alerted to the possibilities of feelings of possessiveness and to the "need fulfillment work." Their attitudes and feelings are not all termed "transference."

The policies are based on fairly simple philosophical and psychological tenets. In the center there is a general attitude of acceptance, warmth and understanding. In view of the child's experiential world to date, he is entitled to be as he is—unhappy and disturbed. At the same time certain limits are necessary as a basic frame of reference and a baseline of values. The child may not infringe upon the other children, the staff, or upon the physical property.

Housekeeping Program

Another important part of the nursing staff's job is the coordination of daily living with the therapeutic housekeeping program. As the staff does not subscribe to the peculiar notion that the assignment of work activities might infringe on the child labor laws, the children are not kept away from any type of household chores. Even though the housekeeping staff is sufficient to provide cleaning service, housekeeping jobs are given to children to meet their need for similar duties which they might have in their own homes. Supervisors help in the work program along with the children.

Regular daily household chores can be annexed in the way of providing lessons in self-discipline. Chores do not serve any real purpose if they are used as props or punishment. The nursing staff supports the child's desire to participate and contribute to residence living; they help him to develop a sense of belonging and of responsibility. Even though a child may complain about doing chores, the nursing staff insists on having them done when they have been assigned.

Chores are allotted in relation to an individual child's age, capacity, emotional readiness for such responsibility, and ability to carry it through successfully. Housekeeping work assignments are discussed with the nursing staff and are given to children on a rotating basis, and they are changed about so that no child has a chore for too long a time. Some children with compulsive symptoms are apt to volunteer more than is considered advisable, and their activities are redirected whenever possible. The housekeeping work in which the children engage includes helping in cleaning bathrooms, vacuuming, washing windows on the inside and outside, sorting laundry, etc.

Residence life is somewhat different for girls. In their unit, the girls take care of some of their own clothing, are engaged in cleaning, and also do some embroidering, sewing and ironing.

Maintenance of Residence Grounds

Each residence is held accountable for the upkeep of its immediate grounds. This, like housekeeping, is done by the children and staff. Even though maintenance staff is sufficient to keep the grounds in good condition, the children and nursing staff participate in straightening the playground, in felling trees, cleaning up the bushes, etc. Children under the guidance and supervision of the industrial therapist also help with painting, carpentry and other minor repair work.

On Saturdays, small cleaning jobs such as car-washing are available for those children who wish to earn money and supplement allowances. Children are paid for their work and a time slip is submitted to the administrative assistant who controls the children's fund. The staff supervises this job and makes a report about the children's efficiency. No child is allowed to have a job outside the center's grounds.

Children's Council

A formal structure which is called the Children's Council operates in each residence. Its purpose is to allow some self-government to the children as a group and to enable them to carry out responsible residence functions. As with other group treatment methods, this, too, is expected to develop better relationships between the children and staff, not only on a one-to-one basis, but on a group-to-group basis as well, which I believe has important therapeutic relevance.

A meeting of the Children's Council may be called at the suggestion of either the children, the nursing staff, or the psychiatrist. The residence nurse or charge aide always attends the meeting and the children are given the opportunity to air their grievances, discuss matters which may include the use of television, bedtime hours, allowances, permission for outside activities, and ideas about their newspaper (which is written and edited by the children). Many times disciplinary measures are submitted by the group which are quite in proportion to the misdeed and so a form of self-discipline is encouraged.

NURSING SHIFTS (DAY-EVENING-NIGHT)

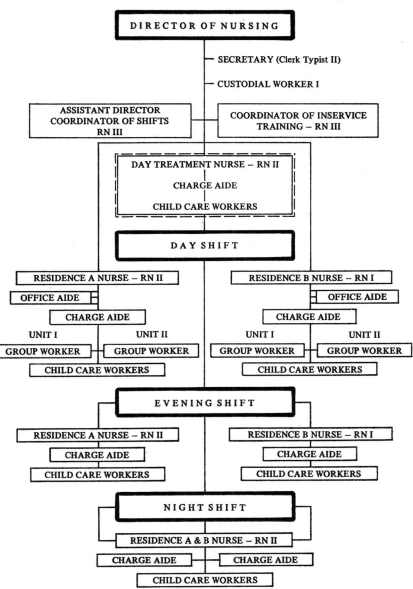

DIRECTOR OF NURSING

— SECRETARY (Clerk Typist II)

— CUSTODIAL WORKER I

ASSISTANT DIRECTOR
COORDINATOR OF SHIFTS
RN III

COORDINATOR OF INSERVICE
TRAINING – RN III

DAY TREATMENT NURSE – RN II

CHARGE AIDE

CHILD CARE WORKERS

DAY SHIFT

RESIDENCE A NURSE – RN II

OFFICE AIDE

CHARGE AIDE

UNIT I

UNIT II

GROUP WORKER

GROUP WORKER

CHILD CARE WORKERS

RESIDENCE B NURSE – RN I

OFFICE AIDE

CHARGE AIDE

UNIT I

UNIT II

GROUP WORKER

GROUP WORKER

CHILD CARE WORKERS

EVENING SHIFT

RESIDENCE A NURSE – RN II

CHARGE AIDE

CHILD CARE WORKERS

RESIDENCE B NURSE – RN I

CHARGE AIDE

CHILD CARE WORKERS

NIGHT SHIFT

RESIDENCE A & B NURSE – RN II

CHARGE AIDE

CHARGE AIDE

CHILD CARE WORKERS

Day Shift 7:00 AM to 3:00 PM

For sufficient staff coverage, the hours of work are strictly observed in order to provide the adequate number of staff on duty when they are most needed. It is for this reason that the nursing personnel of the incoming shift reports for duty at 6:45 AM to receive the report, and to supplement the outgoing shift in getting the children prepared and share in their supervision.

Change of Night to Day Shift

From 6:45 AM to 7:15 AM the night shift changes to the day shift.

Awakening of Children

On "school days" children are awakened and get up at 7:00 AM. On weekends and holidays they may get up between 7:30 AM and 8:30 AM, but breakfast time remains the same—8:00 AM to 8:30 AM.

Morning Report

When indicated, special trips, appointments, lab, X-ray, immunizations, restrictions, change in schedule, etc. are discussed on an individual basis with each child by the group worker.

Residence B Basic Personal Hygiene

The children in Residence B (younger children) are helped with basic personal hygiene matters (wash faces, use of bathroom, etc.).

Bedroom Straightening Tasks

From 7:10 AM to 7:30 AM the children return to their rooms and remain there getting dressed in their own clothes; picking up other clothes; straightening their closets; keeping their toys, games and other possessions in order; and cleaning their room on their own without help given from staff unless there is specific reason. Children are expected to make their own beds; other children are assisted and supervised for bedmaking and straightening of their rooms.

Work Program

From 7:30 AM to 7:50 AM all children are out of their rooms. Every child is expected to participate in the housekeeping work program. He is given routine duties which are set up on a rotating weekly basis by his group worker, and the work is done with the active participation and supervision of nursing staff.

Breakfast

From 8:00 AM to 8:30 AM the children of both Residences A and B go to breakfast with their group worker accompanying and supervising them to insure their arriving at breakfast on time, eat breakfast, and return to residence on time. The time limit is thirty minutes.

General Personal Hygiene—Inspection

From 8:30 AM to 8:50 AM the children, helped by their group worker and child care workers, attend to their general personal hygiene—brushing teeth; combing hair; proper clothing, including shoes; check for sharps, crayons and chewing gum; and prepare for scheduled activities. Children who have completed their room work go to the playground until it is time for bedroom inspection by the charge aide. Formal sick-call is not scheduled. Instead, the residence nurse calls the psychiatrist to report any child who needs medical attention.

Accounting for Children

From 8:50 AM to 9:00 AM an accounting for all children is held and all children line up for scheduled activities. The residence nurse and her staff determine the number of children able to participate in the daily therapeutic and educational activities.

Flag Detail—General Assembly

On a rotational basis two children from each residence are chosen to raise the flag. Each group worker accompanies her children in an organized fashion to the designated assembly area. The residence nurse instructs one or two child care workers to walk towards the assembly area. In case a child care worker is needed, the child's group worker may request his services. The children and their supervisors gather around the flagpole. The two assigned children raise the flag and all present say the Pledge of Allegiance. Following this the group workers send (or accompany) their children to their scheduled activities. The group workers see that their children are in their designated place (school, preparatory program, etc.) by 9:00 AM. The majority of nursing staff may use these ten minutes for planning classes for the preparatory program.

Attendance of Scheduled Activities

Every week a schedule is made by the Director of Nursing Service, which includes all appointments for both children and nursing staff.

Whenever possible children have their individual psychotherapy sessions at 9:00 AM (or 1:00 PM) in order to keep at a minimum the time missed from school and adjunctive therapies. A limited number of psychotherapy sessions are scheduled throughout the day, and the school and other scheduled activities for each child are arranged in such a way to provide for the individual and group psychotherapy periods.

Children who have individual and group psychotherapy appointments during the day do so with a pass from the residence's nursing office. Group workers are responsible for knowing if a child has gone to his appointment and if he has not, for reminding him of his appointment.

Preparatory Program

Some children who are not able to attend school classes and some who cannot profit from a prescribed adjunctive therapy program attend the preparatory program which is a modified treatment and education program conducted by nursing staff. As with the children who are regularly scheduled for education and other classes, the children in the preparatory program, after the general assembly at 9:00 AM, are accompanied to the scheduled classes in the preparatory program and are kept under unobtrusive observation at all times.

Occasionally, a child who is not able to attend any of the programs is placed on a one-to-one escort status prescribed by his psychiatrist.

The Twenty-four-Hour Clinical Report

At 9:00 AM each nurse goes to the psychiatrist's office to give a verbal report of her children's activities and of problems encountered during the past twenty-four-hour period. The official twenty-four-hour clinical report is submitted to the Director's office by 9:00 AM and then circulated among directors of services and psychotherapists.

Nursing Staff's Duties

During the morning period, when the children are in their scheduled activities, a number of nursing staff attend to different residence duties and household tasks such as inspecting children's clothes to determine if articles should be sent to the laundry or if others need buttons or mending and checking through the children's dresser drawers and closets. These, when found out of order, are not straightened by nursing staff. Instead, children are required to straighten them satisfactorily after scheduled activities hours. Other staff duties include securing supplies, preparing reports, reviewing of records, supervising housekeeping, taking a child for a dental appointment, accompanying him for examinations or visits with parents, caring for a physically ill child in residence, etc.

Nursing staff also use the morning time to confer with the residence nurse and other members of the treatment team and attend in-service training classes. These do not last for more than an hour each.

Nursing Staff's Lunch Period

From 11:00 AM to 12:00 the nursing staff, divided in two groups, have their lunch.

Children's Lunch and Lunch Time

From 11:40 AM to 12:15 PM there is preparation for lunch and lunch time for the children. The majority of children are able to return to the residence by themselves. Some, however, need to be supervised and their group worker sees that they are in their quarters for preparation for lunch (washing up, appropriately dressed, check for sharps and other hazardous items). Lunch is served at 11:50 AM. Several child care workers are on duty to be available for any help the children may need over the lunch time as a result of difficulty from scheduled activities.

Relaxation—Free Time

From 12:15 PM to 12:55 PM the children have a period of relaxation or free time. Some engage in freeplay according to their own interests, others serving restrictions, etc.

Accounting for Children

From 12:55 PM to 1:00 PM an accounting for all children is held and all children line up for inspection by the charge aide and are sent or accompanied to their scheduled activities.

Attendance of Scheduled Activities

From 1:00 PM to 2:20 PM all children attend their scheduled activities.

Return from Scheduled Activities

From 2:20 PM to 2:30 PM the children return from their scheduled activities and have their juice break. The group worker sees that all her children have returned from scheduled activities unless they have previously obtained permission from their nurse to go for tutoring, psychotherapy appointment or another appointment.

Group Discussion of Day Activities

From 2:45 PM to 3:00 PM the children meet in the residence privilege (or hobby) room to briefly discuss their activities of the day with the charge aide of the 7:00 AM to 3:00 PM shift. All nursing staff of both day and evening shifts are present.

Change of Day to Evening Shift

From 3:00 PM to 3:15 PM merging of the day and evening shifts takes place.

TABLE VI
SUMMARY FOR DAY SHIFT

6:45 A.M.– 7:15 A.M.	Merging of night and day shifts
7:00 A.M.– 7:10 A.M.	Awakening of children
	Residence B: basic personal hygiene
7:10 A.M.– 7:30 A.M.	Children in their rooms (dressing, bedmaking, cleaning, straightening of rooms)
7:30 A.M.– 7:50 A.M.	Children out of their rooms. Household tasks
8:00 A.M.– 8:30 A.M.	Residences A and B breakfast
8:30 A.M.– 8:50 A.M.	Children's personal hygiene, preparation for scheduled activities, bedrooms inspection
8:50 A.M.– 9:00 A.M.	Assembly around flag pole
9:00 A.M.–11:40 A.M.	Attendance of scheduled activities
11:40 A.M.–12:15 P.M.	Preparation for lunch and lunchtime
12:15 P.M.–12:55 P.M.	Relaxation, free time, serving restrictions
12:55 P.M.– 1:00 P.M.	Preparation for scheduled activities, inspection
1:00 P.M.– 2:20 P.M.	Attendance of scheduled activities
2:20 P.M.– 2:30 P.M.	Return from scheduled activities, juice break
2:30 P.M.– 3:00 P.M.	Washing cups, socializing or quiet time
	Some children in interviews, tutoring, therapy
2:45 P.M.– 3:00 P.M.	Discussion of day activities
3:00 P.M.– 3:15 P.M.	Merging of day and evening shifts

Evening Shift 3:00 PM to 11:30 PM

From 2:45 PM to 3:00 PM the day shift changes to the evening shift. Reports on children are given by the day shift. Nursing staff of both shifts under the evening shift nurse's or designate's supervision, check for sharps and key count, security and contraband.

Residence Group Meeting

From 3:00 PM to 3:45 PM the majority of children are not in organized activities and are closely supervised in the residences, with the exception of those who have scheduled activities or appointments (interviews with their caseworkers, tutoring or psychotherapy). The children remain in the residences until 3:45 PM and participate in a group meeting where they relate their day's activities to the nursing staff. Any information regarding change in routine or scheduling is discussed with the children. After the meeting the children are encouraged to find their companion and engage in free play, except those who serve restriction.

Nursing Staff's Dinner Time

From 4:00 PM to 5:00 PM the nursing staff divided in two groups have their dinner (4:00-4:30 and 4:30-5:00).

Children's Dinner

From 5:00 PM to 5:30 PM the children have their dinner.

Playground Free Play

From 5:30 PM to 6:00 PM (winter) and from 5:30 PM to 7:00 PM (summer) the children are encouraged for free play on the playground. Some group themselves according to their interests or the plan of their supervisors. The children are at liberty to use the various facilities, games and materials (softball, basketball, swings, monkeybars, slide, etc.).

Evening Activities

Often there are a number of regularly planned small group activities and programs in the evening. These include co-educational parties, Saturday night picnics, Sunday outings and movies. Some children may be taken to outside events accompanied by nursing staff members. On Sunday evenings each residence has its meal cookout on grounds.

Shower Time

From 6:00 PM to 7:00 PM (winter) and from 7:00 PM to 8:00 PM (summer) the children have their showers. All children are required to have showers every night and are encouraged to be as independent as possible while taking their shower. They return to the hobbyroom in pajamas and robe. The children have daily changes of clothing, excluding sleepwear which changes three to four times a week.

After showers, the nursing staff is responsible for the cleanliness of bathrooms.

The need to use the largest number of staff at the time when there are no scheduled activities seems to indicate that less supervision is necessary when there is careful grouping and planned activity. The purpose of having this free time is both to avoid regimentation and to provide opportunities for the children to learn to relate to adults.

Bedroom Inspection

At 7:00 PM (winter)-8:00 PM (summer) there is bedroom inspection by the charge aide.

Snack Time—Quiet Period

From 8:00 PM to 8:30 PM the children go to the specially designated place for snacks. Treats are arranged on special occasions for all children. For younger children (Residence B) this is quiet period (reading, watching TV, nonphysical games). Bedtime hours are scheduled according to the ages of different children. Some children who tire easily voluntarily go to bed earlier. Others are sent up earlier when they are observed to be overly excited.

Younger Children's Bedtime

Before bedtime, group discussion of evening activities takes place in Residence B, Unit II.

At 8:30 PM younger girls and boys go to bed.

Older Children's Quiet Period (Homework, Club Activities, Letter Writing, Haircut)

From 8:30 PM to 9:30 PM there is a quiet period for older children, i.e. study hour for those who have homework (usually children in higher grades) and quiet activities for those who do not have homework (watching TV, listening to radio or records, reading books, magazines, playing nonphysical games). Club activities are also planned for some children at this time (stamp collecting, chess, bingo, etc.). The nursing staff helps with homework when help is required. They take measures to make it free from distractions from the other children and television, encouraging the child to use the time fully for his schoolwork without interference. Some children study in their rooms, while others use the hobbyroom.

Before weekends and holidays, this hour is generally used for letter writing. Also, assigned staff members give regular haircuts to children whose parents are unable to do so. Since there is more staff during evening hours, it is possible for the residence staff to spend more time with the children as they are using their quiet hour and gradually preparing for bed.

Group Discussion of Evening Activities Residences A and B

Group meeting with children and evening shift of each residence takes place before bedtime.

Bedtime

At 9:30 PM the children in Residence B and Residence A Unit II (younger children) and 10:00 PM the children in Residence A Unit I (older children) go to bed. On weekends and holidays they may stay up until 10:30 PM.

For all groups lights are supposed to be out one-half hour after bedtime. During periods of tension or emotional outbursts children may be allowed to stay up with the nursing staff past bedtime, or the nursing staff will sit in a child's room until he is able to fall asleep. The nursing staff are expected to stay in the residence (charting, cleaning, etc.) or to secure coverage if they need to visit elsewhere on the grounds.

Change of Evening to Night Shift

From 10:45 PM to 11:15 PM merging of the evening and night shifts takes place.

Night Shift 11:00 PM to 7:00 AM

From 10:45 PM to 11:15 PM the evening shift changes to the night shift. Report on children is given by the evening shift. Staff of both shifts under night shift nurse's or designate's supervision check for patient face, security, contraband, and sharp count. Also the "Midnight Census Report" is prepared.

Attending Children's Needs—Periodic Observation

From 11:15 PM to 6:45 AM any children's physical complaints and other needs, comfort and reassurances are taken care of by the nursing staff. Children are observed on thirty-minute intervals.

TABLE VII

SUMMARY FOR EVENING SHIFT

2:45 P.M.– 3:00 P.M.	Merging of day and evening shifts
	Report on children
	Sharp and key count
3:00 P.M.– 3:45 P.M.	Children's staff group meeting—report read and discussed.
	Free play
	Some children in scheduled appointments (tutoring, etc.)
4:00 P.M.– 5:00 P.M.	Nursing staff dinner (4:00–4:30 and 4:30–5:00)
5:00 P.M.– 5:30 P.M.	Children's dinner
5:30 P.M.– 6:00 P.M.	(Winter) Playground free play
6:00 P.M.– 7:00 P.M.	(Summer)
6:00 P.M.– 7:00 P.M.	(Winter) Children's showers
7:00 P.M.– 8:00 P.M.	(Summer)
7:00 P.M.– (Winter)	Bedrooms inspection
8:00 P.M.– (Summer)	
8:00 P.M.– 8:30 P.M.	Snack time
8:30 P.M.	Group discussion of evening activities
	Bedtime for younger boys and girls
8:30 P.M.– 9:30 P.M.	Quiet period of activities for older boys and girls
9:30 P.M.	Group discussion of evening activities
	Bedtime Residence A Unit II and Residence B
10:00 P.M.	Bedtime Residence A Unit I
10:00 P.M.–11:15 P.M.	Nursing staff charting, cleaning, etc.
10:45 P.M.–11:15 P.M.	Merging of evening and night shifts

Attending Special Children's Needs

When a child is fairly new to the residence, or during a period when a child is particularly upset, he may need more attention after the other children are asleep. A nursing staff member will then sit with the child in his room and let him talk if he wants to, or just let him know she is there until he falls asleep. Other children may awaken in the night and call the staff if they are frightened or cannot sleep. The rooms of all the children are close enough to the Nurse's Office so that any child who awakens can be heard.

Enuretic or encopretic children have showers and clean clothing. The sheets are changed routinely every day by the nursing personnel. Their beds may also be changed in the middle of the night by the staff if the children are uncomfortable. No emphasis is placed by staff on dry or wet beds, unless the children show that they want recognition for a dry bed.

An effort is made to keep the children in bed until all awaken at 7:00 AM. Children unable to sleep are allowed to play quietly in bed until it is time to get up.

Nursing Staff's Housekeeping Duties

Night shift personnel also attend to the children's laundry (washing, drying and folding). Also they are responsible for the cleaning and sanitizing of the residence (including day rooms, nurse's office, hobbyroom) and the maintenance of the infirmary (including supplies).

Every week a list of needed cleaning supplies is submitted to Nursing Administration.

Every third week of each month a list of cleaning supplies for the residences is submitted to Housekeeping Department.

Change of Night Shift to Day Shift

From 6:45 PM to 7:15 AM the night shift changes to the day shift. Report on children is given by night shift. Staff of both shifts under day shift nurse's or designate supervision check for patient face, security, contraband and sharp count.

TABLE VIII

SUMMARY FOR NIGHT SHIFT

10:45 P.M.–11:15 P.M.	Merging of evening and night shifts
11:15 P.M.– 6:45 A.M.	Attendance of children with difficulties
	General observance every thirty minutes
	Attendance of children's laundry
	Cleaning and sanitizing residence
	Maintenance of infirmary
	Prepare weekly list for cleaning supplies
	Prepare every third week of each month list for cleaning supplies
6:45 A.M.– 7:15 A.M.	Merging of night and day shifts

Dining Room, Meals, Special Nourishment

As a part of the total treatment milieu at the center, the policies and procedures pertinent to the operation of the dining rooms and the provision of a balanced and attractive diet enable the children to improve their eating manners, to carry out responsible functions, and receive all the essential nutrients of a daily menu, through proper quality and adequate quantities of all classes of foods.

Kitchen and Dining Rooms

Food is prepared in the central kitchen of the center and is served in the two dining rooms, one for Residence A (Units I and II, older boys) and one for Residence B (Unit I, girls, and Unit II, younger boys).

The keys for the dining rooms are kept in Residences A and B and are used only during dining hours (doors open before meals and locked after meals) by nursing staff designated by the residence nurse.

Policies and Procedures

The children are encouraged to be clean, to dress neatly and attractively, and to develop socially acceptable manners and habits. Before and after meals they attend to their personal hygiene.

Before going to meals an assembly for the purpose of inspection of appearance and accounting for all children is held inside the residence by the charge aide.

All meal times are considered potentially a period when tensions can be anticipated. The hyperactivity to be expected from the children can be controlled by maintaining steady staff coverage. An average of one assigned group worker per unit can adequately cover the group.

Each unit's group worker accompanies the children in an organized manner to the dining room. Breakfast begins at 8:00 AM, lunch at 11:50 AM and dinner at 5:00 PM.

All children attend meals even if they do not choose to eat. They are not forced to eat and are not spoon-fed.

Food is not served in the dining room for those are are late for meals. Individual situations are referred to the residence nurse.

Special diets are prescribed only by the individual child's psychiatrist (low-calorie diet for overweight, etc.).

Children are not permitted to choose what they want. Food is plentiful and all foods are encouraged. Seconds and desserts and other items which the children particularly enjoy are available.

Children on residence restriction are escorted to meals. Food is not served in the residence except for physically ill children who cannot go to the dining room or in cases indicated by the child's psychiatrist's order.

If a child is unable to go on an off-grounds pass (due to restriction, absence of parent, etc.) the Dietary Department is notified by 10:00 AM and this information is communicated through the "Shift Report."

Dietary personnel remain in the kitchen and do not involve themselves with the children.

Staff members have their meal in the staff's cafeteria before or after the children's meals. They serve the children and do not partake in the meal. They also help those children most acutely disturbed and unable to help themselves.

Each meal begins with grace being offered by the child who volunteers. The group then in unison begins with a prayer, e.g. "God is great, God is good, God we thank you for this food. Amen."

Children are encouraged to learn and practice good table manners by the assisting staff and the more mannerly children in the group. Dietary practices of the children are noted and when indicated reported to their nurse. Discussion concerning the food, except for occasional favorable passing comments, is avoided. Conversation is encouraged on subjects of interest to the entire group. This seems to help the children, and meals are peaceful and orderly without repressive measures necessary from the staff.

Places in the dining room are assigned. There is no getting up and down during the meal and children are not allowed to alternate seating and tables. Consideration of group tensions is the major factor in the seating arrangement to protect children as much as possible from disturbances during meals. Children whose behavior is unacceptable for group eating are assigned to individual tables.

One table in each dining room is reserved as an "honor table." Two children, one from each residence unit, are chosen by the nursing staff to sit there. The selection of the children and the duration of their honor status is based on their effort to reach acceptable standards in dining room behavior.

An unusually disturbed child who upsets others may be removed and escorted to the residence. He may return at the discretion of the residence nurse or charge aide.

Clearing of dishes and order of the dining room is attended to by the nursing staff. Children selected by staff help with after-meal chores (clean the tables, load the carts with soiled dishes, straighten tables and chairs). Staff is responsible for accounting of silverware.

Steak knives are made available only for nursing staff use. Children under no circumstances are permitted the use of steak knives.

Utensil Count

The Dietary Department keeps an accurate count of all utensils dispensed (eating and serving). Replacements are exchanged on a one-for-one basis, the soiled item passed through the appropriate window. A three-canister receptacle is placed by the exits of both residence dining rooms. Each child is responsible for his utensils and must demonstrate and deposit same before leaving the dining room. The group worker is stationed at this area to supervise as children from each table leave. If any utensil is not accounted for at a table, the children remain until the utensil is found.

At the termination of their meal, children from Residence A —Unit I leave the dining room first. The other children follow after their entire unit has completed the meal and is in order.

Special Nourishments

AFTERNOON SNACK. Juice is served in the afternoon in both residences after the school and adjunctive therapy classes are over.

REGULAR EVENING SNACKS. Food supplements such as bread, peanut butter, jelly sandwiches and milk are given to children in the evening.

THURSDAY EVENING SPECIAL SNACK. This special treat is purchased by the children's fund and may consist of pizza, soda, ice cream, etc. It is given in addition to the regular evening nourishment to children whose improvement in their functioning was noted and discussed by nursing staff at the weekly staff meeting.

FIELD TRIP LUNCHES. When a field trip is scheduled, a final "Field Trip List" is prepared by the nursing service and on Friday is sent to the Dietary Department. If any change is made, the Dietary Department is informed by the charge aide no later than 8:00 AM Saturday, Sunday or holiday.

Field trip lunches are prepared and packed only by the Dietary Department personnel. Freezer packs are returned immediately and food chests are cleaned before returning to the nursing building adjacent to dining rooms.

BIRTHDAY CAKES. For the "Birthday Child," a cake is purchased by the children's fund and is presented in the dining room as a dessert at the noon meal.

If the "Birthday Child" is on an off-ground pass status, the cake is presented the day before his departure or the day after his return.

Health Program

The medical and nursing staff of the center place considerable emphasis on the health program, which includes prevention of illness and physical and dental care of all children.

All children must meet certain health requirements before they are accepted at the center.

Admission

On the day of admission, the admitting psychiatrist, in the presence of a nurse, gives a thorough physical and neurological examination to the child. Weight and height are also measured. The examination takes place in the examination room which is located in the infirmary area.

Before the examination the nurse prepares the necessary equipment (stethoscope, blood pressure apparatus, tongue blades, percussion hammer, tuning fork, flashlight, ophthalmoscope with otoscope attachment), and the child's residence chart.

The nurse informs the child of the procedure and sees that he is dressed appropriately. She reassures the child and brings the child to the examination room only after the examining psychiatrist has arrived there.

After the examination and weight and height measurements, the nurse accompanies the child to the residence and returns to the examination room where she confers with the psychiatrist, who writes the physical findings on a special form.

The psychiatrist also writes admission orders, such as admission to residence, diet (regular or special), escort status (1:1), precautions, visiting status, special privileges, attitudes, routine laboratory work (urinalysis, hemogram, serology, blood type, feces, chest and skull X-ray, and bone age). Routine laboratory studies may be omitted if they have been done within fifteen days before admission. The admitting psychiatrist determines the need for special consultations and laboratory examinations (neurological, otological, ophthalmological, EEG, EKG, and others). He prepares a consultation request which is forwarded to the director of the center for approval.

The admitting psychiatrist writes the admission note on the day of admission.

Discharge

At the time of discharge every child is also physically examined and the examining psychiatrist states his findings in the Discharge Note.

Health While in Residence

Prevention of illness is the major focus of the health program. For that reason routine physical examinations are given at six-month intervals. The residence nurse is responsible for scheduling such periodic examinations.

Weight and height are checked monthly. Excessive differences in measurements are reported to the child's psychiatrist.

The child also receives any immunizations which have not been completed.

Each morning the residence nurse checks the children for scratches, bruises and other physical complaints. Because of the need some disturbed children have to exaggerate minor illnesses, nursing staff are often misinterpreting these as psychosomatic complaints and discourage children from discussing them. Nursing staff are requested to observe the children closely and listen attentively without asking too many questions. When there is any real possibility of illness, they refer the children to the residence nurse for an initial checkup before having their psychiatrist see them. If the nurse determines that a child needs medical attention, she reports this to his psychiatrist who thoroughly examines the child.

Children with minor illnesses are usually kept in residence, put to bed in their bedrooms, and attended by the nursing staff. Others with common childhood contagious diseases are cared for in the infirmary which has a capacity of two beds.

Children may be referred to a hospital or clinic only after having been examined by their psychiatrist who writes his findings and tentative diagnosis in a special consultation form.

Children can be taken to the emergency room of a hospital or clinic for first aid when necessary.

The center has access to a consulting staff of medical and surgical specialists and uses the services of the dental and laboratory facilities.

Children in cases of emergency and children with serious illnesses are transferred to a hospital or clinic only after consultation between the child's psychiatrist and chief of the medical or surgical section of the hospital or clinic.

Even though the child's medical record contains a signed statement by each child's parents giving the center permission to provide medical care for the child, the parents are informed if an operation or major medical treatment is required.

When children have parents who are able to take care of surgery in their community, they are encouraged to take the child home for this purpose. A consultation is usually arranged with the child's psychiatrist to determine if such a procedure would be detrimental to the child at that time in terms of his total treatment.

Dental Health

Dental care is provided by the center's affiliated dentist, who once a week provides preventive and corrective work. When oral surgical work is indicated, parental authorization is necessary.

When parents or agencies desire and/or are able to pay for dental services, they are informed of the child's needs and asked to take the child to their family dentist.

PSYCHIATRIST'S ORDERS

The psychiatrist's orders are written on the "Doctor's Orders" form which is kept in the child's residence chart. When a page of this form is filled, all orders still in effect are rewritten at the top of a new page. When both sides are filled, the form is transferred by the office aide to the child's Master Chart which is kept in the medical records library.

Renewal of Orders

The psychiatrist and nurse set aside a definite period of time to review, rewrite or write new orders.

Medication not specifically limited as to time or number of doses, when ordered, is AUTOMATICALLY STOPPED as follows:

Narcotics, Class II	24 hours
Non-narcotics, Class II	7 days
Antibiotics/Sulfa	5 days
Hypnotics	7 days
PRN	7 days
Other Orders	15 days

Orders for Narcotics and Non-Narcotics under Narcotic Control

Orders for narcotics and non-narcotics under narcotic control are co-signed by the registered nurse.

Monday through Friday

In case the center is a state facility and when a narcotic or non-narcotic under narcotic control is ordered to be administered, the center's residence registered nurse on duty proceeds to the Surgical Unit of the state hospital with the child's chart.

The R.N. responsible for the narcotic key checks the order and opens the narcotic box. The R.N. obtaining the drug removes the drug from the narcotic box, signs for it, and counts the remainder with the other R.N. before returning it to the narcotic box. The residence R.N. returns to the residence and administers the medication.

Analogous procedures can be agreed upon in case the center is a private facility.

Orders on Management and Control

Such orders are not given or written under the stereotype "administer as necessary."

The "Number ONE" restriction order is written only by the child's psychiatrist who also determines its duration.

Verbal (V.O.) or Telephone (T.O.) Orders

In case of an emergency and during weekends and holidays the psychiatrist may give verbal or telephone orders to the nurse. These orders are marked as V.O. (verbal) or T.O. (telephone) orders and are signed by the psychiatrist within twenty-four hours.

Orders for Off-grounds Visits (Passes)

Orders for children's visits are written by the child's psychiatrist as follows:

Off-ground Visit Limited (e.g. from 1:00 PM to 6:00 PM)

Off-ground Overnight (specify date)

Off-ground weekend or holiday (specify dates)

Based on the psychiatrist's orders the weekly suggested passes are forwarded to Social Work Service, finalized and initialed by the individual child's social worker, and returned for the signature of Director of Nursing Service.

Medication (Charting—Samples—Return)

The office aide transcribes all "doctor's orders" to the Kardex, Medicine Cards and Medication Book. This includes date, child's name, medication instructions and discontinuation date.

The medication card is initialed by the office aide and nurse.

Medication orders written after 2:30 PM are not picked up until the following morning unless ordered "stat" (Exception: anti-biotics). All medication must be obtained from the drug room stock or pharmacy.

Samples and outside sources of medication are not permitted for children's use.

Any medication returned to the center from pass, leave of absence or any other source is returned to the pharmacy. This medication cannot be returned to stock.

Preparation and Administration of Medication

Check medicine card, prepare medication, identify the child, and give one medication at a time with a paper cup of water. Always remain with the child until medication is swallowed. Check the child's mouth with a tongue blade if necessary.

Refusal of Medication

If medication is refused by the child, return it to medication cabinet and destroy, reporting same to charge aide or nurse and chart the incident. If the medication is a count drug it is held and destroyed only in the presence of charge aide or nurse and is documented on the reverse side of the count sheet. Signature is witnessed by both individuals.

Errors in Medication

In the event an error in medication is made, the error is reported immediately to the nurse in charge, and an incident report is made out. The nurse reports the error to the psychiatrist.

Placebo

Placebos are ordered only by the child's psychiatrist. The nursing staff are alerted to the fact that placebo can cause unwanted effects which are neither serious nor long-lived, but they cannot be ignored. These are: nausea, tachycardia, excessive sweating, epigastric disturbance with diarrhea, dryness of the mouth, headache, easy fatigue and somnolence.

Nursing staff informs the child's psychiatrist on any of the above described symptoms.

Medication for Children Going on Pass and Ten-day Leave of Absence (LOA)

An effort is made not to send children off grounds on drugs.

Medication for children going on pass is prepared by the pharmacy aide.

Ordering Drugs

The residences order all drugs through the central pharmacy by the pharmacy aide.

a. *Weekly:* Monday 8:30 AM—The residences submit pharmacy requisitions, drug tally sheets and empty drug bottles (Exception: empty concentrate bottles are picked up by transportation for disposal) via the courier-office aide to the pharmacy. 10:00 AM— a twenty-four-hour supply of medications is returned to respective residence by courier-office aide.

b. *Daily:* Monday, Wednesday, Friday drug tally sheets, pass medication envelopes and empty medication bottles sent to the pharmacy, replenished and returned to the residence by 10:00 AM.

Medication Changed

Monday through Friday 8:00 AM-4:00 PM—any medication change ordered by the psychiatrist is immediately telephoned to the pharmacy aide for delivery and the tally sheet updated.

IMMUNIZATION

The protective shield of immunization guards children against many infections and helps to keep the community at the center free from epidemics. The children's resistance to disease is also fortified with good care, nutritious meals, clean surroundings, adequate clothing, enough fresh air, exercise and rest. A strong and healthy body is a child's best defense against sickness. His natural resistance can usually overcome exposure to many disease germs.

The child's psychiatrist reviews the newly admitted child's (and periodically all children's) record of immunization and determines the type of immunization required for the child. If additional information is necessary, he makes efforts to obtain it from every possible source.

The psychiatrist is responsible for relaying immunization information to the residence nurse who promptly records it on the child's immunization chart. The psychiatrist writes the order for the type of immunization required and the residence nurse notifies the Medical Clinic Nurse. When scheduling is agreed the office aide is responsible for getting the child to the clinic at the specified time.

The psychiatrist, at the time of the child's discharge, includes in the discharge summary any immunizations the child has received at the center and makes sure that this information is communicated to the family physician.

All children are immunized against diphtheria, tetanus, polio, measles and rubella. Smallpox vaccination and typhoid immunization are not recommended.

The following schedule is recommended:

On admission: 1. Diphtheria/Tetanus Toxoid, 2. First dose oral polio vaccine (if not previously immunized).

One month after admission: 1. Diphtheria/Tetanus Toxoid, 2. Measles/Rubella combined vaccine (if indicated by history).

Two months after admission: 1. Second dose oral polio vaccine.

Fourteen months after admission: 1. Diphtheria/Tetanus Toxoid, 2. Third dose polio vaccine.

Immunization Dosage Schedule—two intramuscular injections of 0.5 ml each at intervals of one to four months.

Booster Interval—twelve months after initial series, then every ten years or upon exposure. To be given at time of traumatic injury, but no more than one in any twelve-month period. Alum-precipitated toxoid preferred for routine immunization.

Standing Orders

Medications and procedures involved in standing orders can only be given under the direction of the nurse in charge. The nurse informs the residence psychiatrist (or O.D. in case of weekends and holidays) within a period of twenty-four hours that these medications and procedures have been undertaken. The psychiatrist may give permission to the nurse to continue these orders for a longer period of time.

Following is a list of approved standing orders. From time to time other standing orders may need to be added, others to be modified and some to be deleted from the list by the residence psychiatrists with the approval of the director of the center.

TABLE IX

STANDING ORDERS

Common Cold—Nasal Congestion

Under eight years of age:

 A.S.A. gr. V q 4 h PRN
 T.P.R. b.i.d.
 Neo-Synephrine® ¼% q 3-4 h (PRN)
 2/G Expectorant® (Glyceryl Guaiacolate) 1 tsp. q 4 h. (PRN) for cough
 Force fluids—no milk
 Limit activities
 Bed rest

Over eight years of age:

 Increase A.S.A. gr. X q 4 h (PRN)
 Follow orders as for under eight years

Sore Throat

 Warm salt water gargle q 4 h
 Cepacol® Lozenges
 A.S.A. as per age (see common cold)
 Limit activities
 Bed rest

Indigestion

Gelusil® tabs I or II q 3-4 hrs. (PRN)
Nothing cold, fried or fatty
Notify physician if pain increases or persists longer than hour or two, or patient
 begins to vomit or show other symptoms

Diarrhea

Age five to twelve years:

 Kaopectate® tablespoon I q 2 hr—Day 1.
 Kaopectate tablespoon q 3 hr—PRN after.
 No fruits, juices or roughage
 No too hot or too cold food or drinks until diarrhea subsides
 If diarrhea persists more than forty-eight hours, notify residence physician
  specifically.

Toothache

Ice packs
A.S.A. gr V, q 4 hr (PRN) under eight years of age
A.S.A. gr X q 4 hr (PRN) over eight years of age

Stings (Bee, Wasp, Hornet)

Chlor-Trimeton® 4 mg tab STAT
Remove stinger
Ice pack—on and off
Notify residence physician (or any available physician) IMMEDIATELY of any
systemic reaction

Abrasions (Minor Cuts)

Wash with soap and water, pat dry gently
Rinse with peroxide
Paint with Merthiolate
Apply dry sterile dressing

Sores

For weeping, pustular, open lesions and Florida sores.

Wash gently with liquid soap three times daily
Pat dry gently
Apply aqueous solution gentian violet 1% with applicators
Allow to dry, no bandage, except on those lesions where trauma may occur, such
as heel, bottom of feet, etc.
If lesion is dry and healing, use gentian violet only
Keep nails cut short

Miscellaneous

Menstrual Pain	APC tab. 1 q 4 h (PRN)
Athlete's Foot	Daliderm® Powder
Hot Soaks	Epsom Salt, 2 T./qt. water
Dandruff	Sebulex® Shampoo (Max. 2 times weekly)
Constipation	Absence of abdominal pain—Milk of Magnesia®, 1-2 tblsp.
Minor Ear Ache	Auralgan ear drops (warm)
Minor Eye Irritation	Boric Acid solution 2%
Allergy to Aspirin	Children under 75 lbs. Tempera® tsp. I q 4 hrs.
	Children over 75 lbs. Tempera® tsp. II q 4 hrs.

Count Drugs—Described in the Center's Formulary

1. Count drugs counted each shift and initialed by nurse and/or charge aide on
the on-coming shift.
2. Count drugs poured, if not used for any reason, must be accounted for on
reverse side of Form, # . . . . . ., written and acknowledged by both, medication
aide and nurse.
3. Count Drugs—Pass-L.O.A. must be charted as Pass-L.O.A. at time medication
dispensed.
4. Count Drug Sheet to be sent to Pharmacy by the fifteenth of each month, listing
all count drugs—dose and amounts remaining.

Commonly Used Abbreviations in Metric System

Full Wording	Abbreviations
One Milligram	1 mg.
Ten Milligrams	10 mg. (No "s" is added to signify plural)
One Gram	1 Gm.*
One Cubic Centimeter	1cc†
One Milliliter	1 ml.

* In the abbreviation for one gram (1 Gm.) Capital "G" should always be used.
This is very important as otherwise it may be confused with the abbreviation for
1 grain (1 gr.).

† 1 Cubic centimeter (1cc) is more or less equal to 1 milliliter (1 ml.). Cubic
centimeter (cc) is a term more commonly used in the hospital practice.

Kardex Card

Purpose: This card is used as a quick reference regarding medications and treatments ordered for patients.

Order of Card: List medications ordered, beginning with top of card. List treatment orders starting at bottom of card and work up. Use separate line for each medication or treatment.

Use of Ink: Ink (blue or black) is used for *everything* on this card except: (1) age—pencil (2) date of Rx expiration—pencil (3) *Red ink* for: (a) discontinued order (draw line), (b) write in discontinued date above old one, (c) Rx other than those done daily (e.g. drug free weekend, etc., (d) concentrates, I.M., P.R.N., less than one tablet.

"Stat" Orders: These are *not* listed on Kardex.

P.R.N.: These are *not* charted on the Medication and Treatment record until given.

Supplemental Kardex Card

Purpose: This card is to be used as a quick reference guide regarding information about each patient.

Placement: Kardex File above regular Kardex card.

Note: Due to changing information, all writing on this card is to be in pencil *except* for the name, admission date, birth date which are to be written in blue or black ink. Allergies in *red ink.* Abbreviations to be used for legal status: (a) Co. Ct.—County Court, (b) Cert. 6 mon.—Certified 6 months, (c) Vol. —Voluntary admission, (d) Cr. Ct.—Criminal Court, (e) Cit. Ct.—Circuit Court. Exceptions to above: (1) Use *red pencil* if patient is court hold, suicidal, eloped or homicidal. (2) Write special consults and laboratory work in ink and indicate date requested with abbreviations "req." Write in pencil the date executed. Check type of admission, include under miscellaneous other items of importance.

EMERGENCY PROCEDURES

Classification of Emergencies

Unforeseen events requiring immediate attention occur in the center although great effort is made for the anticipation and prevention of their occurrence. Most of the emergencies that occur are included in the general classifications of (1) accidents, (2) overly expressed hostilities between clashing personalities, (3) attempts by children to harm themselves (climbing walls, trees, roofs, etc.).

Prevention

Prevention rather than treatment of the emergency is the method of choice. To facilitate the prevention aspect of the emergency it is the concept and practice of the center's staff that

a. all children are considered potentially homicidal and self-destructive.

b. all glass, metals or objects that can be used as weapons be removed from the immediate possession of children and their usage be governed by personnel.

c. periodic investigations of all children's possessions be conducted to reduce the hoarding of contraband materials.

d. thorough search of a child upon his return from off-ground pass be made.

Procedures for Emergencies

a. *Keep calm.* Excitement is contagious and reduces the efficiency and the effective functioning of those that may be of assistance.

b. *Immediately remove the child from danger.* If you are not able to do this alone, support the child and first call for help and then ask another child capable of following your directions to notify your assistants, in the event your call was not heard. Avoid the delays involved in telephoning or running to secure help. The delay may result in further injury or death of the child.

c. *Administer first aid.* If there is cessation of breathing; begin artificial respiration without delay.

Hemorrhage: Use either direct pressure or digital pressure.

Fracture: Keep the child flat and prevent movement of the affected area.

Traumatic shock: Whenever the body is affected adversely, shock may result. To prevent or combat this condition, cover the child as soon as possible.

d. *Obtain immediate assistance of physician or nurse.* If there are two or more personnel, one remains with the child, the other obtains help. Under some circumstances, it may be necessary that the child be left unattended while assistance is sought. In either situation, clear the area of milling children before you leave.

If medical help is not readily available at the center, you may call the switchboard operator to obtain the needed medical assistance from the community.

e. *Keep the child quiet.* Remaining with the child will greatly aid in abetting excitement. Discuss the child's injury with him and if asked, permit him to see injury.

f. *Assist when help arrives.*

g. *Note details of circumstances for recording and reporting* (see charting).

Emergency Tray

The emergency tray is available at all times and includes:

1. suture tray and suture, novocaine, sterile gloves, alcohol sponges, bandage, adhesive tape, rolled gauze, Merthiolate® and green soap.

2. suture removal and dressing tray.

3. gavage tray.

Also available are sterile syringes and needles, ampule file; cardiac and respiratory stimulants; oxygen, resuscitation and suction equipment; and tetanus toxoid and record of tetanus injection.

First Aid Kit

Each residence has its own first aid kit.

Contents

1. Adhesive on tongue blades—½-1-2″
2. Applicators—3
3. Bandage 2″—1 roll
4. Bandaids®—10
5. Medicine glass
6. Sponge topper 4x3—3
7. Seizure gags—1
8. Mouth thermometer—1
9. Rectal thermometer—1

RESIDENCE MANAGEMENT
Charting

Purposes

To maintain a continuous record of the child's condition and progress which will assist in planning the most effective treatment and care for him.

To serve as an official record of medications, treatment and care given the child in case of legal proceedings.

To be used as reference for research work.

Important Aspects of Charting on "Nursing Notes"
(Form # . . .)

These notes are to be written by each shift, daily. Suggestions about material to observe in chart are: appearance, appetite, eating and sleeping habits; orientation, attention and understanding; attitudes; bodily state; conduct, conversation (actual quotations are always good); reactions to medication, to visitors, to personnel, to other children; self-control, delusions, hallucinations, inappropriateness, irritability, memory, judgement, liability of affect; measures taken in response to the complaints.

General Requirements for Charting

—Accuracy and objectivity. Write neatly and clearly. Keep charts up to date.

—Do not abbreviate.

—Blue or black ink or pencils are necessary.

—Fill chart pages in completely, do not leave any black spaces, and do not indent.

—Indicate quotations by using proper punctuation marks.

—Do *not* use other children's names on charts. Substitute "male peer/female peer."

—Do not use diagnostic terms. *Do not interpret* behavior demonstrated. No impressions.

—Record only what you see or indicate by quotations what someone else has reported.

—Sign recorded material with first initial and last name and position.

—Date and indicate time material was charted.

—Accumulated notes are removed by the office aide from the residence chart and placed in the child's Master Chart (Medical Records Office).

Child's Residence Chart Contents

Obtain "made up" chart which includes approved forms and clinical reports.

Admission Face Sheet
Admission Note
Doctor's Orders
Doctor's Progress Notes
Nursing Notes
Diagnostic and Appraisal Conference Note
Consultation Sheet
Report on Accident, Assault, Injury or Elopement
Physical Examination
Laboratory Reports
Radiographic Reports
Medication and Treatment Record
Temperature, Pulse, Respiration and Blood Pressure Record
Weight Record
Nursing Admission Record
Clothing Inventory Proof
Clothing Record
Immunization Record
Report of Seriously Ill

REPORTS

Written and Oral

A. *Written Reports*

1. *Reports Which the Charge Aide is Responsible for at the Close of Each Shift.*

    a. *Patient count.* This is done with the relieving charge aide. The face check is used.

    b. *Sharp count.* This procedure is done by two charge

aides. All sharps are accounted for before nursing personnel report off duty. Sharps are checked with a charge aide of the oncoming shift and charted.

   c. *Sedation and narcotic count.* The sedative or narcotic is counted, recorded and checked by the nurse.

2. *Reports for Which the Nurse Is Responsible at the Close of Each Shift* (add notes and co-sign the "twenty-four-hour Clinical Report").

   a. *Day Shift.* Nurses on Residence A and Residence B report on their residence to the nurses on the evening shift (at 3:00 PM).

   b. *Evening Shift.* Nurses on evening shift report on their residence to the nurses on night shift (11:00 PM).

   c. *Night Shift.* Nurses on night shift report on their residence to the nurses on day shift (7:00 AM).

   Both evening and night shift nurses' reports are brought by the day shift nurses to the Director of Nursing for review. Each residence nurse in turn reviews the "Twenty-four-Hour Clinical Report" with the psychiatrist. The "Twenty-four-Hour Clinical Report" is forwarded to the office of the director and then to the directors of services.

B. *Oral Reports*

   Oral reports are given at 7:00 AM, 3:00 PM, 11:00 PM by the charge aide on duty to the charge aide who is relieving from the oncoming staff. The reports are given at the residence office. Most oncoming personnel is present.

   Included in the reports are:

   a. Complete report on each child.
   b. Activities for day: lab, X-rays, etc.
   c. Admissions, discharges, transfers.
   d. All new orders.
   e. Behavior, special precautions, etc.

   Informal discussion also takes place with the children and charge aide during the 2:45 PM change of shifts and before bedtime. Specific incidents of children's behavior are reported, as well as imposed restrictions, their justification and clarifications of understandings between children and the relieving shift.

TRANSFERS

Intraresidence Transfer (only for Residence A)

Residence A consists of two units of twelve beds each, Unit I "open" or "privilege unit" and Unit II "closed" or "admission unit."

Newly admitted children reside in Unit II until their inpatient diagnostic evaluation is completed and their adjustment to the treatment programs is satisfactory. Also in Unit II are children whose response to treatment is slow and their needs for closer supervision are more pronounced.

In Unit I reside children whose response to treatment is satisfactory, their needs for supervision are less pronounced, and who are able to assume greater responsibility in their conduct. The unit is considered as an open unit and is used as a goal which children are trying to reach. In this unit the group remains fairly stable which enables the children to establish status in the residence and to form meaningful relationships not only with the nursing staff but also with their group mates.

Children may be moved from Unit II to Unit I if it is felt by their psychiatrist and nursing staff that (a) they have become sufficiently adjusted to the residence and to the aggression of other children their age and are able to compete with them and would not need so much protection; (b) they need more mature companionship and an opportunity to emulate older children; and (c) there is vacant bed in Unit I.

Transfers within the Residence A must be approved by the psychiatrist who also writes the order.

The director's secretary is notified on the transfer and the child is listed on the midnight census.

Interresidence Transfer

The majority of children remain in the same residence throughout their stay at the center. However, children may be moved from Unit II of Residence B to Unit II of Residence A if it is felt by their psychiatrist and nursing staff that (a) they have outgrown the unit; (b) they need more mature companionship and an opportunity to emulate older children.

Transfer of children from Residence B to Residence A must be approved by the director of the center always in consultation with the psychiatrists of both Residence A and Residence B. The transferring psychiatrist writes the order and the transfer note.

The residence is called before the transfer; the child's clothing card, account of all clothing and possessions is listed; and a check is made for eyeglasses and other valuables.

The child is asked to have a shower and dress appropriately. He is never transferred if he is not clean.

Transfer is not made at meal time, before 3:00 PM, or at change of shifts.

The child and the residence chart is transferred at the same time. The charge aide on the receiving residence accepts the child and acknowledges on the transfer form all received property and complete records of the child.

The child is made to feel welcome and is helped in orienting himself in the new residence.

The director's secretary is notified on the transfer and the child is listed on the midnight census.

Center to Hospital Transfer of Seriously Ill Children

Seriously ill children are transferred to the medical or surgical section of a hospital by arrangement between the residence psychiatrist, the director of the center, and the director of the medical or surgical section of the hospital. An effort is made to transfer before 4:30 PM. During evenings, nights, holidays and weekends, this arrangement is made between the center's psychiatrist and the physician on duty (O.D.) of the hospital.

The child's residence chart accompanies the child to the medical or surgical section. If possible, whatever laboratory work is necessary is done before the transfer.

The director's secretary is informed on such transfers.

The parents of critically ill children are notified by their social worker after directions given by the child's psychiatrist.

METHODS OF MANAGEMENT AND CONTROL

In the center, for the proper management and control of children, a degree of reasonable permissiveness within the limitations of a group structure common to everyday living is found to be satisfactory.

Experience has shown that staff members develop effective limit-setting measures only within an administratively determined framework. The most effective controls are believed to be those which derive from good relationships between adult and child.

However experience has also shown that the staff's understanding attitudes towards the children's problems, acceptance of them, and willingness to give endless attention and affection are not enough. Often tensions build up among the children to such a degree that some of them become almost completely out of control.

The value of limits-setting has been proven by the children's positive response to it. As the children recognize that the staff are in control of the situation and that limits are meant to be enforced, there seems to be less need for disciplinary measures. The limits also permit some children to become less overanxious about their own behavior when they realize the use of external controls is present for their benefit.

When the staff can accept the fact that limit-setting is as necessary to a child's development as love and security, they are ready to make every effort to assume the responsibility for implementing controls without defensiveness, apology or irritability.

I believe the goals of discipline are the anticipation of problems and their prevention by distraction, the use of guidance and the removal of certain privileges rather than punishment.

General Policies and Guidelines

The following are considered general guidelines for the children's management and control.

Privileges—Restrictions

Privileges, in order to be valued by the child, should not be given lightly. The child learns about privileges from the residence nurse at the time of admission. He also learns early that the giving or withholding of privileges is a staff decision and that he will be guided in earning most of the privileges. He also learns that he is not allowed to injure himself, to injure other children or staff members, and to destroy property.

Limits—Deprivations

The child's need for reasonable limits is explained to new staff members who are encouraged to help a child understand the reasons for restrictions, e.g. concern for the welfare of the group. Staff also point out the child's need for firmness and strength from the outside when he himself does not have it. Timing of this kind of explanation is very important. Staff members are instructed to wait until a child is calm enough to listen and understand these explanations.

Prohibition of Physical Punishment

Any limits-setting methods involving corporal punishment are prohibited at the center. All staff are informed of this policy when employed and also during their employment. Any staff who violates this policy is reported and an incident report is prepared by the supervisor and forwarded to the director of the center. An investigation is held and the staff member found guilty is immediately terminated from employment.

Authority of Nursing Staff

It is administrative policy to stabilize and maintain the authority of nursing staff, the people who live with the children. When a child's behavior and disposition has been such as to require controls, the nurse upholds the nursing staff even when there are objectional questions by others who are related to and working with the child. Such questions are later discussed among staff involved. This often makes for increased integration among staff and affords guideposts for future action.

Specific Policies and Guidelines

Staff always attempts to make it clear that discipline is not associated with rejection, and contact with the staff continues even when activities are restricted.

In order for the staff to become more effective and have less need to use strict corrective measures, the following specific guidelines for general limit-setting actions are accepted at the center.

"First Aid"

When the child begins to feel that he will overstep the simple limits or become upset in the residence, he is encouraged to go to his room until he feels ready to rejoin the group. Thus, immediate attention is given the child in such situations in the form of "psychiatric first aid."

Verbal Control—Temporary Removal from Activity

Staff sets firm limits whenever they feel a child is infringing on the rights of others through whims, temper outbursts, disrespectful behavior, or self-belittling actions. The staff can limit him with a firm "no." If he persists, he can be temporarily removed from an activity (school, adjunctive therapy, dining room, etc.) and referred to his group worker who takes him to a room, playroom or corridor, or for a walk until he has quieted down and is ready to rejoin the activity. In some cases the teacher might request that the child makes up time in school.

"Holding" Control (Physical-Verbal)

When a child is out of control but manageable, the staff member holds him gently but firmly. He estimates whether the child can regain control of himself and remain with the group or whether he must be removed. Staff members are urged when speaking to children about their behavior to do so in a low, calm voice and to avoid making issues of situations. An adult who screams puts himself on the child's level and becomes the "ineffective parent."

Removal from Activity

When the child is out of control and unmanageable and a disruptive influence for the rest of the group, he is brought by the group worker to the campus O.D. nurse who talks with the child and decides whether he needs residence restriction or is ready to return to his scheduled activity. In acute situations, as when a child becomes recalcitrant or harmful to others, he has to be handled immediately and at times in a forceful manner. Then it may become necessary to remove the child bodily to his room.

Theft—Careless Loss of Property

When a child takes something that does not belong to him or carelessly loses another's property, the staff sees that he makes at least partial, if not complete, restitution. Moderate restriction can be ordered by his nurse.

Witness and Help in Repair of Property

When a child is destructive, he is expected, with the help of the staff, to repair as much of the damage as possible. When maintenance staff are to repair the damage, the child is kept from his regularly scheduled activity to witness and help in the repair. He also serves moderate restriction.

Help in Clean-up and Order

When a child urinates or defecates in areas other than the toilet, he is expected to help the staff clean up. When he forcibly vomits or spits or throws food, he is expected to help staff clean up. When he disturbs the educational, recreational and other equipment such as furniture or clothing, he is expected to help the staff put things in order. He also serves moderate restriction.

Refusal to Leave Residence

When a child refuses to leave the residence for school or other scheduled activity, the nurse talks to the child and attempts to get him to attend. If this fails, she keeps the child in the residence and notifies his psychiatrist, principal, psychotherapist and adjunctive therapist.

Refusal to Attend Psychotherapy

When a child refuses to attend his individual or group psychotherapy session the individual or group psychotherapist is informed. He might decide to talk to the child or ask the staff member who is with the child to call the O.D. nurse who will receive the child or ask his group worker to be with the child for the entire period of the session.

Refusal to Attend School or Adjunctive Therapy

When a child refuses to attend a school class while in school or A.T. (adjunctive therapy), the teacher or A.T. aide notifies the principal or A.T. director who talks to the child. If this doesn't produce results, the O.D. nurse is called and receives the child *or* asks his group worker to be with the child for the entire period of the class. The child can return to his next scheduled class. If he is not able to do so, the child's psychiatrist is called.

Truancy—Running Away

When the child is truant from his regularly scheduled activities or runs away, a child care worker usually escorts him to the activity for awhile. Similarly, when he does not return from school, A.T., or his psychotherapy session, he is not allowed to leave his activity without being escorted by a child care worker. Teachers, A.T., and psychotherapists make sure that such a child is accompanied by a child care worker. Such a child could serve complete restriction ordered by his psychiatrist.

Staff's Infringement Versus Children's Free Play

Other than firm limits to behavior and assignment of scheduled activities, the staff lets the child go from their anxious concerns. This is because it is realized that staff can infringe just as readily with their anxious concerns and lectures as a child can with his immature impulsiveness. Through free play the child benefits from relief from the staff's pressure about habits, personal accomplishments, health, food, clothing and friends and is actively involved in developing his own judgement.

Staff's Inability for Management and Control

These guidelines for assessing, managing and controlling the children's emotional imbalance are helpful in a great percentage in "families" where childhood behavior problems prevail. Some staff members, however, are not able to accept and follow management suggestions because of deeply rooted emotional conflicts of their own, often going back to their childhood. These staff members are best served by being asked to seek another job.

Summary of Restrictions

Major behavior problems are usually handled by restriction of activities or deprivation of privileges.

For the purpose of better communication, the children and nursing staff name the various degrees of restriction as "Number Three," "Number Two," and "Number One."

"Number THREE" Restriction (mild restriction)

—*Ordered* by nursing staff member. May be recommended by group worker through charge aide.
—*Duration:* Not more than one hour.
—*Withdrawal of privileges:* Loss of dessert or snacks or period of playtime.
—*TV time, R.T. movies:* Child remains in residence from 12:20 PM to 1:00 PM and from 3:00 PM to 5:00 PM.

"Number TWO" Restriction (moderate restriction)

—*Ordered* by residence nurse or charge aide with approval of nurse.
—*Duration:* For more than one hour and from one shift to next. It may be extended up to two days and always with the knowledge of the following shift nurse.
—*Escort* to and from the dining room, scheduled activities, psychotherapy and other appointments.
—*Withdrawal of privileges:* All "Number Three" privilege restrictions. In addition, no field trips and on-grounds and off-grounds visits.

"Number ONE" Restriction (only on very rare occasions)

—*Ordered* only by the child's psychiatrist.
—*Duration:* As prescribed by the child's psychiatrist.
—*Escort* to and from the dining room (if child able to go for meals).

—*Withdrawal of privileges:* All "Number Three" and "Number Two" restrictions. No school, adjunctive therapy or other scheduled activities.

For the psychotherapy appointment, the nurse informs the psychotherapist on the child's "Number One" restriction. If the psychotherapist wishes to see the child he confers with the child's psychiatrist. If the decision reached is that the psychotherapist should see the child, the child's psychiatrist notifies the nurse.

PROHIBITION OF ISOLATION ROOMS

In some residential treatment centers what is gracefully called "Quiet Room," "Blue Room," "Time-Out Room," "Seclusion Room," "Isolation Room," and more recently "Aversion Room," is prohibited in the center.

The theories that "isolation of a child can be used as protective device in controlling his disturbed behavior" and "isolation therapy contributes to the recompensation of defenses" have proved to be psychiatric fantasies.

In my experience, doubts have developed as to the faith in the sanctity of the prescribed "isolation." I believe that instead of isolation rooms, normal living areas can be provided where the child and a staff member can sit and talk. Thus, the whole concept of isolation and a room designated for such purpose becomes unnecessary.

I also believe that the existence of such rooms in reality limits operational flexibility and creates an environment in which the staff is prone to treat "behavior" rather than treating people. When there is a standard procedure for isolation, there is also expected standardized behavior quickly learned by children that provokes isolation. Thus, children who might desire to be alone learn to exhibit and utilize purposefully the very behavior which we consider pathological and which may actually be initiated or molded by the practice of isolation.

In the center, the nonexistence of isolation rooms constitutes a statement about the children's expected acceptable behavior, a statement about the staff's expected judicious and prompt response to the individual child's physical and emotional needs for control, and a statement about the humanness of the treatment milieu.

SEARCH FOR LOST ARTICLES

1. *General Instructions*

    a. Sharp and hazardous articles are checked routinely at the end of each shift.

    b. Loss of any articles, including keys, is reported immediately to the nurse in charge.

    c. No member of the personnel leaves the residence until the lost article has been recovered or accounted for. At termination of shift child care workers may leave.

    d. If the article is not recovered, this is reported and an incident form is made out and submitted to the director of nursing service.

2. *The Search*

    a. The search should be systematized.

    b. Know what is lost, when and by whom it was last seen.

    c. Look in the obvious places first.

    d. Keep children occupied and away from the area being searched.

    e. Check every possible area before reporting failure.

    f. Children may be searched without the psychiatrist's permission.

CONTRABAND MATERIAL INTRODUCED IN CENTER

The safety and welfare of the children is somewhat jeopardized by carelessness. Contraband material appears from time to time in the premises of the center and on the children. Contraband includes items such as gum, matches, cigarettes, knives, and other material which might be considered dangerous to the children and possibly destructive to the physical plant.

Sources of Contraband

1) Children returning from home visits.
2) Careless staff (offices, unlocked parked cars).
3) Careless maintenance personnel.
4) Other children and visitors on the grounds.

Instructions to All Staff and Parents

a. Instruct the parents early at the time of admission and afterwards to set standards for the child and not permit him to bring contraband material on the premises.

b. Thorough observation of returning child from home visit (some children hide contraband while on their way to the residence).

c. Thorough search of the child in the residence before he mixes with his peer group.

d. Emphasize to the staff during the in-service training the dangers from contraband introduced to the center and teach them pertinent methods of preventing the introduction as well as searching, discovering and disposing of contraband material.

e. Refer the involved child to his psychiatrist.

f. Keep contraband material; chart, date and tag it for presentation to the members of the treatment team.

g. The child's social worker shall discuss the matter with the child's parents. If parents are unwilling or unable to control the child's repeated contraband introduction to the center this might be a valid reason for the child's termination of treatment.

ELOPEMENT

Elopement Period

Whenever a child (or children) is discovered or assumed to have eloped, the incident is faced by all personnel as calmly and objectively as possible so that routine functioning of the program is not interrupted.

Between the Hours of 8:00 AM and 4:30 PM

The person discovering the elopement immediately notifies the residence nurse (or charge aide). The nurse or charge aide verifies the child's name and, if possible, the area from which the child eloped and instructs the available child care workers (other child care workers do not interrupt their duties unless otherwise instructed) to search for the child on the grounds of the center. Staff members are not permitted to leave the grounds searching or running after a child. The nurse (or charge aide) notifies the center's security office (giving the name and individual description of the child, age, height, weight, color of hair and eyes, clothing, any distinguishing features), the office of the administrative assistant, the child's psychiatrist, and the child's social worker and the director of nursing.

Note: The center's security officers are not allowed to search for the child outside the center's grounds.

If the child is not found within one hour, the nurse notifies the city's police and, if requested, the sheriff's office.

If the child is not found within four hours, the psychiatrist, social worker and nurse determine whether the parents should be notified or not. When the child is found, the nurse notifies all persons involved. Privately owned cars are not used to pick up eloped children.

Between the Hours of 4:30 PM and 8:00 AM, Weekends and Holidays

The same procedure as above except that the nurse, instead of notifying the administrative assistant, psychiatrist and social worker, notifies the director of nursing and the "doctor on call" of the center. She also notifies the center's security office.

When the child is found the nurse informs all persons involved. If a child eloped and returned to his home, the parents are advised to bring him back. If they fail to do so the child may be automatically discharged "against medical advice." There is no form to be signed. In case the child is committed, he is kept on the records for one year "AWOL status" after allowing forty-eight hours to elapse from stated return date and time. The social worker, the child's psychiatrist and the director of the center confer on the case and decide according to the policies of the center pertaining to "Involuntary Patients."

Postelopement Period

A child returned from elopement is searched and given a shower, liquids and food and is physically examined by his psychiatrist.

In case the parents call back to learn about the details of the incident, they are referred to the child's social worker. She may refer them to the psychiatrist whenever she feels this is necessary.

Residence personnel secure broken doors, windows, etc.; remove all harmful objects; and maintain proper physical and emotional climate in the residence, acknowledging the elopement to children and avoiding criticism and preoccupation with the incident.

Unless otherwise prescribed by the psychiatrist, the child is returned to his regular activities, does not miss meals, and is not deprived of privileges.

If the child is in need of restriction, the rules for such measure are followed.

Investigation of Incident

A special "Patient Incident Form" for each elopement is completed and signed by the staff member primarily involved in the incident. The nurse and charge aide investigate the incident, determine the cause, recommend measures for preventing such incidents and sign the form.

If a staff member's negligence has been determined, the staff member involved completes the "Employee Incident Form # . . . ."

The elopement is charted on the nursing notes and also noted on the "twenty-four-hour clinical report."

All forms are submitted to the director of nursing and then to the residence psychiatrist who reports on the child's physical and mental condition and makes the necessary recommendations. All completed forms are finally forwarded to the director's office, and after consultation with both residence nurse and psychiatrist, the forms are filed in the child's records (original copy to Master Chart and copy to Residence Chart).

CLOTHING

Preadmission

When a child is scheduled for admission a list of clothing needs is sent to the parents by the Child Study Unit (Admissions Office).

It is the responsibility of the parents, responsible relatives or

TABLE X

The following list is forwarded to the boy's parents before admission.

Admission List: Personal Items and Clothing for Boys

Following is a suggested list of clothing and personal items your child will need during his residential treatment at the Center. Please furnish as many of these items as you are able to. This list may be supplemented at any time by you according to our inventory procedure.

Kindly identify all personal belongings clearly with a marking pen in order to facilitate proper care and handling.

Marking Procedure:

Socks—on toes
Shoes—indentation on sole
Shirts—tails
Trousers—waist seam
Underwear—waist seam
Wherever remainder of items indicated for convenience

Boys—All Clothing to Be Machine Washable With Little or No Ironing.

1 pair bedroom slippers
2 pairs tennis shoes: Prefer slip on—no ties
1 pair shoes—no ties
12 pair socks
4 pair pajamas
12-15 undershorts
1 robe
5 trousers—Perma-Press® or dress jeans
8 pair shorts or trousers (casual wear)
2 bathing suits
1 baseball cap
2 wash sweaters—NO WOOL
1 jacket
1 raincoat and hat
2 ties
2 dress shirts
1 suit or dress trousers and jacket (for dress-up occasions)
7 shirts, sport

Personal Items:

Stationery and stamps
Medicated powder, deodorant and hair care items
Shoe polish
2 toothbrushes (not electric) and toothpaste
2 comb and brush
Shampoo, if child has preference
Soap, if child has preference
NOTE: Toilet articles should not be in glass containers

Prohibited Are:

Razors, pocket knives, jewelry, nail files, scissors, eyebrow tweezers and personal items of a like nature. This restriction is necessary to assure safety for all the children.

TABLE XI

The following list is forwarded to the girl's parents before admission.

Admission List: Personal Items and Clothing for Girls

Following is a suggested list of clothing and personal items your child will need during her residential treatment at the Center. Please furnish as many of these items as you are able to. This list may be supplemented at any time by you according to our inventory procedures.

Kindly identify all personal belongings clearly with a marking pen in order to facilitate proper care and handling.

Marking Procedure:

Socks—on toes
Shoes—indentation on sole
Dresses—neckband seam
Blouses—neckband seam
Skirts—waist seam
Underwear—waist seam
Wherever remainder of items indicated for convenience

Girls: (All Clothing to Be Machine Washable With Little or No Ironing)

1 pair bedroom slippers
1 pair shoes—regular school wear—no ties
2 pair tennis shoes—play—no ties if possible
12 pairs socks or Peds®
2 robes
3 pair pajamas
pantihose for dress occasions
2 slips or pettipants
bras and garter belts as needed
12 pairs underwear (briefs)
5 skirts ⎫
8 blouses ⎬ or any combination
3 dresses—casual
1 party dress
8 short sets or casual wear
2 sweaters—NO WOOL
2 bathing suits
1 bathing cap
1 hat
1 raincoat and hat
1 jacket or coat
handbags

Personal Items:

Stationery and stamps
Medicated powder, deodorant and hair care items
4 toothbrushes (not electric) and toothpaste
2 comb and brush
Shoe polish
Shampoo and soap, if child has preference
Sanitary belts
NOTE: Toilet articles should not be in glass containers

Prohibited Are:

Razors, pocket knives, jewelry, nail files, scissors, eyebrow tweezers, and personal items of a like nature. This restriction is necessary to assure safety for all the children.

legal guardians to supply the clothing and personal items. However, when parents are unable to provide clothing, as determined by the administrative assistant, it is provided by the center.

Admission

Clothing is counted in the presence of a parent and is itemized on the clothing card, which is kept in the residence where the child will reside (Clothing Record # . . .) after being acknowledged by the signature of the parent. Clothing is marked by the Nursing Staff. Marking ink is not used on clothing.

Replacement of Clothing

1. *When the parents are unable to provide clothing and other personal items (e.g. deodorant, dusting powder).* The residence nurse, assisted by the charge aide

a. Lists clothing, etc. needed on the form in duplicate (one requisition original, and one copy is filled out for each person).

b. Makes an appointment with the Housekeeping Department and takes the child—one child per week—for replacement of clothing.

2. *When the parents are able to provide clothing and other personal items.* The residence nurse submits a list of needed personal clothing to the social worker, who writes a letter to the parents. When no appropriate clothing is found for the child (whether from the center or the parents) the residence nurse submits a list identifying the clothing needed to the Housekeeping Department and to the administrative assistant of the center.

Washing of Clothing by Parents

When parents are willing and able to provide for washing of their children's clothing they are allowed to do so.

Nonusable Clothing

Clothing no longer usable, whether worn out, destroyed or outgrown, is reported to the parents and their wishes are carried out in regard to the disposition. Written and signed permission for disposition of clothing is obtained from the parents, legal guardians or responsible relatives. Clothing is not to be destroyed until this permission is granted. When clothing is disposed of, it is to be accounted on the clothing card.

Excess Clothing

An attempt is made to keep amounts of clothing at a minimum in order to avoid loss and also to conserve space. Seven changes are adequate. Excess clothing is sent home at frequent intervals.

Minor Repairs and Maintenance of Clothing

Minor repairs and maintenance is done by the Nursing Staff.

Donated Clothing

All donated clothing is directed to the volunteer services of the center.

Disposition of Discharged Child's Clothing

All clothing is accumulated a week prior to discharge date and is given to the parents when the child is discharged.

Any clothing left after the child's discharge is mailed to the parents through the office of the administrative assistant.

If parents insist on leaving the child's clothing at the center after the child is discharged, they can do so provided that they have signed the appropriate form at the time of admission. This clothing is washed, has minor repairs and is kept in the office of the administrative assistant.

CORRESPONDENCE

General Instructions

Writing supplies, paper, one stamp and envelope are obtained from the residence office.

Know if a child has a pencil or pen and whether or not he must be supervised.

No child may have stamps in his possession.

Under no circumstances is any staff member to mail a letter for a child.

Children are allowed one letter to be mailed per week at center's expense.

Children must have stamps (kept at the residence office) if they wish to mail more than one letter.

Outgoing Mail

The children's outgoing mail is not censored. Only when there is specific written order of his psychiatrist, letters which might unduly disturb or mislead the addressee or contain obvious distortions of fact, may be returned to the child with a thorough discussion. The social work service should be notified if any problems arise.

No letter is destroyed, but is given to the parents with the knowledge and consent of the child.

In some instances, a child's letter may accompany the psychiatrist's letter of explanation enclosed.

Letters must carry a legible return address: child's name, center's name, address, zip code.

The mail is forwarded to the office of the administrative assistant.

Letters written after 8:30 AM each day are not mailed until the next day, unless a staff member brings them to the center's post office in the administration building.

Children are not allowed to correspond with other children in treatment, staff, or discharged children.

Letters addressed to the director of the center are forwarded directly.

Incoming Mail

All incoming mail for children is received at the administrative assistant's office and is picked up by the Nursing Office Aide and is given to the child at noon or evening hours. Incoming letters are not censored. Only packages are opened in the presence of the child and of the nurse or charge aide, in order to check the contents. For individual children the physician may give different instructions.

CHILDREN'S TELEPHONE CALLS AND TELEGRAMS

Children are allowed to make a telephone call or to send a telegram only with the consent of their psychiatrist. If such consent is obtained, all telephone calls or telegrams must be made at a pay phone in the presence of a nursing staff member.

CHILDREN'S TOYS

Parents are encouraged to allow their children to bring a few of their favorite toys which are acceptable and approved by the nurse according to a prepared list. They should be such that can be readily cleaned and disinfected.

Radios should be small and inexpensive. Electric trains, bicycles or other expensive toys are not allowed.

RESIDENCE TV PROCEDURES

Television sets are kept in the residence hobby room. They are turned off at 9:00 PM except for Friday and Saturday night when they may be left on until 10:00 PM. Television is kept at a normal tone and the program is selected by the majority of children who are present in the hobby room, always with the permission of the charge aide. If no children are watching the television, it is turned off.

CHILDREN'S GIFTS, PRESENTS, CARDS ON BIRTHDAYS, HOLIDAYS, ETC.

On his birthday, the child is presented with (1) a birthday cake supplied by the center or by parents and is shared with the other children at noon meal, (2) one gift from the center and (3) one present from his parents.

Gifts, money, etc. are not allowed to be given to the children by individual staff members. This policy is enforced by the entire staff. Birthday cards may be sent to the child by any service of the center, not by individual staff members.

CHILDREN'S MONEY

Parents or legal guardians who send money for the child are instructed to forward it to the Office of Administrative Assistant and make it payable to the center.

Money which comes directly to the residence is taken to the Office of Cashier with requisition in duplicate and deposited to the child's account. The child is allowed up to $1.00 at a time.

THE USE OF EDIBLE ITEMS

The dispensing of edibles to individual children before, during and after evaluation, individual and group psychotherapy sessions, school, and adjunctive therapy classes is prohibited. The directors of services are held responsible for the implementation of this policy.

The dispensing of edibles to groups of children is allowed only during weekends and holiday group programs, special group events, midmorning snacks, bedtime snacks and for medically prescribed dietary supplements. The director of the nursing service, with the cooperation of other services, is responsible for determining the frequency, time, place, quantity and quality of the edible items given to the group of children.

PHOTOGRAPHS

A picture of the child received before or after admission is kept in his medical record.

The taking of photographs in the center is not allowed unless permission is given by the director; (e.g. for public information, for special prescribed activity, or for record-keeping). The directors of services may call the director of adjunctive therapies to take pictures or slides (35 mm) depicting typical activities within their areas of responsibility. The director of adjunctive therapies is reimbursed for personal expenditures on the project upon application to the Office of the Administrative Assistant. The director of adjunctive therapies maintains a general file of slides from which slides can be withdrawn by the director of education and placed in the projector reels designated for one of the varieties of subjects to be shown. Photographs taken by staff members (after permission given by the director of the center) are collected by the director of adjunctive therapies and on a monthly basis are given to the librarian who places them in the library's photograph book.

OFF-GROUND ACTIVITIES (FIELD TRIPS, CLOTHES PURCHASING TRIPS, ETC.)

No staff member, or a relative of a staff member, is allowed to take children for off-ground visits.

During field trips, nursing staff are instructed not to provide snacks or ice cream if it is not listed in the field trip agenda. A staff member does not give money to a child on a field trip for any reason. A refund will not be given to a staff member.

A clothes purchasing trip is limited to the purchasing only. No treats. Psychotherapists and scheduled activity areas are notified if scheduled hours will be missed.

Medication is prepared by the residence nurse and administered by the nurse or charge aide accompanying the children if they will be off the grounds for a period of more than six hours.

TRANSPORTATION OF CHILDREN

Only center-owned vehicles are used in transporting children off the grounds when it is necessary for them to leave the center's grounds for authorized activities or for treatment. Staff members are not allowed to transport children in their privately owned vehicles.

The request for transportation of children is made by the administrative assistant and only an authorized person should drive the center's vehicle.

Permission from the parents or legal guardian is obtained before transporting the child off the center's grounds.

VISITING ON GROUNDS

In determining visiting privileges we consider the treatment program of the center, the parent and the individual child. Most important, we feel the visit is part of the treatment program and must benefit the child.

A child's "visitor" is defined as the parent, a legal guardian, a relative, or a friend. In case of a relative or friend, he should be of legal age and have a written permission from the parents or guardians to visit the child, or to take the child for an off-grounds visit.

Children's relatives under twelve years of age are not permitted on the grounds of the center unless this is prescribed by the child's psychiatrist.

Newly admitted children are not allowed visitors for three weeks, unless otherwise authorized by their psychiatrist through a written permission. This authorization is communicated to the child's social worker and residence nurse.

After the first three weeks, visiting privileges are determined by order of the child's psychiatrist. This will depend upon the progress of the child and understanding of the family circumstances, strengths and weaknesses. On a twice-a-month basis the child's psychiatrist renews the orders for visits. The nursing office prepares a weekly list of the children who are allowed visits on the grounds and off the grounds. This list is signed by the director of nursing or the children's psychiatrist.

A suggested list for children who might not be allowed visitors and passes is submitted by the residence nurse to the child's psychiatrist who communicates this information to the team members. Also, if in the opinion of treatment team members, a child is too disturbed to receive visitors or go on an off-ground visit, the psychiatrist is notified before the visit takes place. He communicates this information to the child's social worker, who in turn notifies the parents for the change of visiting status.

In order not to disrupt the treatment and education programs, visits are encouraged only for weekends and holidays. If a visit is allowed during weekdays (with the specific permission of the psychiatrist) the visitor is asked to wait until the child's activities are over. Exceptions to this are allowed by the child's psychiatrist. The child will be escorted to the visitor by nursing personnel. All visitors must sign in and out at the receptionist's desk (administration building). If this is closed, the signing may be done at the residence. The "Visitor's Record" form (# . . .) is to be completed.

Visitors are not allowed to visit the children on the residence, dining room or other activities unless written permission is granted by the director of the center or his delegate. Visiting areas include the reception room and the center's grounds. In case of rain and during weekends and holidays visitors can visit with the child at the Nursing Service Building (day room-lounge). The school can be shown the visitor after school hours and with the permission of the principal or his delegate.

Other "visitors" such as former employees or their relatives may not visit a child. Present or former employees may not take a child off grounds for shopping, entertainment, etc., unless otherwise authorized by the child's psychiatrist.

Employees wishing to bring their own relatives or friends to the center to look over various areas are to contact the office of the director of the center.

VISITING OFF GROUNDS (PASSES)

After a brief initial period of visiting in residence (on grounds) a child is permitted to go home for visits.

Passes are another important aspect of the overall treatment program and are not to be construed as a vacation from treatment. The amount of time spent at home is considered in relation to the child's use of treatment. For example, it might be considered injudicious to arrange a prolonged visit home shortly after he has come into residence if he was having a great deal of difficulty in making an adjustment or becoming involved in treatment. In my experience such instances are very few, and the weekend and/or holiday visit is strongly encouraged after the first three weeks in residence. It is the responsibility of the psychiatrist to determine, in collaboration with the members of the treatment team and particularly the social worker who is working with the parents, what is the best plan for each individual child. Passes are given in order to obtain information in terms of the child's behavior with the family away from the center. Any increased visiting is based on the belief that if a child goes home frequently, he does not become so divorced from his problems with his family that there is spurious improvement in residence. It keeps the family fully aware of the child's problems and their own feelings about them. In this way, casework with the parents can be carried out more realistically. It is also my experience that when the parents see the child frequently at home, the period of planning for his return is shorter and less difficult for both parents and child. I also believe that children feel less rejected by placement at the center if they are taken home by parents for weekends, and that children should have an opportunity to check their fantasies about their home situation against the reality during treatment.

When it is possible and advisable, children may go home for two weeks vacation in the summer.

All weekend passes (under seventy-two hours) or a leave of absence (LOA) (over seventy-two hours) are listed on Form # . . . .

In case a parent or guardian is allowed by the child's psychiatrist to take the child off-grounds, he is required to sign the "Responsibility for Supervision of Patient" (Form # . . .).

Passes may be designated by the psychiatrist

1) for a period of time off the center's grounds during the day.

2) for twenty-four hours.

3) for a weekend from 12:00 noon Friday to 6:00 PM Sunday.

4) for ten days. By the director's order this can be renewed for an additional ten days.

Permission for returning at a later hour must be requested from the child's psychiatrist and will be granted at his discretion.

In order to serve the best interests of all the children, the parents are asked to cooperate and to notify the center by phone if they are detained and cannot pick up the child immediately.

They should follow the physician's orders for medication and treatment and report on their observations of any unusual behavior on the child's part during the visit.

AWOL (Absent Without Official Leave)

If a child does not return from a pass or leave of absence (LOA) within forty-eight hours of the midnight census of the day he was to return, the child is classified as AWOL. If the director extends the pass (which he may do for a ten-day period) the residence is notified.

A voluntary patient on AWOL must be returned within the next two weeks or he will be given a discharge while on AWOL status.

RELIGIOUS SERVICES

As it happens with adults, children too are influenced in some degree by religion. Whether this influence is healthy or not to the child's personality development depends upon his general ability to understand and interpret basic teachings and observances as well as the attitudes towards these by adults important to him.

Religion and the Normal Child

In childhood, religion has a social as well as a divine meaning. Some children are able to perceive certain similarities in the religious attitudes of their parents, regardless of the faith to which they belong. Children frequently ask about the mysteries of birth, growth and death through their questions about religion. Hirschberg (1) in an excellent paper writes that

in childhood . . . religion is so concretely conceived that one of the problems in early religious education is to translate religious concepts into a meaningful communication for the child. The child's religious ideas relate to his everyday experiences, especially those occurring within the family; many concepts of God are gained through experiences with his parents; many ideas of sin flow from experience with parental authority; grief and remorse arise with parental distress; guilt and forgiveness are experienced out of distance or closeness in the parental relationship.

In later childhood years, as identification becomes more firm, the child's religion gives him an awareness of standards that come from outside the immediate family and allow him an identification with figures other than his parents. Although still as realistic and concrete as it was in early childhood, the religious attitudes are not so entirely self-centered and egocentric. The child who was so very strong on getting, now gives some thought to giving. Furthermore, additional meanings are found in his religion; healthy religious development now adds the securities of a sense of belongingness, of group unity, of shared ritual, and of group forgiveness. Along with this, the religious experience becomes somewhat less unique and somewhat more impersonal; it is a bit less "mystical" and more a means to a desired end. God is visualized as a person who will do things for or against the child. There is some confused questioning, some vague doubts about the "inadequacies" of the Creator and some attempt to reconcile these with the earlier ideals, but all this does not distress the usual grade school child as it does the usual adolescent. God is still omnipotent and omniscient, offering to the healthy child the sense of intimate, close, secure safeguards against aloneness or want and providing secure, noncompulsive control of impulse.

In later childhood, both the family and religion offer a basis for structuralized organization of experience. The offer of limits and discipline by religion coincide with the search of the child for such securities. By not allowing an avoidance of responsibility, by requiring that some difficulties be faced personally, a healthy religion favors growth.

During adolescence, the reorganization of individual and social experience that takes place is also reflected in the reconstruction of religious beliefs which occur. Not until adolescence does religion become truly personal and subjective. Although this will finally result in an increase in reverence when the change in attitude is completed, nonetheless it brings about the discard of certain of the religious beliefs of childhood as the adolescent struggles through his search for identity. Eventually the integrating effects of a healthy religion will aid the adolescent to mobilize and concentrate capacities now seemingly dispersed, but this can only occur if the religious attitudes themselves are reconstructed. In order to become emancipated fully from the parents, many an adolescent also doubts the religious attitudes and standards of his parents, for his own real distress as well as that of his family and church. For a period of time the need for identification with and support from his peers involves the adolescent in a comparison of his religious beliefs with those of others; resulting sometimes in abandonment, sometimes in renewed intensity, but always resulting in some change.

In childhood, religion is often felt as a contrast between a maternal principle and a paternal one. It is a part of healthy growth during adolescence that the child comes to terms with this conflict both within himself and within his faith. Through such growth the religious attitudes of childhood which depended so much on parental authority acquire the dignity and conviction of the religious beliefs of independent maturity. This becomes even more important when we realize how relatively seldom it is that religious beliefs are altered later in life.

Religion and the Emotionally Disturbed Child

Emotionally disturbed children are often very hostile towards religion as something superimposed upon them by adults or else misuse it as an avoidance of personal responsibility. In my experience, there is wide divergence of interest among the children in religion. Some resist it and seem to resent others practicing it. Some children show anxiety at the prospect of having non-Protestant or non-Catholic or non-Jewish staff on the grounds as they do not think that such staff could understand them.

From a therapeutic standpoint, I consider it desirable that children have the opportunity to attend religious classes and services and to explore what religion means to them and be helped to understand it. I also believe that unduly restrictive or punitive attitudes towards religion which cause confusion should be avoided.

Role of the Chaplain—Director of Nursing Services—
Psychiatrist

Within the limitations of the treatment program, the center's chaplain is responsible for religious services to children, providing such services for Protestant children, and serving as liaison with the visiting Roman Catholic Priest and Rabbi. Notices regarding regular services of worship, sacramental observance, and other religious group meetings appear in the daily bulletin of the center.

The religious services at the center are under the supervision of the director of nursing service who is helped by the chaplain.

The chaplain is available to children seeking the traditional clerical relationship of counsel and guidance. Such a request is reported to the child's psychiatrist who then communicates with the director of nursing. She also notifies the center's chaplain when arrangements need to be made for religious services.

The chaplain is also available to interpret the treatment program of the center to visiting clergymen. Pastors, priests and rabbis who come to the center to see children are expected to obtain the usual visitor's permission. If these clergymen have specific questions about a child they are referred to the child's psychiatrist.

Procedures

The center is nonsectarian, and all three major religious groups are represented at any one time (Protestant, Catholic, Jewish). Religious instruction, observances, and attendance at church, Sunday school or synagogue is required as it is considered an essential activity in the normal life of children. The center tries to give children the feeling of positive identification with their parents' major faith. Exceptions are made of those whose emotional maladjustment makes such an effort inadvisable and when parents ask that no religious instruction be given to their children.

The decision as to whether a child in residence shall participate in religious observances or attend church is made on the basis of his emotional capacity for such an experience. This is a treatment team staff's decision made in collaboration with the child's parents.

When the child is ready and able to participate in religious education, instruction and services, he is assigned to classes conducted by clergymen of one of each major faith. Religious instruction and services are conducted in residence. As children stabilize and are able to assimilate experiences outside the center they are allowed to attend the church of their parents' selection.

At the center all Christian and Jewish holidays are appropriately observed.

The Protestant and Catholic clergy meet separately with the children every Tuesday evening for one hour. The Protestant services are held with the center's chaplain in the nursing building and during this time hymns may be sung and Bible stories may be read and discussed.

The Catholic children go to Mass regularly on Sunday accompanied by a Catholic nursing staff member. They receive Holy Communion and are confirmed when, in the opinion of their psychiatrist, their priest and their parents they are ready for the ceremony. The children attend Friday night chapel services (Nursing Building). From a children's prayer book, they may choose the service and bring in their own variations and interpretations of certain parts of the service. Frequently there are new songs and sermons given by the children.

When indicated, arrangements are made with the center's chaplain for children to attend the nearby churches in the community. Children are supervised and transported by the nursing personnel. They attend the Church of their parents' particular preference or religious faith.

Jewish studies are offered every other Saturday at the center.

Some older children attend the weekly synagogue services conducted on Saturday mornings. A junior service is conducted for younger boys and girls where the emphasis is on Biblical materials and chanting of the Blessings. Another service is conducted for young boys and girls where the focus is on preparation for young adult synagogue participation.

No pressure is placed on the child (male or female) to be bar or bas mitzvah or confirmed. However, if the child and his family wish it and the center staff consider that the child is able to incorporate this experience, then the center arranges for their formal preparations by the visiting rabbi. In most cases the family provides the celebrations of the ceremony in the child's home after the religious services at the synagogue. When the child has no home, the celebration is held at the center residence. All the churches and synagogues in the community make a concerted effort to welcome the children and often visit the center to personally invite them to attend religious services and other of their institutional activities.

RESIDENCE HOUSEKEEPING

General Principles

a. It is the responsibility of all the nursing personnel to keep the residence clean. Children help in the process.

b. Make a general plan of all cleaning to be done and make assignments to cover this plan by using teams of personnel and children to carry out activities in each area.

c. Use all possible precautions to provide safety for both children and personnel, especially on wet and freshly waxed floors. Remove hazards, such as broken furniture, broken glass, loose articles which may be used as a weapon, etc.

Ventilation

Open doors and air residence thoroughly at intervals. If residence is too cold or too hot, notify residence nurse and administrative assistant.

Floors

All floors are scrubbed daily—PRN (as circumstances may require) at least every other day. Always dust floors before scrubbing. Wax residence floors a minimum of once a month.

Furniture Arrangement

Arrange furniture to provide a homelike atmosphere.

Care of Rooms

a. *Bedrooms:* Help children to keep bedrooms clean and orderly. Empty beds should be kept in their places and with all of their accessories (mattresses, pillow, cover).

Lock dormitory doors when children are in residence and off-residence activities. Do not allow pasting of various clippings from newspapers, magazines, etc. on the walls. A special board on the wall is used for such purposes.

b. *Bathrooms:* Tubs and showers are scrubbed with appropriate disinfectant and hot, soapy water after using.

The lavatories are cleaned twice daily and PRN.

Toilets are scrubbed thoroughly with brush and powder, twice daily.

Toilets are checked frequently to see if they are stopped up. Report to residence nurse if toilet is clogged.

Dirty linens are kept off the floor at all times. Place in linen bag.

Care of Cleaning Materials

When residence housekeeping is completed be sure that articles used in cleaning are thoroughly cleaned, rinsed, shaken out, dried, and replaced in the place provided for storage on the residence.

DAILY CLEANING SUPPLIES

6 face soap	1 can cleaner
6 toilet tissue	1 toilet brush
½ gallon of floor cleaner	1 dust pan
2 mops	1 bag utility crystals
2 buckets	sanitizer
4 straw brooms	closet bowl cleaner
4 push brooms	pine oil
	bleach for laundry

RESIDENCE PROPERTY

1. *Responsibility for Residence Property*

a. All center's property is numbered and charged by location.

b. A property inventory is maintained for each residence and service.

c. No property is removed or transferred from its assigned location until a transfer request has been submitted to the office of the administrative assistant and authorization granted for the transfer.

d. The residence nurse on each residence is responsible for the state of accounting for all property in the residence to which she is assigned.

2. *Disposition of Residence Property*

Residence nonusable property is reported by the residence nurse to the office of the administrative assistant.

Check on classification of property (expendible or nonexpendible) with the office of administrative assistant.

3. *Requisitions for Repair*

When repair work is needed, a special form is filled out by the office aide and sent to the office of the director of nursing service. The form is forwarded to the office of the administrative assistant.

4. *Requisitions for Medical Supplies and Equipment*

All requisitions for medical supplies carry the signature of the residence psychiatrist. Needs for new equipment originate from the residence nurse who notifies the director of nursing service. The director of nursing service requests approval from the residence psychiatrist and the director of the center.

REFERENCE

1. Hirschberg, J. Cotter: Some comments on religion and childhood. *Bull Menninger Clin, 19*:6, 227-228, 1955.

DAY TREATMENT PROGRAM

INTRODUCTION

Philosophy of Day Treatment

THE SETTING WHERE DAY TREATMENT is provided has been variously named "Day Hospital," "Day Ward," "Day Care Unit," "Day Care Clinic" and "Day Care Center." It may be defined as a clinical setting where full hospital treatment is given under medical supervision and the patients return to their homes each night. Such an arrangement offers an alternative to inpatient treatment for those patients for whom outpatient treatment is not helpful, yet suitable for those of the mentally ill who are well enough and do not need inpatient hospital setting. The day hospital does not isolate them from home, family and community.

Although many decades ago other small countries pioneered and implemented the concept of day psychiatric treatment, the "Day Hospital" was founded (1958) through the evangelism of the British and the Canadians. It had many expectations, among which was the hope of circumventing inpatient hospitalization, thus avoiding the "undesirable" aspect of inpatient confinement. This, of course, implied that the patients coming for treatment were representative of inpatient admissions. However, an evaluation of the experience with the day hospital concept indicates that only a segment of admissions are representative of residential patients with many other day treatment patients differing in degree and/or nature of psychopathology. It has been demonstrated that children's day treatment programs have prevented many admissions to inpatient settings; they have also been used to provide treatment for children with different or lesser psychopathology as a transition between residential treatment and full return to the community and even as a transitional adjustment phase from the community into residential treatment.

In the United States the concept of day treatment is presently expanding. The public is becoming more sophisticated in the matters of mental health and less content with the kind of care and treatment offered by some institutions. Also the monetary cost of building and operating mental institutions is itself a factor forcing citizens and lawmakers to seek other less expensive and more productive ways of doing the job. Day treatment centers do seem to offer opportunity for savings by providing day places rather than inpatient beds.

Operational Costs

The expense of operating such a program includes education facilities; salaries of professional and other personnel; food; educational and adjunctive therapy equipment and supplies; laundry, telephone and office operational costs. The combination of day and residential treatment affords the greatest savings inasmuch as some costs are shared.

It goes without question that in order for a children's day treatment program to function as a partial alternative to a residential or outpatient program, produce the best results, and be of the greatest service to the community and to the state, it needs adequate facilities, adequate staff, and financial support from its incipiency.

Day Treatment Versus Day Care

The concept of "day treatment" is often confused with the concept of the "day care." A children's day care center is usually a service for children two and one-half to five years old which substitutes for home care or provides enrichment programs. Often their purpose is to make jobs possible for mothers who, without day care arrangements, might have to stay home with their children and subsist at a poverty level. The day treatment program, on the other hand, is active and treatment oriented, geared to the needs of emotionally disturbed children, and is far removed from a custodial or "baby-sitting approach."

FORM OF ORGANIZATION

The need for a service which can offer a therapeutic and educational program for disturbed children on a day treatment basis should be met with understanding and good will on the part of the center's staff. Ideally, a staff of eighteen members under the leadership of a child psychiatrist (psychologist, two social workers, four teachers, three adjunctive therapists, nurse, five child care workers, and secretary) should offer the day treatment program.

In addition, staff from the residential treatment program should contribute in the implementation of the day treatment program which should be able to service up to thirty children. This seems to be more in line with the reality of staff allocation, space and transportation.

PURPOSE

1. *Treatment—Education*

a. To provide day psychiatric treatment for the disturbed child under the supervision of the child psychiatrist. Treatment consists of a therapeutic milieu; individual and group psychotherapy; social group work; recreational, industrial and music therapy; and if necessary, chemotherapy.

b. To provide ongoing casework, parental counseling and family therapy for the parents of the child.

c. To also provide a well-rounded educationally therapeutic program where (under the supervision of certified school-teachers) the child will have the opportunity to experience educational success and greater socialization.

2. *Further Knowledge*

a. To develop knowledge of the best techniques of day treatment for helping the child to make a more adequate social adjustment and thus become better prepared for school programs in the community.

b. To better define and delineate the types of children that will be included in this program on the basis of need and on a scientific rationale.

c. To develop the most efficient and useful methods for providing casework process and family or parental counseling wherein the troubled family group will be aided in their adjustment to the problems presented by the presence of a disturbed child.

3. *Community Relations*

a. To develop closer coordination of community resources in order to provide the best possible medical, psychosocial and educational evaluation of the child who is presented for this program.

b. To develop the best method of publicizing this program so that those parents in need of such services will use them. An ongoing public relations program designed to present the benefits of day treatment to the community should be maintained.

4. *Professional Education-Training*

a. To be used as a teaching and training resource for the community's special education teachers as well as resident psychiatrists and social work, psychology, and nursing students, and mental health technicians.

5. *Contributions to Future Directions*

a. To make recommendations for future directions to the director of the center.

PHYSICAL PLANT—SUPPLIES EQUIPMENT

The day treatment program is conducted on the grounds of the residential treatment center. It uses all the facilities and equipment of the center and is provided with operating space for the daily program, educational and adjunctive therapy supplies, and janitorial service.

PROGRAM

The day treatment program is a functioning part of the residential treatment program, and follows the residential treatment program of evaluation, diagnosis and treatment.

It is believed that the child can be helped to reach his highest potential of functioning through a program best designed for his special needs. This approach will enable him to become more self-sufficient and effective as a healthy, functioning individual.

All adjunctive therapies (recreational, industrial, music, etc.) as well as therapeutic-educational programs contribute to the philosophy which is both child-centered and parent-centered. These two services are emphasized in children's psychiatric services.

The psychotherapy programs are planned on three levels—individual, group and family. Child psychiatrists, psychologists and social workers see the children in individual psychotherapy, in group psychotherapy, and, when indicated, in family therapy. The treatment is basically directed toward facilitating adjustment to family and community living.

Parental guidance and counseling are vital parts of this program. These contribute to the betterment of the health of the family as a whole and to each individual component. Opportunities are also provided for the family to re-evaluate the impact of the problem child on each member of the family and vice versa. Families are assisted in this re-evaluation and in planning for subsequent changes in the home management of the disturbed child.

One distinctive aspect of the day treatment program is the utilization of group processes for treatment, another effort to enhance the therapeutic milieu. Each group of children has a group worker who is involved with his group throughout the day. A brief meeting of the group at the beginning and end of each program day is held to help in the development of group relatedness as well as to allow the children's expression of thoughts, feelings and self-evaluation within the supportive environment.

STAFF—ADMINISTRATIVE—CLINICAL—
FUNCTIONS—DUTIES

The budgeted staff for the center's day treatment program thus far consists of one child psychiatrist, psychologist, schoolteacher, social worker, clerk-typist, recreational therapy aide and two child care workers. Staff from the residential treatment program augment the day treatment program. All members from the various services are involved in in-service education and training.

Child Psychiatrist—Chief

He is the official head of the day treatment program and all staff assigned to it for both internal and external functions and relationships. He is charged with the administration of all aspects of day treatment of children. He is directly responsible to the director of the center for carrying out the following duties.

Administrative Duties—Functions

1. Directs, coordinates and supervises the functional assignments of staff members as related to their participation in the day treatment program.

2. Promotes the day treatment program.

3. Plans the most effective utilization and maintenance of existing facilities within the center.

4. Encourages the development and implementation of the treatment programs for children within the framework of existing policies and procedures developed by the advisory council and approved by the director of the center.

5. Communicates with the directors of the services (psychology, social work, adjunctive therapy, school, etc.) and encourages the professional discipline representative assigned to the day treatment program to do likewise.

6. Shares authority with the directors of the services (psychology, social work, adjunctive therapy, school, etc.) for discipline assignments to the day treatment staff; for promotions, demotions, terminations; for coordination of vacations, time off; for performance evaluations and for salary adjustments.

7. Confers and collaborates with the chiefs of Residence A and Residence B for the comprehensive integration of the residential and day treatment programs.

8. Coordinates children's admission to the day treatment program with the Child Study Unit (admissions office).

9. Assists in the interpretation and re-evaluation of the center's policies and procedures and prepares budgetary and other administrative requests.

10. Submits to the director the monthly and the final annual report on the administrative and clinical activities of the day treatment program and recommendations for optimal range of its functions.

Clinical Duties—Functions

1. Participates in the pre-admission evaluation and selection of children for admission to the day treatment program.

2. Admits and completes the work-up of a new child.

3. Presides at the Initial (and Progress) Diagnostic and Appraisal Conferences, the discharge planning, as well as in the treatment team meetings.

4. Shares the responsibility for Interpretation Conferences with the parents.

5. Prescribes appropriate medical and psychiatric treatment for children.

6. Provides psychotherapy (individual, group).

7. Supervises other psychotherapists.

Educational Duties—Functions

1. Confers and collaborates with the director of education in developing the education and training programs for professional and nonprofessional personnel of the center.

2. Exerts whatever effort is necessary to maintain a balance between the creation of new knowledge and the practical application of such knowledge to the delivery of services.

3. Provides individualized and continuing education and training for the staff of the center.

4. Provides education and training for members from various community mental health services.

Psychologist

He provides psychological evaluations to aid in admission decisions, in diagnostic and treatment formulations, and in discharge planning.

The psychologist provides psychotherapy in various settings (individual, group, family).

Social Worker

1. Provides evaluation of the family's strengths, weaknesses and treatment needs during the child's initial evaluation period, during the course of his treatment and during discharge planning.

2. Shares the responsibility for an interpretation conference with the family.

3. Provides individual and group psychotherapy for the child and child-centered treatment for the family using casework,

groupwork and family therapy or any combination that is necessary and appropriate.

4. Helps families find and make use of existing community resources during the period of day treatment.

5. Participates in liaison activities for the interpretation of the day treatment program to community agencies.

Schoolteacher

1. Organizes and implements appropriate educational procedures for children admitted to the day treatment program. These encompass therapeutic education, tutorial services and speech therapy if needed.

2. Provides educational testing and evaluation services for admission, placement and discharge purposes.

3. Integrates day treatment children into school programs together with residential treatment children.

4. Recommends special services for children having speech defects or other physical problems beyond the scope of the school.

5. Reports periodic academic and behavioral observations of day treatment.

6. Makes recommendations for the educational needs of day treatment children upon discharge.

Adjunctive Therapist (Recreational, Industrial, Music)

1. Is a member of the treatment and administrative team.

2. Assists with personality evaluation and treatment recommendations through observation of the child while he is participating in activities.

3. Aids the child in developing a proper attitude toward himself and others.

4. In liaison with the nursing services, he organizes activities for day treatment children for the period from 2:30 to 4:30 PM.

5. Helps the child develop skills that allow him to pursue activities of interest to him upon return to his home.

6. Plans and organizes special activities.

Nurse

1. Is a member of the treatment team.

2. Serves as clinical assistant to the child psychiatrist.

3. Serves as liaison with RT (*Residential Treatment*) nursing service.

4. Functions as a co-therapist under the direction of psychotherapist.

5. Supervises the child care personnel, delegating authority and responsibilities to them according to their capacity.

6. Obtains and supervises medication.

7. Assigns and supervises the charting and related materials on children, and the "Twenty-four-Hour Clinical Report."

Child Care Worker

1. Receives and notes communications from parents about the children when they are brought to the program in the morning. Records this information in the "Twenty-four-Hour Clinical Report."

2. Supervises children's schedules and activities.

3. In liaison with the Adjunctive Therapies Service he conducts small group meetings daily at the beginning and end of the program day with the purpose of improving group and peer relations and of allowing expression of thoughts, feelings and self-evaluation within a supportive, reality oriented environment.

INTEGRATIVE METHODS

Communication among staff members and between staff and the family is extremely important for the children's treatment. A variety of formal and informal channels of communication are used.

a. Regular casework sessions held by the social work service are a primary source of information on family interaction.

b. Parents inform the day treatment staff to unusual or significant occurrences in the family situation.

c. Staff is available to the family during times of crisis either by phone or in special interviews during working hours.

d. Information regarding the family situation is shared with the treatment team

during weekly team meetings

via the day treatment "Twenty-Four-Hour Clinical Report"

information regarding crisis situations, either at home or in the day treatment setting, is shared immediately with the day treatment chief who in turn informs members of the treatment team.

e. Sharing of information by the various disciplines at the regularly scheduled diagnostic and appraisal conferences.

ADMISSION
Criteria for Admission
Child

a. Ages six to twelve.

b. Unable to function adequately in a regular school environment.

c. Does not suffer from brain damage, convulsive disorder or severe physical handicap which significantly impairs his performance.

d. Is not chronically and severely psychotic or mentally retarded.

e. Does not have severe acting out behavior problems (extremely hostile, belligerent or negativistic).

f. Does not have drug addiction problems.

g. Has enough inner control that he will not hurt himself or others (suicidal-homicidal).

Parents or Legal Guardians

a. Must be available, cooperative and willing to participate in the child's treatment program.

b. Must be willing to keep the child at home in the evening and night, and on weekends and holidays.

c. Must live within a reasonable commuting distance of the center.

d. Must provide transportation to and from the center on a schedule determined by the staff.

e. Must legally authorize other adults (not staff members) or agencies to provide transportation for the child in case they themselves cannot provide such transportation.

Procedures for Admission
Referrals

a. The Child Study Unit of the center handles all referrals. These are made by medical or nonmedical practitioners (private physicians, educators, social workers, psychologists) as well as by parents. Preadmission evaluations from outside sources are desirable, but if they are not available the center administers the necessary examinations (psychiatric, psychological, educational and social evaluation).

b. *Admission Decision:* The Child Study Unit, through its admissions committee makes the decision as to whether the child and parents meet the criteria for admission to the day treatment program. The Child Study Unit notifies the parents and referral sources.

If necessary, the parents and the child are evaluated by the staff (psychiatric, psychological, social, educational evaluation).

c. *Admission:* On the day of admission the parents and child are received by the child psychiatrist, nurse, and social worker.

The social worker conducts an intake interview during which the list of "Regulations and Suggestions for Parents" is given to them and is reviewed, the family involvement in treatment is re-emphasized, and the appropriate legal forms are signed by the parents.

The admission examination is conducted by the child psychiatrist on the day of admission and an admission note is written within twenty-four hours. The child is oriented to school and other activities.

On the second day the child can continue in the school, adjunctive therapies and other programs as recommended by the treatment team. The initial diagnostic and appraisal conference is held within the third week after admission so as to further evaluate the child and the treatment plan. For the admission to the day treatment program from the residential treatment, the final diagnostic and appraisal (D&A) for residential treatment serves as the initial D&A for day treatment with evaluations geared toward recommendations for the day treatment program follow-up.

GENERAL POLICIES—PROCEDURES

Attendance

The day treatment program runs on a five-day-per-week basis (Monday through Friday) from 8:30 AM to 4:00 PM. It operates twelve months each year, as with the residential treatment program, but is closed on state designated legal holidays and other days specified in the day treatment calendar. A copy of the calendar is given to the parents and any changes are promptly acknowledged. Extended holiday periods, such as during the Christmas season and the summer, may be granted to individual children at the discretion of the treatment team.

Treatment Modalities

Day treatment includes individual psychotherapy, group psychotherapy, family therapy, counseling, chemotherapy, educational experience, and adjunctive therapies (recreational, industrial, music) as found in the programs of the residential treatment center.

Medication—Physical Illness

Medication relative to the psychiatric treatment of the child can be prescribed. If the child becomes physically ill, the necessary examination and treatment is given by the family physician.

Meals—Beverages—Snacks

Lunches are provided by parents. Beverages are supplied by the day treatment program. Small midmorning snacks are provided for children ages five to seven.

Parent Volunteers

Parent volunteers are not used.

Fees

The reimbursement from parents of children at the day treatment program is at a rate specified on the governing body of the center.

ANTICIPATED PROBLEMS AND METHODS OF MANAGEMENT AND CONTROL

Difficulty in Fully Evaluating the Child's Progress

As the child is at home from 4:00 PM to 8:30 AM and is not an inpatient, it is difficult to accumulate behavioral observations. Therefore, the treatment team members must maintain consistent contact with people with whom the child spends his evenings, nights, weekends and holidays.

Failure of the Parents to Bring the Child to the Day Treatment Program Each Morning

It is the parents' responsibility to notify the day treatment nurse by 9:00 AM if the child cannot report for day treatment.

If the child is absent for twenty-four hours without notification, the nurse informs the chief of the day treatment program and telephones the child's parent. Excessive absences are also reported to the child psychiatrist.

When the child is absent due to physical illness for more than three consecutive days, upon his return the parents are asked to obtain a note from the family physician stating the reason for the absence and that he is well enough to return to day treatment program. In general, the family must have a clear, bona fide reason for the child remaining at home during the day treatment period.

Failure of the Parents to Pick Up the Child in the Afternoon from the Day Treatment Program

It is the parents' responsibility to pick up the child from the day treatment program not later than 4:00 PM. As "guesting" is not allowed, the child cannot be kept as an inpatient in the residence.

If a child is not called for and parents or other relatives cannot be located, the day treatment nurse informs the psychiatrist, social worker for a decision-making conference.

In case an admission to the residential center is recommended, it must be approved by the chief of residence and the director of the center. The secretary is notified (admission papers, midnight census, etc.).

Threatened Suicide

Although threatened suicide is infrequent in day treatment programs, when threats do occur it is of sufficient concern to call an emergency meeting of the treatment team. If a day treatment child is diagnosed as not safe to remain at home, he is re-evaluated and may be considered for residential treatment or any other plan.

Child's and Parents' Misconceptions about Day Treatment

For the child the day treatment program may be seen as a way of getting away from the family, the teacher or as a means of obtaining recreational activities. *For the family* the day treatment program may be seen as a type of "hospitalization" which creates little guilt or shame because it is less of a stigma than "inpatient commitment" and does not exile a child from the home.

If it appears that the child or his parents have lost sight of the goals, it is important for the staff to confer with them either to confirm the original goals or establish new ones.

If all efforts fail to spur progress after a six-month period, the effectiveness of day treatment should be re-evaluated according to the needs of the child and his accessability to day treatment. A diagnostic and appraisal conference is held to decide whether the child should continue in the program, be transferred to another program, or terminate his treatment at the center and be referred to an outpatient program.

CRITERIA FOR DISCHARGE

a. Child is functioning in a socially acceptable manner.

b. Child can function in a regular or special school setting.

c. The family is ready to keep the child at home without undue anxiety.

d. Treatment can be reduced to outpatient basis.

e. Child is in need of a longer or more structured program than provided in day treatment, or the home situation is no longer adequate for, or able to cope with, the child's needs; thus transfer to a residential setting is indicated.

INFORMATION FOR PARENTS

The support of every parent is necessary in order to help the child receive maximum benefit from his experiences in the day treatment program. Your use and support of the following list of suggestions and regulations will be helpful to all of us—you, your child, and the staff.

1. Children are expected to attend every day (Monday through Friday), 8:30 AM to 4:00 PM. In the event of absence, you should notify the day treatment nurse by 9:00 AM.

2. The day treatment staff should be notified by the parent about any change in behavior or unusual incidents at home which could affect the child's behavior for the day. This should be done at the time the child is brought to the day treatment program.

3. Children are to be brought to the day treatment building at 8:30 AM and received there by parents at 4:00 PM.

4. When the child is absent due to physical illness for more than three consecutive days, his parents should obtain a note from the family physician, stating the cause and that the child may return to the day treatment program.

5. Every child should have a full breakfast before coming to the day treatment program.

6. Each child must bring an ample lunch. A beverage will be provided through the day treatment program. A small midmorning snack is provided for children age five to seven.

7. Children are to be dressed appropriately.

8. Articles not related to the day treatment program should not be brought in, e.g. radios, tape recorders, skates, cigarettes, matches, sharp objects, chewing gum, marbles, etc.

9. Children are responsible for the deliberate destruction of the property of other children, the staff and the center. For therapeutic purposes, the item should be repaired or replaced or an amount paid as determined by the treatment team members.

APPENDICES

I N THIS SECTION ARE INCLUDED forms which I have used in actual practice. Their layout varies from the original in some instances and spacing between items has been occasionally reduced. This is in order to make these reproductions conform to the page size of the book. The actual forms are on standard size, 8½ x 11 inch sheets, with sufficient space between items to allow for complete entry of data.

APPENDIX A
PRE-INTAKE DATA

(Drop-in) (Phone Call)   Taken By: ....

Date: ....

Child's Name: .... Age: .... d/o/b/: ....
(Last) (First) (Middle)

Parent or Guardian   Address   Telephone

Informant: Name .... Address: ....

Problem: (Both as seen by informant and by interviewer. Include previous treatment and responses)
Family Situation: (As relates to problem)
Plans made with informant or interviewer? (Add any impressions)

APPENDIX B
INSTRUCTIONS TO PARENTS OR LEGAL GUARDIANS
Dear Mr. and Mrs. ....

In response to your inquiry regarding the services of the Residential and Day Treatment Center of ...., we enclose an application form, a questionnaire titled "Our Child's Life History," a note for the referring or family physician, a medical records form, an educational information form and an authorization for release of information form.

The *application form* should be completed and signed by the parent or the legal guardian of the child or in the absence of such, by the person or agency having custody of the child. It should be witnessed, notarized and returned directly to us.

The *questionnaire* titled "Our Child's Life History" is a detailed record with many questions which should be answered as completely as possible. It has been designed as simply as possible, just to give us an understanding of the child and to help us to know something of what has occurred in the child's life. Through a better understanding of the child's past and present it will be possible for us to determine if the child is in need of our services and will benefit from them.

The *note for the referring or family physician* should be given to the physician who has conducted an examination of the child not less than fifteen days prior to the date of the application.

The *medical record form* should be filled out by the referring or family physician. The physician's certificate and medical record form should be forwarded by the physician to the director of the center.

The *educational information form* should be given to your child's present school principal for completion or if not enrolled now, then given to the principal of the last school he attended.

The *authorization for release of information form* will make it possible for us to obtain pertinent information from professional people, clinics and agencies which have had contact with the child and his family.

As soon as all these reports have been received, they will be presented for review and study to the Admissions Committee. The decision as to whether the child is accepted or not will be made known to you as soon as possible. If you have any questions, you may contact the Coordinator of the Child Study Unit, Phone number . . . ., between 8 AM and 5 PM.

Sincerely,

. . . .

Director

APPENDIX C

APPLICATION FOR VOLUNTARY ADMISSION

I/we .... and ....

parents or legal guardians of .... sex ......

birthdate .... address ....
                                       (Street or Route)

....

    (City or Town)   (County)   (State)
hereby request his/her admission to the Residential and Day Treatment Center of .... for observation, diagnosis, care, treatment and education as provided by the organizational policies and procedures of the center.

If our child is accepted for admission to the center as a voluntary patient, I/we give my/our consent in his/her behalf for his/her total treatment as may be prescribed by members of the medical and psychiatric staff and to abide by the rules and regulations of the center.

....
(Signature of father)

....
(Signature of mother)

....
(Signature of guardian)
The above named party (parties) personally appeared before me, and who, being duly sworn, says (say) on oath that the statements contained in the foregoing application are true and correct to the best of his (their) knowledge and belief.

Sworn to and subscribed before me this ...... day of ......
19... at ....

....
(Officer Administrating Oath)

APPENDIX D

(To be filled out by the parents)
OUR CHILD'S LIFE HISTORY

NAME:

    (last)   (first)   (middle)

                                           Attach
                                           Recent
                                           Photo

BIRTHDATE:
BIRTHPLACE:
HOME ADDRESS:
RESIDENCE: YEARS IN STATE: COUNTY:
CITIZEN: YES   NO

1. What is it about your child with which you would like help? How do you see the problem? What you hope the residential (or day) treatment could accomplish for the child?
2. What was it about your child that first made you feel that he was having difficulty in his development? How old was the child when this happened?
3. FAMILY HISTORY: Are the persons listed below living and well?

    a. Child's mother
    b. Child's father
    c. Mother's brothers and sisters
    d. Father's brothers and sisters

    e. Maternal grandmother
    f. Maternal grandfather
    g. Paternal grandmother
    h. Paternal grandfather

4. Any history of diabetes, rheumatic fever, allergies, cancer, epilepsy, syphilis, tuberculosis, endocrinopathy, mental illness, or mental retardation? Any other illnesses you wish to mention?
5. Parents' Present Marriage (date):
    Natural Father's name: Age:
        Schooling: Occupation:

Natural Mother's name: Age:

    Schooling: Occupation:

Divorced ( ) Separated ( ) Re-married ( ) Widowed ( )

Stepfather: Stepmother:

Adopted: Date: Agency:

6. Previous and subsequent pregnancies. List all children in order of birth:

Name	Sex	Birthdate	Pregnancy Full Term	Present Health	Grade School
. . . .	. . . .	. . . .	. . . .	. . . .	. . . .

Others at home: Name, Age, Relation to Child:

7. Mother's general health before pregnancy with this child? How was her menstrual cycle in general? Were there any illnesses? Any blood abnormalities? Miscarriages?

   Did the mother work during pregnancy?   How long?
      Type of work:

   Was this a financial necessity or by choice?

   Was this child planned?

8. Mother's first examination by a physician during pregnancy:
   Name and address of physician caring for mother during pregnancy:

9. Did mother have any infection, bleeding (spotting), high blood pressure, swelling of feet, convulsions, pain, contractions, fever, accidents, falls, vomiting, unusual worries, depression?

   During the first three months: During the last six months:

10. How was mother's diet?   Was she on a special diet?
    Did she receive any medications?   What kind?
    Was she examined by x-rays?   How were the urine and blood tests?

11. How was the living situation or events in the home during this period?

12. Length of pregnancy. How much earlier or later than expected did the baby arrive?
    Name and address of hospital. Physician attending at birth:
    Age of Mother   Age of Father   at birth of child.
    Was the father present in the hospital?

13. Length of active labor: Was the labor difficult or easy? Did the doctor have to start the labor? Were instruments used? Were drugs used?
14. Type of delivery: Spontaneous   Breech   Caesarean
    Any anesthetic used?   Gas   Local
15. Weight   Length   of baby at birth.
16. Condition of baby. Did the baby breathe quickly and easily? Was oxygen used or other medical assistance given to baby after delivery?
    Was there anything unusual in the baby's condition such as blueness, injury, paralysis, excessive crying?
17. Did the mother have unusual bleeding, temperature, convulsions, nervousness, fears or anything else just *before* or *at* or *soon after* baby's birth?
18. How soon after delivery did the mother see the baby?
19. What was the appearance of the baby (jaundice, blue, bronze color of skin; weak or strong cry, convulsions, bleeding, feeding difficulties)?
20. Nutritional history of the child:

    a. Breast fed   For how long?
    b. Bottle fed   What was the formula?
    c. Both types of feeding:
    d. Other foods   When added
    e. Vitamins:

    If breast fed (partially or completely) did the mother experience any difficulty with milk supply, nursing painful, cracked or inverted nipples, etc.?
21. Does the mother recall the baby's response to feeding (active, eager, had to be encouraged)?
22. What were the mother's feelings about the nursing experience?
23. Were there times when the baby had frequent spells of colic, constipation, or diarrhea?
24. What attitude or mood did the baby seem to express most of the time? (Happy, smiling, laughing, "cuddly," whiney, seemed in pain, sad, unresponsive, fearful, fussy?)

25. Did the parents follow a baby book in bringing up the child? If yes, name author and title.

26. At what age did the child: hold head up .... follow objects with eyes .... notice noises .... roll over alone from back to stomach .... crawl .... play with hands .... reach for objects .... reach for familiar persons .... sit unsupported .... get the first tooth .... stand alone .... first steps .... speak a few isolated words .... walk about room unattended .... "talk" (in short sentences) .... follow simple instructions .... eat alone with spoon .... dress-undress self ....

27. At what age was child's bladder training started?
    At what age was child's bowel training started?
       Were they complete or partial?
    What were the child's reactions and attitudes toward this training?

28. Unusual behavior patterns of the child:
    How did he get along with brothers, sisters, father, mother, others:

29. Any hearing or visual difficulty?

30. Were there any speech difficulties?

31. Any temper tantrums; breath-holding; sleep disturbances; wetting at night, in the daytime; masturbation; finger-sucking; nail biting; nightmares; fears of darkness or animals?
    Did the child have daydreams, imaginary companions, unusual fantasies?
    Under what circumstances did they seem to occur most frequently?

32. What were the parents' reactions to these?

33. What methods were used to deal with them? (Talked to? Picked up and fondled? Left to cry it out? Scolded or spanked? Other?)
    Did the child seem to know what he was doing?
    How did the child respond to discipline?

34. Did the parents agree with each other on methods of discipline used? Who ordinarily disciplined the child?

35. Were there any deaths in the family? Did the child ever lose

any person with whom he seemed to have a close relationship? What was the child's reaction?

36. During the early years (under three) of the child's life was either parent absent from the house for more than a week at a time?

37. When did the child start attending school (nursery school, kindergarten, grade school, special class)?
Please give name and address of school:
Were there any reading, writing, learning difficulties?
Did he stop attending school?   What grade was the child in?
Reason for stopping:

38. Has the child done any outside work for wages?   What work and wages?

39. Did the child seem to have a closer attachment to one parent than the other?
Which one?   Were there any changes in his attachments and if so, when did they occur?

40. Did the child require his parents or others to do things for him which he was capable of doing for himself?

41. Did the child have any frightening experiences?   Describe the age, the experience and his reaction:

42. How did the child react to the birth of brothers or sisters?

43. Did he show marked preference or dislikes for any of his brothers & sisters?
How was this expressed?
How are these feelings expressed now?

44. Has the child shown curiosity in regard to the bodily differences between boys and girls?   Age?   What has he said or asked about this and how did he understand this?

45. At what age did the child reach puberty?   If female, was she prepared for menstruation?   At what age?
How was she told?
At the onset of menses was she shocked?   Tearful?
Casual?   Pleased?

46. Does the child have any motor coordination difficulties such as confusion in regard to left-handedness or right-handed-

ness or frequent falling, awkwardness in throwing a ball or riding a bicycle, etc.?

47. What illnesses has the child had previously? Age at which each occurred. How long each illness lasted. What treatment was given. Was the child hospitalized or cared for at home? Were there any unusual reactions or after-affects?   Give name and address of physician.

48. Did the child have any operations?   Specify:
   At what age?
   Name and address of physician:
   Was the recovery uneventful ?   Or complicated?
   Type of anesthetic used: Was the child hospitalized and for how long?
   What was the child told about operation before hand?
   Did the child show fearfulness, temper tantrums, increased shyness after the operation?   Specify:

49. What accidents did the child have?
   At what age?   Was he unconscious as a result and for how long?
   Was a physician called?   What treatment was given?
   Did the child have a fracture?   Did the child show any behavior after the accident which seemed to be reaction to it such as fearfulness, sleep disturbances, speech disturbances, nervousness, etc.?

50. Does the child have convulsive seizures? When did they first appear?
   Describe the seizures: before   now
   Any change in temperament noticed before the seizure? Is his whole body or part of the body involved in the seizure? Which part? How many times a day, week or month does he have seizures?
   What kind of medication (and the amount) is given now?
   What kind of medication (and the amount) has been given in the past?
   Does the medication help?

51. List medical and psychological examinations child has had

and when. Also list the results of the examinations. Name
and address of examiners.

52. Does the child feed himself? Does he dress and undress himself alone? Can he tie a shoelace?

53. What is the general health of the child?

54. Describe any deformity now present:
Is there any abnormality in his walking? If so, explain:
In his other body movements:

55. Has the child undergone any psychiatric treatment in the
past?   Present?
If yes, date: Psychiatrist's Name: Address:
Outpatient: Inpatient:

56. Is the child taking any medication at the present time?
If so, what kind, dosage, for what was it prescribed?

57. Please describe what your child is able to do and his play in-
terests.
Does he play with any other children?
In general, how does he spend his day?

58. In what activities do the mother and child engage?
In what activities do the father and child engage?

59. Immunizations: Has your child had the following immuni-
zations?
Diphtheria (give date)
Whooping cough (give date)
Tetanus (give date)
Booster shots for the above (give date)
Smallpox (give date)
Polio Shots (give date) 1.   2.   3.   4.
Polio Oral/Sabin (give date) 1.   2.   3.   4.
Tuberculin Test and Result (give date)
Measles (give date)
Allergy to penicillin or other medication, foods, etc.
Name and address of the physician now caring for the child:

60. Are you willing to participate in your child's treatment program?

Name of person filling out this child's life history:

Relation to the child:

I/we understand that this information will be used in the evaluation of our child and will be included in the Center's Medical Records thereof:

Date: Signed:

APPENDIX E

(To be sent to the referring or family physician)

INFORMATION AND INSTRUCTIONS FOR CHILD'S ADMISSION

According to the Policies of the Center:

The application shall be accompanied by a certificate of at least one licensed physician in good professional standing and a graduate of a school of medicine recognized by the American Medical Association and shall state that the child has been examined by the physician and it is the opinion of the physician that the child is severely emotionally disturbed or mentally ill and is in need of and will benefit from intensive care and treatment at the Center. The certificate shall also contain a diagnosis and history of the child's condition. The certificate shall be based on an examination conducted not less than fifteen days prior to the date of the application.

Upon receipt of the application, the Admissions Committee of the Center or its designated authority will, on the basis of the certificate of examination, reject or accept the applicant as a patient at the Center. The Director of the Center or his designated authority has the sole discretion of determining the order of admission of applicants based on the type of case, the urgency and facilities available.

The Medical Record Form shall be filled out by the child's family physician.

Both the Medical Certificate and the Medical Record Form should be forwarded to the Director of the Center.

APPENDIX F

(To be filled out by family physician)
MEDICAL RECORD

Name of Child: .... Sex: ... Age: ...
  (Last) (First) (Middle)

I. PAST MEDICAL HISTORY

1) *Family History:* Speech, visual, or hearing handicaps; tuberculosis, diabetes, mental illness, epilepsy, or other illnesses in the family?

2) *Previous illnesses*

	Age		Age
Chickenpox		Rheumatic fever	
Measles		Nephritis	
Whooping Cough		Poliomyelitis	
German Measles		Meningitis	
Mumps		Encephalitis	
Diphtheria		Typhoid	
Scarlet Fever		Mononucleosis	
Frequent Colds		Bleeding tendencies	
Earaches		Hay fever	
Draining ears		Asthma	
Frequent sore throats		Eczema	
Pneumonia		Foreign protein or serum sensitivity	

Convulsive disorders: Type:
        Age of onset:
        Frequency:
        Date of last seizure:
        Present medication, if any:
        Dosage, time given, etc.

3) *Significant Health Data:* Include other serious illnesses, hospitalizations, accidents, injuries, or operation, drug or serum reactions, medications, known defects, menstrual history, nutritional history, etc.

II. PRESENT PHYSICAL STATUS:

Date of Examination: Height   Weight   B.P.

General Appearance: Blood Type: RH Factor

Eyes   Vision

Ears   Hearing

Lymph nodes   Thyroid

Nose   Throat

Gums   Teeth

Heart   Lungs

Abdomen   Nutrition

Skin   Sec. Sexual charact.

Orthopedic

Nervous system

Speech   Other

X-rays: Chest (last)

        Skull (last)

Recent laboratory tests: Urinalysis:

                         Hemogram:

EEG

ECG

Is further examination or laboratory test recommended?

     (Reverse side may be used for additional data)

. . . .

     Name of Physician   Address

. . . .

     Signature of Physician

. . . .   Date:

     License No.   Date

APPENDIX G

(Letter to School Principal)

EDUCATION INFORMATION

Dear Principal:

. . . . is being considered for admission to the Residential and Day Treatment Center. In order to evaluate this child's educational achievement, we are asking that you kindly forward to us the following:

1. A transcript of grades
2. Standardized test results and interpretation
3. Health sheets
4. Teacher comments
5. Any other information which you feel might help us in our evaluation

Our school is a vital part of the treatment program. It consists of a full school program plus tutoring in remedial and accelerated areas. Your information will also help us provide proper grade placement and curriculum. The material should be addressed to: Director, Residential and Day Treatment Center.

Thank you for your cooperation in this matter.

> Sincerely,
> Director,
> Residential and Day Treatment
> Center

APPENDIX H

(To be filled out by parents or agency)

AUTHORIZATION FOR RELEASE OF INFORMATION

In order that we may know as much as possible about your child's problem, it is desirable that we contact the professional persons who have seen him/her. For example, these may be psychiatrists, physicians, psychologists, social workers, teachers, hospitals, child guidance clinics, social agencies, Juvenile courts, etc. Please list below.

NAME   Date of Contact
Address
NAME   Date of Contact
Address
NAME   Date of Contact
Address
NAME   Date of Contact
Address

NAME   Date of Contact
Address
NAME   Date of Contact
Address

Please complete the following authorization for the release of information:

I hereby authorize the above persons and agencies to release their information concerning my child   to the Residential and Day Treatment Center of
Date:
Witness
Signed

Parent or Legal Guardian

Address of Witness

APPENDIX I

(To be filled out by parents or legal guardian)

PARENT'S OR LEGAL GUARDIAN'S AGREEMENT

As the policies, practices and procedures of the Residential and Day Treatment Center of .... have been fully discussed with me/us,

A. I/We hereby understand that the Center is a State (or County or private) facility which offers residential and day psychiatric treatment to children; that it is located on .... ; that its primary purpose is to offer professional evaluation, care, treatment and education services to severely emotionally disturbed or psychotic children between the ages of six and twelve years inclusive; that its secondary purpose is to educate and train specialists in the fields related to the diagnosis, care, treatment and therapeutic education of children and to advance knowledge by research in the fields of the emotionally disturbed children; that the integrity and dignity of the children and their families is held in the utmost regard by the staff members of the Center; that the staff exercises every possible care and precaution in the interest of the children's safety and well being; therefore,

B. I/We .... and .... parents

or legal guardians of .... acknowledging that he/she being a minor and unable to consent, do hereby give permission and consent in his/her behalf to the staff of the Center:

 a) To admit the child to the Residential and Day Treatment Center of ....
 b) To carry out the necessary procedures for physical, psychological, psychiatric and educational examinations of the child.
 c) To provide the child with appropriate emergency treatment, and to remove the child to a special hospital when in the judgement of the medical staff it is deemed necessary.
 d) To arrange for the use of such necessary routine and special tests and treatments which in the opinion of the medical staff of the Center are deemed advisable.
 e) To provide for personal grooming as necessary for the child.
 f) To use research materials gathered from the care, treatment and education of the child at the Center.

C. I/We also agree:

 a) To concur in good faith in the visitation requirements of the Center.
 b) To cooperate with the staff of the Center, as they request it in my/our part of the child's overall treatment program.
 c) To observe the rules and regulations pertaining to the release of the child from the Center and to remove the child immediately upon a written request for his release issued by the Director of the Center or remove the child on my/our will from the Center after giving a notice in writing.

....

| Father | Mother | Legal Guardian |

Sworn to and subscribed before me this ...... day of ....
19 ... at .... •

....

(Officer Administrating Oath)

APPENDIX J

(To be filled out by parents or agency)

GENERAL AUTHORIZATION

I/we, ... parent(s) or legal guardian(s) of
.... do give my (our) authorization to the
residential and day treatment center of .... for my
(our) child to:

... ... A. Receive all immunizations deemed necessary by
Yes No physicians of the Center.

... ... B. Transport off Center's grounds when necessary.
Yes No

... ... C. Participate in supervised activities off Center's
Yes No grounds. These activities are part of the total therapeutic program (shopping trips, visits, picnics,
swimming, etc.).

... ... D. Receive on grounds visits and/or visit the homes
Yes No of approved volunteer visiting families—visiting
friends in the community. Such visits are part of
the therapeutic program and are prescribed at the
discretion of the physician.

DATE: .... SIGNED: ....

Parent/Legal Guardian

I have this date witnessed the signature of the above parent/legal
guardian. I am not related to either the above child, parent or
legal guardian.

DATE: .... SIGNED: ....

Witness

....

Address of Witness

APPENDIX K

(To be filled out by parents)

FINANCIAL STATEMENT

Name of Child: *Date of Birth:*   *Admission Date:*
Address:

No. Street   City or Town   State   Zip Code

Parents: *Name*   *Employed*   *Occupation*
                                Yes   No

1. Father:
2. Mother:
3. Stepfather:
4. Stepmother:

Number of other dependents in home:

Employment: Give information on each person checked above as employed:

Employer's Name and Address: *Salary*
                                              $ per

Home: Owned   Rented   Payment: $ per

Support and/or Alimony payments: Yes   No

If yes, indicate for whom   Amount: $

If other regular payments, give amount and for what:

Does patient have income?   No   Yes

If yes, give amount: $ Source

Medical Insurance: Is child included?   No   Yes

If yes, give name and address of company:

Has child had inpatient psychiatric treatment in past year?

No   Yes

If yes, where?

Charges: $ per

Has child had outpatient psychiatric treatment in past year?

No   Yes

If yes, where?

Charges: $ per

Have you had counseling or therapy in past year?

No   Yes

If yes, where?

Charges: $ per

Name of Parent
Signature of Parent

INDEX

359

N

O